D0940582

PRAYER FOR THE CITY
Bootcamp for Urban Mission

by John F. Smed, with Justine Hwang

Copyright © 2011 by John F. Smed

Published by Prayer Current
106 – 1033 Haro Street
Vancouver, BC V6E 1C8
CANADA

info@prayercurrent.com

All rights reserved.
No part of this publication may be reproduced, stored in
a retrieval system, or transmitted in any form or by any means –
electronic, mechanical, photocopy, recording, or any other –
except for brief quotations in printed reviews, without
the prior permission of the publisher.

Prayer Current
Navigating Life Through Prayer

WWW.PRAYERCURRENT.COM

Encouraging Word on the Street about Prayer for the City:

"Kingdom-centered prayer is a battlefield. To grow and mature in prayer warfare we need the Spirit's urging and guidance. We also seek intercessors who stand with us encouraging and opening our understanding to the truths of Scripture. John Smed and his team enter this arena with humility, wisdom and confidence. They teach prayer through praxis, a process of praying with reflection. They explore biblical content on prayer and then apply it immediately in small group praying. As a result praxis becomes an ongoing process of listening to God through the Word, reflecting on its implications, and responding in joyful prayer."

~Allen Thompson, President, International Church Planting Center, New York

"The Urban Prayer Bootcamp, hosted by Prayer for the City's John Smed and Justine Hwang is the most intensive, practical and gospel-centered training for developing a life of prayer and a church of prayer that I have ever seen. The modules are biblically sound and personally practiced in the training. The materials and books they have published are easily transferable to others. I encourage all our leaders to get the training. We implement their training in all the Church Planting Networks we facilitate! I highly recommend you attend as soon as possible. As we have heard, "Prayer does not fit us for the greater work, it is the greater work!"

~ Tom Wood, President, Church Multiplication Ministries, Atlanta

"Prayer Bootcamp for Urban Mission training deepens and widens people in biblical, kingdom prayer. However, it does far more: Community develops as groups share and pray together; Repentance begins as heart idolatries are exposed; Individuals initiate in ministry; Expectant prayer leads to evangelistic boldness; An exciting vision for a church in mission is born as a spirit of prayer and the Spirit of God comes upon people. Prayer Training is transforming New City Church."

~Connan Kublik, Church Planter, Hamilton, Ontario

"Thanks so much for taking the time to come share with us. It was extremely timely for us in Camden. God has used the training powerfully in our ministry — each time we go out we pray for boldness (well, actually, most times it's my young daughters who pray for me and ask God to make me bold and open doors) and it's been amazing how he's answered those prayers each and every time. We have not gone out once this week where God hasn't both given the opportunity and the boldness to us to share the gospel with at least one person. Thank you so much for sharing your hearts with us, and for letting God shape you all in the way that he has."

~Daniel Passerelli, Church Planter, United Kingdom

"This training had both vision and practical tools, with an excellent kingdom focus. Most training only focuses on one area."

~Workshop participant

"This combined the eschatologically urgent need/mandate for prayer combined with very practical steps to teach us to pray."

~Workshop participant

PRAYER FOR THE CITY

Bootcamp for Urban Mission

II. How Christ Builds a House of Prayer .... II-i

7. Jesus' Priority in Building a House of Prayer

8. The Power of Praying Together for Renewal and Revival

9. Reaching a World through Prayer

III. Leaders Reach a City through Prayer .... III-i

10. Searching and Serving the City Through Prayer

11. Prayer and Spiritual Warfare

12. Bringing it all together: A day of prayer for the church in the city

Section I
Personal Prayer Life of a Leader

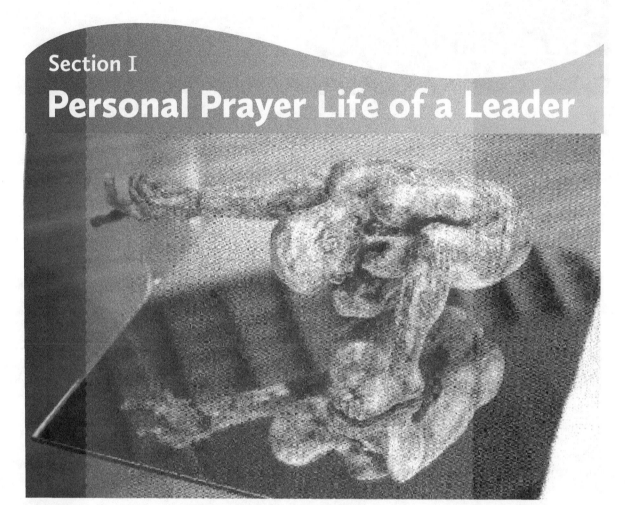

Section I: Introduction
Personal Prayer Life of a Leader

(See DVD Section 1: Lesson 1A)

Learning to pray for the church and city begins with the personal prayer life of the leader. **Leaders lead. By definition, they take responsibility for their people and behave in a way that inspires faith and courage.**

Think of Shakespeare's Henry V. King Henry disguises himself as an ordinary soldier and walks among the troops on the battle front. He assesses the courage and loyalty of his troops when it matters most – the night before the battle. He leads his troops into battle with a firsthand awareness of the challenges they face and the enemy they fear. *This is the kind of leader worth following.*

In Tolkien's Lord of the Rings, King Theodon leads his troops into battle. They are not ready to give their life for the cause until he does. He makes the first assault and he takes the first hit. Stepping up to the front line is the secret of his heroism.

Remember David and Goliath? As long as King Saul hides far from the battle front in the tents of strategy, his soldiers shrink in fear at the taunts of Goliath. Only when a shepherd boy, David, takes up the challenge, with a mere slingshot, are Israel's soldiers ready to join the fight. David proves his leadership by leading!

As long as church leaders retreat to the safe confines of church gatherings and meetings, there is no compelling reason for God's people to enter the fray in the name of Christ.

Jesus is our supreme leader. He goes before us. He leads the assault. He takes the death blow of the enemy for us. He gives us his live and calls us to follow him into the fields of battle. *"My prayer is not that you take them out of the world but that you protect them from the evil one."* ~John 17

From the front line Jesus issues our marching orders.

> *[18] Then Jesus came to them and said, "All authority in heaven and on earth has been given to me. [19] Therefore go and make disciples of all nations, baptizing them in the name of the Father and of the Son and of the Holy Spirit, [20] and teaching them to obey everything I have commanded you. And surely I am with you always, to the very end of the age." ~Matthew 28*

Apply this to prayer. Leaders lead in prayer.

They have a strong prayer relationship with Christ. They derive great joy and strength from this prayer relationship. They learn how to pray at the feet of Jesus (Lesson 1). Their prayers are filled with Christ so they long to be with Christ in the field of battle (Lesson 2). Leaders know Jesus personally – they care about what matters to him so they pray his priorities (Lesson 3). Because they know they are loved by Jesus, they are deeply transformed by the gospel as they pray (Lesson 4). Because they have learned to listen and discern Christ's word and will, as they pray they become clear about their calling (Lesson 5). Indeed, a life of prayer with Christ is indistinguishable from a life of serving Christ in the church and city (Lesson 6).

Leaders teach prayer and model prayer in such a way that encourages and empowers God's people to pray with passion for the world changing purposes of Christ and to courageously follow where he leads.

This diagram helps to illustrate the principle of praying leadership as we have sought to practice it in our church life:

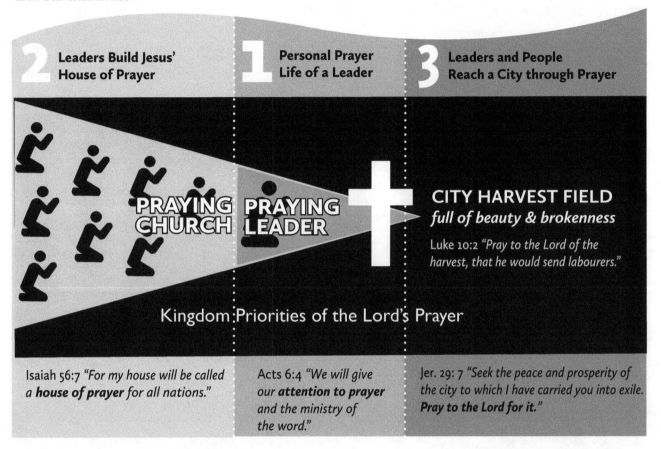

Let us look at this diagram starting in the centre, then moving to the left and ending on the right.

1. Notice first of all in the centre that although the **personal prayer life of a leader** begins in the closet in fellowship with Christ, the outcome of this strong personal prayer life, is that they find they become 'active duty' in the fields of harvest.

2. On the left we see that **leaders lead in prayer.** No one would dispute – a praying church is always lead by praying leaders! People follow their leaders and grow in their personal prayer relationship with Jesus. Now leaders and people are praying together.

3. On the right, we see the result is that praying people led by praying leaders are actively praying for the city – in its beauty and its despair. **God's people are sent out to love and serve the city and its people** as they pray.

Biblical patterns
Teach Kids
Beyond relief
Beyond my inner circle

Why We Train in Prayer

GOALS: In this lesson we will...
- ❑ Explore the priority of prayer related to the gospel and to mission
- ❑ Evaluate your current prayer health and progress
- ❑ Identify and confess your obstacles in prayer

Introduction
(See DVD Section I: Lesson 1A)

This is not a workshop about prayer. It is a prayer workshop where you learn to pray by praying! Nor are we going to pray about prayer.
1. We will pray for spiritual transformation.
2. We will pray for the church.
3. We will pray for the city.

To start or renew prayer in your own life or in a church is not easy. It is a work of Christ's Spirit! It is filled with Christ's Spirit...

"And I will pour out on the house of David and the inhabitants of Jerusalem a spirit of grace and supplication... "On that day a fountain will be opened to the house of David and the inhabitants of Jerusalem, to cleanse them from sin and impurity." Zechariah 12:10

Almost every Christian wants to pray. Why are we not praying?
The ruts of intellectualism run deep.
We have become passive and speculative when we should be active and participative.
Too often, in seminary and church, prayer is not required. Prayer training is seldom provided.
Too often, we haven't got a prayer.

Prayer for the City Bootcamp is a proven means to grow in prayer.
We will pray together. One half of our time together and one half of homework is prayer!
We will pray with focus, purpose and direction. We will follow the pattern of
the Lord's Prayer and other biblical models. We will grow spiritually and in mission.
Prayer Bootcamp for Urban Mission connects prayer to the gospel and prayer to mission.

MY STORY
From my earliest time as a Christian I have been trained in prayer.

Eighteen years old and a brand new Christian travelling around Europe, I come across a Christian community in Switzerland called L'abri. Francis and Edith Shaeffer and others open their homes to any that "God would send." I spend more than three months living, studying and working in the community wood shop.

Each Monday morning, for two or three hours Mrs. Shaeffer would lead all members and visitors in prayer for the community. She taught us what prayer means and models prayer for us.

Once a month she leads the entire community in a day of prayer and fasting. We pray through various scriptures and spend the time asking for the spiritual and practical needs of the community. I imprint on this L'abri pattern of regular prayer and periodic days of prayer. Almost 40 years later this is still my personal habit.

During the same period I am taught how to form and keep a prayer list. Donald Drew, a Christian teacher and scholar, gathers a group of five young men to meet with him for Bible study and prayer one afternoon each week. He shows us his lengthy and tattered prayer list and encourages us to form our own. It sticks. To the present day I use a list for prayer.

Fast forward 15 years to my first pastorate in Calgary, Alberta – Woodgreen Presbyterian Church. My wife Caron and I, with five kids in tow, plant a church by throwing every conceivable strategy and program into the mix. Frankly we are clueless. One great challenge, I find out, is teaching a congregation to pray. We exhaust ourselves, which drives us to our knees in prayer. After four years we form a group for the single purpose of praying to reach our neighbours. We call it, simply, "Prayer and Evangelism Evening." We start with two others. It slowly grows in numbers, strength and vitality. This Sunday evening group increases to about 30 over the next few years. People come because it is a warm energizing meeting. It is here we learn to pray, to love each other and to spread the news to our neighbours. Prayer becomes the spiritual furnace which warms and fuels the growth of the church. We learn an important lesson – spiritual strength and mission momentum rise and fall in relation to prayer.

After seven years, my next leadership opportunity is as church planting director for Mission to North America. We were stationed there for seven years. It did not take long to realize that new church missions might expand quickly but the spiritual fabric is not strong and is easily torn. One disappointed church planter, in a new work in a major urban center, simply reported, "We grew quickly but Satan took us down without much of a fight. We were not spiritually prepared. When the attacks came it was simply too late to get in shape for the fight." Watching this outcome on several fronts, we resolved to invest more time in spiritual growth and development – specifically in prayer training. Our conferences and workshops changed from simple 'how to' talks to spiritual formation workshops. We all agree this was both necessary and fruitful.

Since 1999 we have been planting and growing Grace Vancouver Church. Our first twelve weeks was basically a prayer meeting – as we sought to discern God's call for us in the city. Prayer walks, days of prayer, prayer groups and prayer training are part of our DNA because prayer has been our highest priority from day one. Our first goal is to become a praying church. This prayer training workshop runs every year at Grace. All of our leadership and many of our members have taken this training. Each year we host a prayer training workshop for churches around Vancouver and other cities. Every year we hold one two or three prayer workshops in cities around North America and London England.

As a follow up we have written and distributed a study guide called *Journey in Prayer: Seven Days of Prayer with Jesus*. This is a seven week Bible study patterned on the Lord's Prayer. *Journey in Prayer: Seven Days of Prayer with Jesus* was then simplified to be used as an outreach instrument – our way to teach seekers and young believers how to pray.

We are on a journey of prayer. By taking this prayer training workshop you are this journey with us. It is an immense privilege and joy to encourage you in prayer. Please pray for us as we pray for you.

John Smed

Zechariah 12:10,11 and 13:1-2

God pours out a spirit of prayer

"And <u>I will pour out</u> on the house of David and the inhabitants of Jerusalem a <u>spirit of grace and supplication</u>. They will look on me, the one they have pierced, and they will mourn for him as one mourns for an only child, and grieve bitterly for him as one grieves for a firstborn son.

Outcome of repentant and humble prayer

"On that day a fountain will be opened to the house of David and the inhabitants of Jerusalem, to cleanse them from sin and impurity. "On that day, I will banish the names of the idols from the land, and they will be remembered no more," declares the LORD Almighty. "I will remove both the prophets and the spirit of impurity from the land.

Isaiah 62:1,6,7

God calls out his prayer watchmen

For Zion's sake I will not keep silent, for Jerusalem's sake I will not remain quiet, till her righteousness shines out like the dawn, her salvation like a blazing torch. I have posted watchmen on your walls, O Jerusalem; they will never be silent day or night. You who call on the LORD, give yourselves no rest, and give him no rest till he establishes Jerusalem and makes her the praise of the earth.

QUESTIONS

For Small Group Discussion

1. From the Zechariah passage, how is prayer connected to the Gospel (to Christ's work of salvation)?

2. From the Isaiah passage, how is prayer connected to mission (the missionary nature and result of our prayers)?

PRAYER PRACTICE:
- Praise Jesus for His saving work, greatness and worthiness.
- Confess your past neglect and your powerlessness.
- Pray for a "spirit of grace and supplication." Cry out for it!

Vision: To see a river of prayer, fed by the Spirit, nourished by the Word, filled with the message and mission of Christ – through the church to the community, our city, and the world. Revelation 22:1-2, Ezekiel 47:7-12

Core Values:

1. Gospel
2. Prayer
3. Mission

Desired Outcomes

1. To develop praying leaders
2. To develop praying churches
3. To pray for the city

What You Will Do In This Course

To help bridge the gap between desire/awareness to pray and actual practice of prayer, our aim is to **model** practical tools for prayer and create opportunity for learners to **practice**:

1. *Evaluate* **prayer progress,** including *positive indicators* of healthy prayer and *negative idols*
2. *Practice* **Biblical patterns for prayer** following the Lord's prayer and Paul's prayers
3. *Build* a **prayer list** to balance needs according to Christ's priorities and his specific calling for you
4. *Practice* **prayer accountability** to spur on growth in the gospel and in mission
5. *Practice* **prayer walking** and *create* a **prayer map** to focus prayer in your specific mission field
6. *Practice* principles of **leading others** in prayer
7. *Participate* in a day of **fasting and prayer**
8. *Articulate* a **personal calling/mission statement** to inform the heart of your prayers
9. *Identify* your city's **spiritual strongholds** to commit to prayer

Prayer Bootcamp Preparation

This is Prayer Bootcamp. As bootcamps entail, the work is intensive. Generally, the more you time, energy and prayer you invest in your training, the more you will grow.

> **White "Application Boxes"** throughout the materials encourage personal and small group reflection and discussion.

> **Grey "Prayer Practice" boxes** deliberately lead us to respond in prayer to readings and exercises.

Each session you will be responsible for reading the material prior to meeting with your group. As you go through the material, concentrate your focus on the readings for each lesson, the personal reflection questions and prayer practice points.

PRAYER FOR THE CITY BOOTCAMP APPROACH TO GROUP PRAYER

A Few Principles in Horizontal Prayer

Throughout our time together, we will be aiming to invest half our time in prayer practice. While prayer involves a *vertical dimension* of communicating with our heavenly Father above, there is also an *horizontal dynamic* of which we should be conscious when we gather with others in prayer.

The following guidelines will help our group prayer times to be engaging and fruitful:

- To increase opportunity for each one to pray, we will mostly pray in **small groups of 2 to 4**.

- **Pray in concert** with the person who is currently praying out loud on behalf of the group; pray in the same spirit with them (i.e. fight wandering thoughts or planning what you will pray next)

- **Pray conversationally**, moving from theme to theme, as the Holy Spirit guides.

- **Pray short prayers**, but pray as often as you like (rather than praying a continuous list of requests in one long prayer). Pass it back and forth; keep the ball rolling.

- Remember the **ABCs** of group prayer:
  a. Audible
  b. Brief
  c. Christ-centred

"You have nothing to hide. You are forgiven in Christ
You have nothing to fear. You are eternally loved.
You have nothing to prove. You are righteous in his grace."

Personal Evaluation of Your Prayer Life

Evaluate your <u>present</u> prayer health:

		Ouch, no pulse	Weak	Needs some work	Progressing & growing	Wow, my prayer life is on fire!
1.	When I pray I experience God's delight & pleasure over me as his child........	1	2	3	4	5
2.	I experience great joy in worshipping God as I pray	1	2	3	4	5
3.	My prayers go beyond asking for relief (from stress, illness, financial need) .	1	2	3	4	5
4.	My prayers often follow Scripture or follow Biblical patterns/priorities	1	2	3	4	5
5.	I regularly ask others to pray for me...	1	2	3	4	5
7.	I regularly wait on God in prayer for his vision, action and direction..............	1	2	3	4	5
8.	My personal calling is being deepened and made clear through my prayers..	1	2	3	4	5
9.	God speaks to me with clarity as I pray and read His Word	1	2	3	4	5
10.	I am often burdened to pray throughout the day.................................	1	2	3	4	5
11.	I pray regularly for a time each day	1	2	3	4	5
12.	I practice regular extended times of prayer (monthly day of prayer, etc.)......	1	2	3	4	5
13.	I practice keeping an updated method of praying for many prayer needs of my flock and city (eg. prayer list, prayer journal, etc.)	1	2	3	4	5
14.	I frequently see specific answers to my prayers	1	2	3	4	5
15.	I pray regularly for missionaries, evangelists and my own witness	1	2	3	4	5
16.	There are a number of non-Christians that I pray for regularly	1	2	3	4	5
17.	I pray regularly for my church, neighborhood, workplace and city.................	1	2	3	4	5
18.	I am part of a group of people who pray regularly with & for each other	1	2	3	4	5
19.	I pray regularly with my spouse/children..	1	2	3	4	5
20.	I am teaching others how to pray	1	2	3	4	5

This progress evaluation is a simple tool to help provide a snapshot of the health and pulse of your <u>present</u> prayer life at any given moment in time. You may find it helpful to review this periodically. The indicators listed here can also help us to begin drawing a picture of the signs of a full and rich <u>future</u> prayer life as God grows us.

McGrade – mother, Connie
Grace – chey husband
? – Corry, plan + joy friend
? – 9hre + el babbul

Summarize observations from your progress snapshot

3. What encouraging growth do you see in your prayer life? What other evidences can you see?

4. Which weaknesses do you want to trust God to address and change (choose one or two)?

5. How does the grace of Christ speak to these areas? How can you find encouragement in the gospel in these areas?

6. **Future** Prayer Progress: **Your Prayer Vision and Outcomes**

How do you hope God will grow your prayer life during this time? What do you hope to do with what you learn here?

For Discussion in Pairs: With the person next to you:
- Share *one encouragement* from your prayer progress evaluation.
- Share *one weakness* you are trusting God to change in the coming weeks.
- Share how you *desire to grow* in prayer during this training.

PRAYER PRACTICE:
- Pray for each other by name, to grow in grace and supplication.

Your Commitment to Seek Prayer Transformation

In seeking spiritual transformation and forming new prayer habits, making a commitment to practicing prayer, reading the Word of God (which inspires and teaches us in all matters of prayer), and learning in community is in order.

By God's grace, are you willing to make the effort on keeping the following commitments?

- ❑ I will attend all group meetings on time. My presence and absence is noticed and felt by the group.

- ❑ I will participate in group prayer times and discussions.

- ❑ I will be open to trying new means of prayer for the duration of the training.

- ❑ I will do the homework, readings and assignments each week.

- ❑ I will pray 15 minutes a day (the only way to grow in prayer and in my relationship with God).

- ❑ I will invest in this training my resources of time and money (which covers the cost of materials and furthers the expansion of this ministry so that others are able to benefit from it also).

- ❑ I will participate in my church's worship each week for the duration of our training.

- ❑ _____

- ❑ _____

_____   _____
Signed   Date

PRAYER PRACTICE:
- ▪ On your own, write out a prayer of surrender and commitment:

HOMEWORK:
- • Continue to pray about your prayer vision and flesh it out some more.
- • Read through the material for Lesson 2, concentrating on the readings, the personal reflection questions and prayer practice points.

The Priority of Prayer of an Apostolic Leader

GOALS: In this lesson we will...
- ☐ Practice the connection between prayer and the Word
- ☐ Consider the priority of prayer of leaders in the Bible

Introduction

(See DVD Section 1: Lesson 2)

The personal prayer life of an Apostolic Leader

Learning to pray for the city begins with the personal prayer life of the leader. We want to become 'apostolic' in prayer and in leadership. Simply put, this means to lead like the apostles lead. What do we mean by apostolic leadership?

First, Apostolic leaders lead from the field

The apostle Paul furnishes a specific apostolic example. He leads the church into battle. He is the first to storm the strongholds of every city. He writes missives from the battle field and from prison.

In the midst of mission Paul requisitions missionary prayer from the churches – for boldness, for open doors, and for deliverance. Paul does not stand behind a pulpit encouraging others to preach Christ to a lost world. He is not an expositor of the history of spiritual warfare. He is on the field. He is engaged with the enemy. He takes direct hits, from all sides. An apostolic leader cannot boldly point to the world as the place of mission while remaining secure in church barracks. His chief call is not to preach to the choir but to the lost in the field. It is not enough to sow gospel seed among the already converted. He knows real joy and harvest comes when he leaves the ninety nine and finds the one.

Prayer loses its weight when relegated to a Sunday service. Away from the mission field it sounds sentimental. Like preaching, prayer away from the front is a facsimile – a static likeness of the life-shattering original. Missionary prayer is different. One apostolic leader reports: *As hour after hour goes by, we all sense, prayer by prayer, an increase in spiritual significance and importance. Our prayers are not heavy – but they are weighty. As we progress eyes brighten. Praise of God rises spontaneously. Mutual encouragement becomes profuse as we prayer for each other by name. Confronting our idols, studying our neighborhoods, we pray with renewed passion.*

When a leader steps out and follows Christ into the field of harvest, they quickly learn the power and purpose of prayer. They find there can be no advance without prayer. There is no defense apart from prayer. Prayer is the hand that wields the sword of the Spirit. Like young David finds out, the fear of battle evaporates in the fields of harvest. Tending sheep is important but this is what God's people are about! Followers will notice. They wake up to the reality of the power of God in the gospel. They come out of the safe confines of study groups into the full light of day, and into the mud and blood of loving, serving and saving those who need it.

On your own, read this article on how George Mueller started his day.

While I was staying at Nailsworth, it pleased the Lord to teach me a truth, irrespective of human instrumentality, as far as I know, the benefit of which I have not lost though now…more than forty years have since passed away.

The point is this: I saw more clearly than ever, that the first great and primary business to which I ought to attend every day was, to have my soul happy in the Lord. The first thing to be concerned about was not how much I might serve the Lord, how I might glorify the Lord; but how I might get my soul into a happy state, and how my inner man might be nourished. For I might seek to set the truth before the unconverted, I might seek to benefit believers. I might seek to relieve the distressed, I might in other ways seek to behave myself as it becomes a child or God in this world; and yet not being happy in the Lord, and not being nourished and strengthened in my inner man day by day, all this might not be attended to in a right spirit.

Before this time my practice had been, at least for ten years previously, as an habitual thing, to give myself to prayer, after having dressed in the morning. *Now* I saw, that the most important thing I had to do was to give myself to the reading of the Word of God and to meditation on it, that thus my heart might be comforted, encouraged, warned, reproved, instructed; and that thus, while meditating, my heart might be brought into experimental, communion with the Lord. I began therefore, to meditate on the New Testament, from the beginning, early in the morning.

The first thing I did, after having asked in a few words the Lord's blessing upon His precious Word, was to begin to meditate on the Word of God; searching, as it were, into every verse, to get blessing out of it; not for the sake of the public ministry of the Word; not for the sake of preaching on what I had meditated upon; but for the sake of obtaining food for my own soul. The result I have found to be almost invariably this, that after a very few minutes my soul has been led to confession, or to thanksgiving, or to intercession, or to supplication; so that though I did not, as it were, give myself to prayer; but to meditation, yet it turned almost immediately more or less into prayer.

When thus I have been for awhile making confession, or intercession, or supplication, or have given thanks, I go on to the next words or verse, turning all, as I go on, into prayer for myself or others, as the Word may lead to it; but still continually keeping before me, that food for my own soul is the object of my meditation. The result of this is, that there is always a good deal of confession, thanksgiving, supplication, or intercession mingled with my meditation, and that my inner man almost invariably is even sensibly nourished and strengthened and that by breakfast time, with rare exceptions, I am in a peaceful if not happy state of heart. Thus also the Lord is pleased to communicate unto me that which, very soon after, I have found to become food for other believers, though it was not for the sake of the public ministry of the Word that I gave myself to meditation, but for the profit of my own inner man.

The difference between my former practice and my present one is this. Formerly, when I rose, I began to pray as soon as possible, and generally spent all my time till breakfast in prayer, or almost all the time. At all events I almost invariably began with prayer.…But what was the result? I often spent a quarter of an hour, or half an hour, or even an hour on my knees, before being conscious to myself of having derived comfort, encouragement, humbling of soul, etc.; and often after having suffered much from wandering of mind for the first ten minutes, or a quarter of an hour, or even half an hour, I only then began *really to pray.*

I scarcely ever suffer now in this way. For my heart being nourished by the truth, being brought into experimental fellowship with God, I speak to my Father, and to my Friend (vile though I am, and unworthy of it!) about the things that He has brought before me in His precious Word.

It often now astonishes me that I did not sooner see this. In no book did I ever read about it. No public ministry ever brought the matter before me. No private intercourse with a brother stirred me up to this matter. And yet now, since God had taught me this point, it is as plain to me as anything that the first thing the child of God has to do morning by morning is to *obtain food for his inner man.*

As the outward man is not fit for work of any length of time, except we take food, as this is one of the first things we do in the morning, so it should be with the inner man. We should take food for that, as everyone must allow. Now what is the food for the inner man; not *prayer*, but the *Word of God*; and here again not the simple reading of the Word of God, so that it only passes through our minds, just as water runs through a pipe, but considering what we read, pondering over it, and applying it to our hearts….

I dwell so particularly on this point because of the immense spiritual profit and refreshment I am conscious of having derived from it myself, and I affectionately and solemnly beseech all my fellow believers to ponder this matter. By the blessings of God I ascribe to this mode the help and strength which I have had from God to pass in peace through deeper trials in various ways than I had ever had before; and after having now above forty years tried this way, I can most fully, in the fear of God, commend it. How different when the soul is refreshed and made happy early in the morning, from what it is when, without spiritual preparation, the service, the trials and the temptations of the day come upon one!

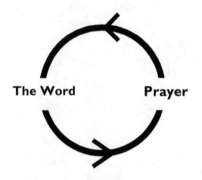

The Word   **Prayer**

As we meditate and feed on the Word of God, the Spirit leads us to prayer and the Word nourishes and guides our prayers. As we continue in prayer, the Spirit leads us back into the Word.

APPLICATION QUESTIONS

For Personal Reflection

1. How can you relate to Mueller's struggles?

For Small Group Discussion

2. *"The first thing the child of God has to do morning by morning is to obtain food for his inner man."* Why is it important to start with obtaining food for the inner man, of finding inner "soul happiness" in the Lord? How have you been doing this?

PRAYER PRACTICE:

On your own: spend a few minutes trying Mueller's method focusing on Psalm 67

¹ May God be gracious to us and bless us and make his face shine upon us,
  Selah ² that your ways may be known on earth,
  your salvation among all nations.
³ May the peoples praise you, may all the peoples praise you.
⁴ May the nations be glad and sing for joy,
  for you rule the peoples justly and guide the nations of the earth.   Selah
⁵ May the peoples praise you, O God; may all the peoples praise you.
⁶ Then the land will yield its harvest, and God, our God, will bless us.
⁷ God will bless us, and all the ends of the earth will fear him.

DEBRIEF QUESTIONS

For Small Group Discussion

3. Debrief your experience using Mueller's method. What did you find helpful?

Borrowing from Jonathan Edwards, we can identify two main hindrances to having a personal prayer life: foolish pride and fear.

1. Foolish Pride

a. We all regularly deal with self-sufficiency.
As a leader, you will be plagued with thoughts that you must work hard, keep blowing air into the balloon and if you stop blowing, it will die. Part of the reason we lack a prayer life is that we falsely believe that we can do it ourselves—we really don't believe we are in that desperate a condition. We need God for some things, but most things in life, well, we can take care of them ourselves.

b. Asking for our own idols and selfish aims to be accomplished.
Most Christians just want God to bless their thing. God doesn't answer prayer that will foster our own idolatry of approval or personal security by having a successful church or ministry.

c. Pray in a legalistic way to get God to do something.
This is the trite saying, "Prayer changes things". So our prayers are limited to telling God what to do and false belief that God has to act on our behalf. We try to put God into our debt, force him to act.

d. Talk about prayer so we can brag about our disciplined life as a leader.
We can make ourselves look good or better than others who don't pray.

Want to experience the presence of God? God is opposed to the proud, self sufficient…but He gives grace to the humble. Be one who wants God to do His Thing through you. So rely on Him in prayer.

2. Fear Factor
The most often repeated command of the Old Testament is "Fear not!"
   a. You find you doubt God. You hear a disturbing little voice in your hearts…*Can you really trust the heart of God? God is not for you. He might be for others, but not you*".
   b. You have a deep sense of disappointment from unanswered prayer
   c. Your sins testify against you.
   d. You are simply not convinced of God's love for you.

3. In contrast, the outcome of gospel prayer is knowing God

"And this is eternal life, that they know you the only True God, and Jesus Christ whom you have sent." John 17:3)

"Prayer increases our capacity for God's gift of himself." Augustine

John Calvin writes that it is vital for us to call or connect to God for several reasons. (re: Institutes 3.20.3)

1. That our hearts may be fired with zealous and burning desire to ever seek, love and serve God.
2. That there may enter our hearts a desire to set all our wishes before his eyes and even pour out our whole hearts to him.
3. That we would be prepared to receive his benefits with true gratitude of heart and thanksgiving.
4. That we would be convinced that what we were seeking did indeed come from his kindness.
5. That we enjoy to a greater degree the things we know came as a result of answered prayer.
6. That God promises never to fail us and extends his hand to help us, defending us with his own presence.

APPLICATION QUESTIONS

For Personal Reflection

7. In these two areas – pride and fear – what are the specific reasons that keep you from praying? What do the expressions of pride and fear look like in your own life?

For Small Group Discussion

8. "Preach the gospel to each other" in response to pride. What is Jesus saying to the proud heart?

9. "Preach the gospel to each other" in response to fear. What is Jesus saying to the fearful heart?

PRAYER PRACTICE:
- Confess and surrender your pride and fear.
- Confess and receive the work of Jesus on the cross on your behalf.
- Ask the Father for a fresh filling of the Spirit and a growing spirit of prayer and dependence.

A. What is an "apostolic" leader?

Apostolic means 'like the apostles', especially Paul.

1. *He is active on the mission field as an evangelist.*
2. *He leads from the field.*
3. *He is an evangelist pastor/ more than a pastor evangelist.*

Personal prayer is at the heart of apostolic mission and ministry
> *"We will devote ourselves to prayer and the ministry of the word"* Acts 6:4

B. Apostolic leaders put prayer first

Apostolic leaders evidence a massive dependency on prayer because they have learned complete dependency on God's Spirit.

> *The soul winner must be a master of the art of prayer. You cannot bring souls to God if you cannot go to God yourself. You must get your battle-ax, and your weapons of war, from the armory of sacred communication with Christ. If you are much alone with Jesus, you will catch his Spirit; you will be fired with the flame that burned in his breast, and consumed with his life. You will weep with the tears that fell upon Jerusalem when He saw it perishing; even if you cannot speak as eloquently as he did, there will be about you somewhat of the same power which in Him thrilled the hearts and awoke the consciences of men."* Charles Spurgeon "The Soul Winner"

Notice how the apostles insist on the priority of prayer (Acts 6:1-7)

> *[1]In those days when the number of disciples was increasing, the Grecian Jews among them complained against the Hebraic Jews because their widows were being overlooked in the daily distribution of food. [2]So the Twelve gathered all the disciples together and said, "It would not be right for us to neglect the ministry of the word of God in order to wait on tables. [3]Brothers, choose seven men from among you who are known to be full of the Spirit and wisdom. <u>We will turn this responsibility over to them [4]and will give our attention to prayer and the ministry of the word."</u>... [7]So the word of God spread. The number of disciples in Jerusalem increased rapidly, and a large number of priests became obedient to the faith.*

Implications of Acts 6 passage:

1. Prayer has equal priority with word ministry
   We will turn this responsibility over to them [4]and will give our attention to prayer and the ministry of the word."...
2. Prayer comes before hands on ministry
   > *"It would not be right for us to neglect the ministry of the word of God in order to wait on tables...we will give our attention to prayer and the ministry of the word"*
   a. Prayer comes first – even though the situation is both urgent and important:
      ...the Grecian Jews among them complained against the Hebraic Jews because their widows were being overlooked in the daily distribution of food.
      Both unity and mercy are at stake here.
   b. In order to create space and time for prayer we need to learn to delegate... "to turn this responsibility over to others..."

How to put the personal priority of prayer into practice

A. Consider Jesus' personal prayer life:

I. Jesus modeled personal prayer
Luke 11:1   One day Jesus was praying in a certain place. When he finished, one of his disciples said to him, "Lord, teach us to pray, just as John taught his disciples."

2. He bathed major decisions in prayer
Luke 6 [12]One of those days Jesus went out to a mountainside to pray, and spent the night praying to God. [13]When morning came, he called his disciples to him and chose twelve of them, whom he also designated apostles

3 . He found restoration with his heavenly father in prayer when ministry became exhausting and chaotic
Luke 5:[15]Yet the news about him spread all the more, so that crowds of people came to hear him and to be healed of their sicknesses. [16]But Jesus often withdrew to lonely places and prayed.

B. Notice the Apostles' prayer life

I. They maintained and modeled that prayer is a highest priority
Acts 1:14 [14]They all joined together constantly in prayer, along with the women and Mary the mother of Jesus, and with his brothers.

Acts 2 [42]They devoted themselves to the apostles' teaching and to the fellowship, to the breaking of bread and to prayer.

Acts 3:1 One day Peter and John were going up to the temple at the time of prayer—at three in the afternoon.

Acts 6:3-4 [3]Brothers, choose seven men from among you who are known to be full of the Spirit and wisdom. We will turn this responsibility over to them [4]and will give our attention to prayer and the ministry of the word.

2. They bathed major decisions in prayer
Acts 13:2,3 [2]While they were worshiping the Lord and fasting, the Holy Spirit said, "Set apart for me Barnabas and Saul for the work to which I have called them." [3]So after they had fasted and prayed, they placed their hands on them and sent them off.

3. The apostles found joy and restoration in the toughest circumstances – in prayer
Acts 16... [22]The crowd joined in the attack against Paul and Silas, and the magistrates ordered them to be stripped and beaten. [23]After they had been severely flogged, they were thrown into prison, and the jailer was commanded to guard them carefully. [24]Upon receiving such orders, he put them in the inner cell and fastened their feet in the stocks. **[25]About midnight Paul and Silas were praying and singing hymns to God, and the other prisoners were listening to them.** *[26]Suddenly there was such a violent earthquake that the foundations of the prison were shaken. At once all the prison doors flew open, and everybody's chains came loose.*

APPLICATION QUESTIONS

For Personal Reflection

4. How well have I placed personal prayer on an equal priority with word ministry?

5. Have I consistently resorted to prayer for important decisions/crossroads?

6. Have I responded to crisis and chaos with seasons of prayer?

For Small Group Discussion

7. Suggest practical ways to avoid the "tyranny of the urgent" in order to maintain the priority of prayer:

    a. When things get busy

    b. When things get overwhelming

PRAYER PRACTICE:
- Confess any neglect of the priority of prayer.
- Thank God for any of the ways that you have been committed to the priority of prayer.
- Pray for a conviction and Spirit of prayer!

HOMEWORK:
- Use Mueller's devotional Word and Prayer method at home this week.
- Read through the material for Lesson 3, concentrating on the readings, the personal reflection questions and prayer practice points.

Leaders Pray the Priorities of the Kingdom

GOALS: In this lesson we will...
- ❑ Explore and pray through the priorities of the Lord's prayer and evaluate our own prayer themes accordingly
- ❑ Build a personal prayer list based on the priorities of the Lord's prayer

Introduction
(See DVD Section 1: Lesson 3A)

Kingdom prayer training brings two things together – the Spirit's passion and the Lord's method. Passion and method go together like a fast flowing river within its banks. The Spirit's passion is the river of prayer. Christ's method is like the banks. To build a river of kingdom passion, we challenge and motivate our heart affections as well as our mind's understanding. The deep and strong love of Jesus leads us to a passionate love for the gospel and for the people we serve in our church and cities. This passion leads to a rigorous gospel analysis, challenging our idols, and prayer walking our city. To build kingdom banks, to guide and direct the Spirit's passion, we apply ourselves to Christ's comprehensive method – the Lord's prayer. Developing a prayer life based on the Lord's prayer directs and sustains a deep and moving prayer life.

Jesus trains his disciples to pray. Jesus often models the practice of prayer which is noticed by the disciples. They notice that John the Baptist trains his disciples to prayer. They want this training too:

> One day Jesus was praying in a certain place. When he finished, one of his disciples
> said to him, "Lord, teach us to pray, just as John taught his disciples."
> He said to them, "When you pray, say:
>> Our father in heaven,
>> Hallowed be your name,
>> Your kingdom come,
>> Your will be done
>> On earth as it is in heaven.
>> Give us this day our daily bread,
>> Forgive us our debts
>> As we forgive our debtors.
>> And lead us not into temptation,
>> But deliver us from the evil one.

The disciples ask Jesus to teach them to pray. They want to learn how to pray. Indeed, they want prayer training. This is what Jesus provides to them and to us.

Like the disciples we need to cry out to Jesus to teach us to pray. We need to review the example and teaching that Jesus provides his disciples. Specifically we need to learn to pray the Lord's Prayer. This article expands the character and application of each petition in the Lord's Prayer.

Priorities in Prayer:
Connecting the Gospel to Prayer and Prayer to Mission
John Smed

The urgent mission of Christ

Once his public ministry starts, Jesus had three years to complete his work of making atonement, and to train the twelve to be fishers of men. To reach a lost world he must engraft in each disciple's mind and soul the inseparable connection between the gospel and prayer, and between prayer and his mission.

Christ's method is people. First, through his disciples, Jesus preaches the wonders of his grace and finished work at the cross. Second, on the readiness of the church to pray to the Lord of the harvest all the hope of the world rests. God has ordained it.

It is no surprise that crucial instruction concerning prayer occurs at the beginning of his training of the disciples. What we call the Lord's prayer – in the Sermon on the Mount (Matthew 6:9-13), comes hard on the heels of the initial call of the disciples (Matthew 4:18-22). This instruction is unsolicited.

We hear this same prayer repeated near the end of their training as well. This time instruction comes at the disciples' urgent request; "Lord, teach us to pray, just as John taught his disciples." (Luke 11:1) Following Jesus, and then going on their own into the harvest, they are now hungry to experience the power and momentum that flow from effective prayer. They have come to realize that the message will stall on frozen lips without the presence and power of Christ's Spirit.

The connection and catalyst which brings gospel understanding and gospel mission together is prayer. *Prayer is the key to boldness, to open doors for the gospel, and to deliverance from evil.*

Not just any prayer will do

Without guidance in this crucial matter of prayer the disciples will flounder in present urgencies and personal problems. To judge from most prayer meetings, the same is true with us. Jesus understands this – <u>we become what we pray</u>. If we pray without aim or purpose our way of life will be directionless. If we pray according to his kingdom priorities and mandate, our life will be transformed into the same.

To encourage and train his followers then and now, Christ gives a comprehensive strategy, a kingdom agenda, and a world-winning purpose in prayer.

> *Our father in heaven,*
> *Hallowed be your name,*
> *Your kingdom come,*
> *Your will be done*
> *On earth as it is in heaven.*
> *Give us this day our daily bread,*
> *Forgive us our debts*
> *As we forgive our debtors.*
> *And lead us not into temptation,*
> *But deliver us from the evil one.*

Before considering each petition separately, it is important to **note the twofold dynamic introduced by Christ in this prayer**. On one hand <u>we pray in order to bring the power and purpose of heaven down to earth.</u> "Thy will be done on earth as it is in heaven." Secondly we are to <u>pray that the coming reality of Christ's future kingdom would be present today.</u> "Thy kingdom come." Essential to purposeful and effective prayer is understanding this: in prayer we bring 'down to earth' the present reign and rule of heaven; in prayer we realize in the present the certain and guaranteed powers of his coming kingdom.

These two forces, from heaven to earth, and from future in time to present in time together inform and energize prayer. The dynamic of the Lord's Prayer can be diagrammed in this way.

How Kingdom Prayer Works
"Thy kingdom come, thy will be done, on earth as it is in heaven."

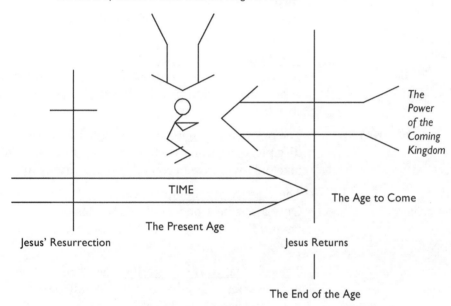

The Power of Christ's Present Rule and Reign in Heaven

The Power of the Coming Kingdom

TIME

The Age to Come

The Present Age

Jesus' Resurrection

Jesus Returns

The End of the Age

> [3]*Praise be to the God and Father of our Lord Jesus Christ, who has blessed us <u>in the heavenly realms with every spiritual blessing</u> in Christ.* [17]*I keep asking that the God of our Lord Jesus Christ, the glorious Father, may give you the Spirit of wisdom and revelation, so that you may know him better.* [18]*I pray also that the eyes of your heart may be enlightened in order that you may know the hope to which he has called you, the riches of his glorious inheritance in the saints,* [19]*and his incomparably great power for us who believe. <u>That power is like the working of his mighty strength,</u>* [20]*<u>which he exerted in Christ when he raised him from the dead and seated him at his right hand in the heavenly realms,</u>* [21]*far above all rule and authority, power and dominion, and every title that can be given, not only in the present age but also in the one to come. ~ Ephesians 1:3, 17-21*

Christ's prayer simply indicates a larger truth; each Christian is, at any and every point, a citizen of God's present and future kingdom. The secret of bold proclamation, indeed of all life and ministry, is to participate in these present and future realities here and now.

All of the priorities of heaven and of Christ's coming kingdom are contained in the petitions of this prayer[1]:

Petition	Priority
Our father in heaven	<u>This is the gospel priority.</u> Before all else we are the legitimate children of God and rightful heirs of his kingdom.
Hallowed be your name	<u>The worship priority.</u> He is the Lord. He is to be revered and obeyed and worshipped before all and in all we do.
Your kingdom come	<u>The evangelism priority.</u> His coming kingdom is surprisingly evidenced in seeing sinners convicted of coming judgement and Christ's atonement.
Your will be done on earth *As it is in heaven*	<u>The priority of obedience especially in mercy and social justice.</u> As with Christ, so with the follower – carrying out and experiencing healing and deliverance in church and society.
Give us this day our daily bread	<u>The priority of generosity and contentment.</u> For a true disciple, everything we have belongs to Christ. We take only what we need and give the rest away.
Forgive us our debts *As we forgive our debtors* our common life.	<u>The priority of redemptive community.</u> Only as we bear one another's burdens will we fulfill the law of Christ and discover the joy of
Lead us not into temptation *from evil*	<u>The spiritual warfare priority.</u> The Christian *deliver us* life is warfare. But the enemy will only be defended against or defeated when the gospel and the mission are connected to prayer.

Concluding applications:

1. Above all we must pray. Here we begin. Here we advance.
2. Not just any prayer will do. Christ has given us the pattern for all prayer.
3. We become what we pray.

---

[1] *For further elaboration on the priorities highlighted here, please see "Seven Days of Prayer with Jesus" by John Smed. Copies of this resource can be ordered by emailing info@prayerforthecity.com*

The Shorter Catechism in Modern English on the Lord's Prayer

This article is a simple memory device for rehearsing the pattern of the Lord's Prayer.

Q. 98. What is prayer?
A.   Prayer is offering our desires to God in the name of Christ for things that agree w[ith His] will, confessing our sins, and thankfully recognizing His mercies.

Q. 99. How does God direct us to pray?
A.   The whole word of God, but especially the Lord's prayer, which Christ taught His disciples, directs our prayers.

Q. 100. What does the beginning of the Lord's prayer teach us?
A.   The beginning of the Lord's prayer *(Our Father in heaven)* teaches us to draw near [to] God with completely holy reverence and confidence, as children to a father who i[s] able and ready to help us. It also teaches that we should pray with and for others.

Q. 101. For what do we pray in the first request?
A.   In the first request *(hallowed be your name)* we pray that God will enable us and oth[ers] to glorify Him in everything He uses to make Himself known and that He will w[ork] out everything to His own glory.

Q. 102. For what do we pray in the second request?
A.   In the second request *(your kingdom come)* we pray that Satan's kingdom may be [destroyed], that the kingdom of grace may be advanced, with ourselves and others brought into and kept in it, and that the kingdom of glory may come quickly.

Q. 103. For what do we pray in the third request?
A.   In the third request *(your will be done on earth as it is in heaven)* we pray that by His grace God would make us have the capability and the will to know, obey, and su[bmit] to His will in everything, as the angels do in heaven.

Q. 104. For what do we pray in the fourth request?
A.   In the fourth request *(Give us today our daily bread)* we pray that we may receive an adequate amount of the good things in this life as a free gift of God and that with them we may enjoy His blessing.

Q. 105. For what do we pray in the fifth request?
A.   In the fifth request *(Forgive us our debts, as we also have forgiven our debtors)*, encouraged by God's grace, which makes it possible for us sincerely to forgive others, we pray that for Christ's sake God would freely pardon all our sins.

Q. 106. For what do we pray in the sixth request?
A.   In the sixth request *(And lead us not into temptation, but deliver us from the evil one)* we pray that God would either keep us from being tempted to sin or support and deliver us when we are tempted.

Q. 107. What does the conclusion of the Lord's prayer teach us?
A.   The conclusion of the Lord's prayer *(for yours is the kingdom and the power and the glory forever)* teaches us to be encouraged only by God in our prayers and to praise Him by acknowledging that kingdom, power, and glory are His. To show that we want to be heard and have confidence that we are, we say *Amen.*

In this article, Martin Luther explains to his barber the power and purpose of praying the Lord's Prayer. His prayers reflect the reality of spiritual warfare being all about the coming kingdom of Christ and his mission. Despite the reality of a fallen world, he yearns for redemption. This is a good example of one expression of praying through the Lord's prayer.

A Simple Way to Pray

Martin Luther in a letter to his barber

Prayer According to God's Command and Promise

I pray in the name of my Lord Jesus Christ together with all your saints and Christians on earth as He has taught us:

Our Father in heaven, Hallowed be Your name. Your kingdom come, Your will be done, On earth as it is in heaven. Give us this day our daily bead. And forgive us our debts, As we forgive our debtors. And do not lead us into temptation, But deliver us from the evil one. For Yours is the kingdom and the power and the glory forever. Amen (Matthew 6:5-13)

The first petition: *Hallowed be your name*

For the Destruction of False Teachings

Yes, Lord God, dear Father, hallowed be Your name, both in us and throughout the whole world. Destroy and root out the abominations, idolatry, and heresy of all false teachers and fanatics who wrongly use Your name in scandalous ways and in vain and horribly blaspheme it. They insistently boast that they teach Your word and the laws of the church, though they really use the devil's deceit and trickery in Your name to wretchedly seduce many poor souls throughout the world, even killing and shedding much innocent blood, and in such persecution they believe that they render You a divine service.

The second petition: *Your Kingdom come*

Dear Lord, God and Father, convert them and defend us. Convert those who are still to become children and members of Your kingdom so that they with us and we with them may serve You in Your kingdom in true faith and unfeigned love and that from Your kingdom which has begun, we may enter into Your eternal kingdom. Defend us against those who will not turn away their might and power from the destruction of Your kingdom so that when they are cast down from their thrones and humbled, they will have to cease from their efforts. Amen.

The third petition: *Your will be done on earth as it is in heaven*

For Help to Do God's Will

O dear Lord, God and Father, You know that the world, if it cannot destroy Your name or root out Your kingdom, is busy day and night with wicked tricks and schemes, strange conspiracies and intrigue, huddling together in secret counsel, giving mutual encouragement and support, raging and threatening and going about with every evil intention to destroy Your name, word, kingdom, and children. Therefore, dear Lord, God and Father, convert them and defend us. Convert those who have yet to acknowledge Your good will that they with us and we with them may obey Your will and for Your sake gladly, patiently, and joyously bear every evil, cross, and adversity, and thereby acknowledge, test, and experience Your benign, gracious and perfect will. But defend us against those who in their rage, fury, hate, threats, and evil desires do not cease to do us harm. Make their wicked schemes, tricks, and devices come to nothing so that these may be turned against them, as we sing, "His mischief returns upon his own head, and on his own pate his violence descends."

The fourth petition: *Give us today our daily bread*
For Peace and Good Government

Dear Lord, God and Father, grant us Your blessing also in this temporal and physical life. Graciously grant us blessed peace. Protect us against war and disorder. Grant to our dear emperor fortune and success against his enemies. Grant him wisdom and understanding to rule over his earthly kingdom in peace and prosperity. Grant to all rulers good counsel and the will to preserve their domains and their subjects in tranquility and justice. Amen.

For Protection for Home and Family

Oh, God, grant that all people – in city and country – be diligent and display charity and loyalty toward each other. Give us favorable weather and good harvest. I commend to You my house and property, wife and children. Grant that I may manage and guide them well, supporting and educating them as a Christian should. Defend us against the Destroyer and all his wicked angels who would do us harm and mischief in this life. Amen.

The fifth petition: *Forgive us our debts as we forgive our debtors*
For God's Mercy

O dear Lord, God and Father, enter not into judgment against us because no person living is justified before You. Do not count it against us as a sin that we are so unthankful for Your ineffable goodness, spiritual and physical, or that we stray into sin many times everyday, more often than we can know or recognize. Do not look upon how good or how wicked we have been but only upon the infinite compassion which You have bestowed upon us in Christ, Your dear Son. Amen.

For Our Enemies

Also grant forgiveness to those who have harmed or wronged us, as we forgive them from our hearts. They inflict the greatest injury upon themselves by arousing Your anger in their actions toward us. We are not helped by their ruin; we would much rather that they be saved with us. Amen.

The sixth petition: *Lead us not into temptation*
For Triumph Over the Devil

Oh dear Lord, Father and God, keep us fit and alert, eager and diligent in Your Word and service, so that we do not become complacent, lazy, and slothful as though we had already achieved everything. In that way the fearful devil cannot fall upon us, surprise us, and deprive us of Your precious Word or stir up strife and factions among us and lead us into other sin and disgrace, both spiritually and physically. Rather grant us wisdom and strength through Your Spirit that we may valiantly resist him and gain the victory. Amen.

The seventh petition: *And deliver us from evil*
For Help to Pass Safely through Dangers

O dear Lord, God and Father, this wretched life is so full of misery and calamity, of danger and uncertainty, so full of malice and faithlessness, as St. Paul says, "The days are evil." We might rightfully grow weary of life and long for death. But You, dear Father, know our frailty; therefore, help us to pass in safety through so much wickedness and villainy; and, when our last hour comes, in Your mercy grant us a blessed departure from this vale of sorrows so that in the face of death we do not become fearful or despondent, but in firm faith commit our souls into Your hands. Amen.

The Amen

Finally, mark this, that you must always speak the Amen firmly. Never doubt that God in His mercy will surely hear you and say "yes" to your prayers. Never think that you are kneeling or standing alone, rather think that the whole of Christendom, all devout Christians, are standing there beside you and you are standing among them in a common, united petition which God cannot disdain. Do not leave your prayer without having said or thought, "Very well, God has heard my prayer; this I know as a certainty and a truth." That is what Amen means.

Concluding Counsel

You should also know that I do not want you to recite all these words in your prayer. That would make it nothing but idle chatter and prattle. Rather do I want your heart to be stirred and guided concerning the thoughts which ought to be comprehended in the Lord's Prayer. These thoughts may be expressed, if your heart is rightly warmed and inclined toward prayer, in many different ways and with more words or fewer.

I do not bind myself to such words or syllables, but say my prayers in one fashion today, in another tomorrow, depending upon my mood and feeling. I stay however, as nearly as I can, with the same general thoughts and ideas. It may happen occasionally that I may get lost among so many ideas in one petition that I forego the other six.

If such an abundance of good thoughts comes to us, we ought to disregard the other petitions, make room for such thoughts, listen in silence, and under no circumstances obstruct them. The Holy Spirit Himself preaches here, and one word of His sermon is far better than a thousand of our prayers. Many times I have learned more from one prayer than I might have learned from much reading and speculation.

It is of great importance that the heart be made ready and eager for prayer. As Sirach says, "Prepare your heart for prayer, and do not tempt God." What else is it but tempting God when your mouth babbles and the mind wanders to other thoughts? Like the cleric who prayed, "Make haste, O God to deliver me. Farmhand, did you unhitch the horses? Make haste, O God to help me, O Lord. Maid, go out and milk the cow. Glory be to the Father and to the Son and to the Holy Spirit. Hurry up, boy, I wish the ague would take you!" I have heard many such prayers in the past. This is blasphemy! It would be better if they played rather than prayed if they cannot or do not care to do better. In my day I have prayed many such canonical hours myself, regrettably, and in such a manner that the psalm or the allotted time came to an end before I even realized whether I was at the beginning or the middle.

It seems to me that if we could see what arises as prayer from a cold and inattentive heart we would conclude that we had never seen a more notorious kind of buffoonery. But, praise God, it is now clear to me that those who forget what they have said have not prayed well. In a good prayer one fully remembers every word and thought from the beginning to the end of the prayer.

So, a good and attentive barber keeps his thoughts, attention, and eyes on the razor and hair and does not forget how far he has gotten with his shaving or cutting. If he wants to engage in too much conversation or let his mind wander or look somewhere else, he is likely to cut his customer's mouth, nose, or even his throat. Thus if anything is to be done well, it requires the full attention of all one's senses and members, as the proverb says, "The one who thinks of many things, thinks of nothing and does nothing right." How much more does prayer call for concentration and singleness of heart if it is to be a good prayer!

This in short is the way I use the Lord's Prayer when I pray it. To this day I suckle at the Lord's Prayer like a child, and as an old man eat and drink from it and never get my fill. It is the very best prayer, even better than the Psalter, which is so very dear to me. It is surely evident that a real master composed and taught it. What a great pity that the prayer of such a master is prattled and chattered so irreverently all over the world! How many pray the Lord's Prayer several thousand times in the course of a year, and if they were to keep on doing so for a thousand years they would not have tasted nor prayed one iota, one "jot and little" of it! In a word, the Lord's Prayer is the greatest martyr on earth (as are the name and word of God). Everybody tortures and abuses it; few take comfort and joy in its proper use.

APPLICATION QUESTIONS
For Personal Reflection

1. What priorities and themes currently drive your prayer life? How do these compare to the priorities in the Lord's Prayer?

2. How do you think your life might change if you pray intentionally and regularly through the priorities of the Lord's prayer?

For Small Group Discussion

3. What priorities and themes currently drive the prayer life of your church/ministry

4. How might your church's life and mission be different if you pray intentionally and regularly toward the kingdom priorities of the Lord's Prayer?

5. Brainstorm ways we can incorporate this pattern in our lives and ministries.

PRAYER PRACTICE:
- **In class,** form in small groups of 3-4 people and <u>pray conversationally</u> through the priorities of the Lord's prayer (one petition per person).
- **On your own at home,** have an extended prayer time once this week using the Lord's prayer pattern by writing your own version, as Luther does here. Alternatively, take a current problem or challenge you are facing personally. Write out a prayer using the Lord's prayer as a lens for praying through the challenge.

- Prayer lists are a helpful tool to help you **map your life** and see God change you (and the world around you) through prayer.

- A prayer list **uses the Lord's prayer as a framework to give direction and purpose** to your prayer life. A prayer list helps you see how the people, places and things you are praying for fit into the bigger picture of God's plan. It guards your prayer life from being overtaken by self-centred prayer or primarily pressing needs.

- **You are what you pray:** A good prayer list will reflect who you are, and the calling, priorities and passions God has shaped in you.

- **What you pray is what you become:** An even better prayer list will reflect who God is shaping you to become. As you meet with God in prayer, He will transform you and motivate you to Kingdom vision, purpose and priorities.

- Like a fitness plan or a carpenter's tool, your prayer list is most useful when you sharpen it continually. Your list will need to be adjusted as God changes you/your heart through prayer, as He makes your passions and calling clearer, and as people, needs and circumstances in your life change.

- A prayer list is in **process** just as we are in process. It is organic. It should be growing and connected to your life. While it is clearly not a substitute for your relationship with God, it is one way of marking growth and alignment of our lives to Christ's priorities.

- A prayer list helps you to simply **manage the volume** of prayer needs, to bless others, and to not "sin against them" by forgetting to pray or to find "you have not because you ask not."

QUESTIONS

For Small Group Discussion

6. What methods have you tried before to keep prayer regular? What help or hindrances did you experience?

7. What other benefits (in addition to those stated above) can you see of using a prayer list?

8. What anticipations/apprehensions do you currently have about using a prayer list?

		Day 1	Day 2	Day 3	Day 4	Day 5	Day 6	Day 7
1	Reminder Row	✓	✓					
2	**Pattern** for request	Our Father in heaven	Our Father, Holy is your name	Our Father, Your kingdom come	Our Father, Your will be done on earth as it is in heaven	Our Father, Give us this day our daily bread	Our Father, Forgive us our debts as we forgive our debtors	Our Father, Lead us not into temptation, deliver us from evil
	Priority of prayer	Sonship	Worship	Evangelism	Mercy Social Justice	Generosity Contentment	Unity Reconciliation	Warfare
3	Prayers for **Passions** of my heart (heart affections)	release guilt embrace joy	see how my sins hurt God's heart	compassion to see people as God does different patience	empathy to relate with others different than me	gratitude release greed	willingness to let go of my grudges	wisdom & strength to make wise choices
4	Key **Person**	Mom	Worship Leader	Spouse	Outreach Leader	sister	church leaders	brother
5	Prayers for **Petitions** (people, plans, etc.)	friend who just became a Christian	worship team community art show	conversations w/ co-workers opportunity to meet my neighbours summer mission trip	friend's depression my sponsor child soup kitchen friends	budgeting volunteer fundraising drive opportunities to give	bible study groups family conflict	resist my temptations friend's struggle with addiction spiritual protection for church
6	**Pressing** urgent requests				friend's struggle with cancer	unemployed friend to find a job	friend's divorce	
7	**Praise** for answers to my prayers	new sense of joy		going out with co-workers for lunch now		friend found work!		

* Handwritten notes are sample items. **For an electronic blank template of the list, email info@prayercurrent.com

This prayer list provides a sequence to pray through one of the Lord's Prayer priorities one day at a time:

1. Reminder Row: Pray through one priority / column a day. Make a check mark at the top of the column to help pray through all priorities in a balanced way. This frees you from a rigid Monday – Sunday schedule and allows the list to be left on some days, with the confidence you will soon get back to it.

2. Pray the Kingdom Pattern/Priority: Meditate on the priority. Your prayer life arranged according to the priorities grows you to see how his kingdom expresses itself uniquely in your life. It is comprehensive enough to include all your requests!

3. Pray for Kingdom Passions (Heart Affections): Next, allow God enough time to thoroughly examine and encourage your heart affections according to His priorities and the values. The goal here is heart transformation through relationship with Jesus.

4. Pray for Key People: Next, pray for the key people you want to spend concentrated prayer on. For example, family members, key ministry leaders, and high priority relationships. Also include a day for just yourself and personal needs.

5. Pray for Petitions (Intercession): Pray for individuals, churches, ministries (including plans), etc., especially those that are related to the priorities (eg. pray for seekers, evangelists and outreaches on "your Kingdom come").

6. Pray for Pressing Needs (Urgent Requests): Pray for urgent needs in your life, of your church and others in your life. Saving these for the end gives them a place without having them dominate your prayer time.

7. Praise (for Answers to Prayer): Recognize that answers to your prayers builds faith and momentum to keep praying. This reminds us of God's character, power and faithfulness.

PRAYER PRACTICE:

The practice of praying through one petition (column) of the Lord's prayer using sequence is a dynamic process of dialogue with God. We will pray through "Your Kingdom Come" (the evangelism priority) to get a taste of the flow of the types of prayer that make up the list.

Use the following guides to lead you through the sequence of the prayer list.
These guidelines are written for use in class time – alternating times of individual and group prayer – but can also be used to guide your personal prayer time.

1. **Pattern and Priority** of Evangelism
   - In groups of 3, pray short sentence "arrow" prayers of praise.
     i. Ponder the kingship and lordship of Jesus in your life and city.
     ii. Consider his heart for people to surrender to Jesus' kingship.
2. **Passions of the Heart** related to Evangelism
   - On your own:
     i. Ask the Holy spirit to *search your heart*
     ii. Thank him for *growth* in concern for the eternal welfare of others
     iii. Confess your *weakness or coldness* of heart
     iv. Ask the Spirit to fill you and *change your heart to align to His heart*
3. **Prayers and Petitions for Other People**
   - In your groups:
     i. Pray for *seekers* you know to be found by the King!
     ii. Pray for *other believers, ministries, churches and outreach initiatives* to be actively sharing Christ (Paul prays for boldness, open doors and protection from evil)
     iii. Pray for *church planting* efforts in your region/nation
4. **Pressing Needs**
   - "Korean style"… everyone out loud all at once:
     i. Pray for *current outreach efforts* and *present opportunities* and *future open doors* you have to share Christ with those around you
5. **Praise**
   - In your groups:
     i. Praise God for his power and *sovereignty in saving* people and answering prayer
     ii. Praise him for any *fruitful conversations* or interactions you have recently seen

DEBRIEF QUESTIONS

For Large Group Discussion

9. What are your observations/reactions to the process of praying through a sequence like this list?

10. What effect did having a clear priority and pattern/sequence have on your prayers?

1. On your own, take a few minutes to begin your prayer list. Start by listing various people and needs as they come to mind. (Do not worry about classifying them just yet; we will do that in the next step).

    Who are the key relationships in your life you desire to regularly pray for (eg. spouse, children, ministry partner, etc.)

    What priorities/passions/issues are naturally and regularly on your heart that you feel burdened to pray for?

    Who are people that God has placed in your sphere of influence to pray for
    (both believers and non-believers)?

    What ministries, churches, groups, missionaries, etc. are you burdened or committed to pray for?

    What other needs do you feel led to pray for?

2. Now begin to place the various items you have listed above into related parts of your list.
   - Organize and complete it in ways that make sense to you.
   - Do not feel pressed to fill every space. Let the Spirit guide you in what to include, add and remove.
   - Try praying through two or three columns this week.
   - Plan when you will pray with the list. Where in the rhythm of your life can you incorporate it? (e.g. during devotions, commuting, at the gym, etc.)

PRAYER LIST							
reminder (x)							
Pattern	Our Father in heaven	Holy is your Name	Your kingdom come	Your will be done on earth	Give us this day our daily br.	Forgive Us our Debts	Lead us deliver us
Priority	Sonship	Worship	Evangelism	Mercy	Today's Needs	Unity	Warfare
Passions (Heart Affections)							
Key Person							
People, Places **Petitions** (Intercession)							
Pressing Needs (Urgent)							
Praise (for Answers)							

A Gospel Reminder

Remain grounded in the gospel as you develop this new habit. It is not unusual to encounter resistance in forming a new habit, especially one with deep spiritual impact such as this one. These are simply tools to serve us, not enslave us.

Remember the goal is to know God and his heart and to let be known by him. Let the Spirit and Scripture lead you – in praise, confession, listening prayer, intercession.

HOMEWORK:

- Pray through the Lord's Prayer in its entirety at least once this week.
- Finish building your prayer list and try praying through more than one priority/column this week.
- Read through the material for Lesson 4, concentrating on the readings, the personal reflection questions and prayer practice points.

Leaders Pray for Gospel Transformation

GOALS: In this lesson we will...
- ❏ Pray Paul's kingdom prayers for spiritual transformation in each other's lives
- ❏ Identify our obstacles to true gospel transformation
- ❏ Confess our challenges in prayer and apply the gospel to them

Introduction   (See DVD Section 1: Lesson 4)

According to Augustine, prayer is "the soul's articulation of its longing for God." He adds, "In prayer God increases our capacity for God's gift of himself." Prayer and spiritual transformation are deeply integrated. In fact, there can be little or no inner renewal apart from prayer.

In this lesson we will learn to focus on praying for spiritual transformation.

We will begin by praying a blessing into each others lives. The Scriptures are filled with prayers of benediction. Benedictions are words of generous blessing from God.

Jesus' high priestly prayer in John 17 is an extended prayer of benediction for his disciples. It is filled with prayers for spiritual transformation.

> [15]*My prayer is not that you take them out of the world but that you protect them from the evil one.* [16]*They are not of the world, even as I am not of it.* [17]*Sanctify them by the truth; your word is truth.* [18]*As you sent me into the world, I have sent them into the world.* [19]*For them I sanctify myself, that they too may be truly sanctified.*

Jesus continues to bless us in prayer today. When Jesus ascends to heaven, we read, 'He lifted up his hands to bless them and was taken up to heaven'. He continues to pray for our transformation today. As he sits at the right hand of God, "He ever lives to make intercession'.

We need to learn to bless each other in prayer. Nothing is more encouraging than when a brother or sister prays for you by name and asks God to fill you with every spiritual blessing. In this lesson we will bless each other in prayer. We will use Paul's many prayers for the churches as a pattern and guide.

As we look at the apostle Paul's prayers for others, in the first exercise of this week, we note virtually all of his prayers are filled with the priority of spiritual transformation for churches and Christians.

Then with the fullness of the Spirit of God in us in answer to these prayers of blessing, we have the confidence and courage to prayerfully search our own hearts and face our own enemies of spiritual transformation. After all, it is spiritual fullness and Christ himself that counters all enemies of the Spirit's work of transformation. The abbreviated "Preface to Galatians" is a vaccine of the soul as we embark on this inner search.

In looking at Paul's prayers for others, we are provided with numerous biblical examples of prayer for spiritual transformation They are notably different than how he prays for himself (see Lesson 6).

PRAYER PRACTICE:

We will learn how to pray kingdom prayers for others by praying through Paul's prayers for others. We will do so in a "concert of prayer" format, alternating back and forth between reading Scripture together and praying the Scripture just read.

For each grouping of Paul's prayers listed here:

- *As a large group,* **read together** the verses and observations listed.
- *In small groups of 3,* **pray in response** to the guidelines listed in each grey "prayer box" corresponding to what was just read.

I Give thanks for other believers

A. He prays for their manifest experience of and growth in faith

- "I thank God, whom I serve, as my forefathers did, with a clear conscience, as night and day I constantly remember you in my prayers…. I have been reminded of your sincere faith, which first lived in your grandmother Lois and in your mother Eunice and, I am persuaded, now lives in you also." – 2 Timothy 1:3, 5

- "We always thank God for all of you, mentioning you in our prayers. We continually remember before our God and Father your work produced by faith, your labour prompted by love and your endurance inspired by hope in our Lord Jesus Christ." – 1 Thessalonians 1:2-3

- "We always thank God, the Father of our Lord Jesus Christ, when we pray for you, because we have heard of your faith in Christ Jesus and of the love you have for all the saints" – Colossians 1:3-4

B. He gives thanks for their "fellowship in the gospel" and for the love they have "for all the saints"

- " I thank my God every time I remember you. In all my prayers for all of you, I always pray with joy because of your partnership in the gospel from the first day until now." – Philippians 1:3-5

- "For this reason, ever since I heard about your faith in the Lord Jesus and your love for all the saints, I have not stopped giving thanks for you, remembering you in our prayers." – Ephesians 1:15-16

- "We ought always to thank God for you, brothers, and rightly so, because your faith is growing more and more, and the love every one of you has for each other is increasing." – 2 Thessalonians 1:3

C. He gives praise and thanks for the word "sounding forth" from them

- "You became a model to all the believers in Macedonia and Achaia. The Lord's message rang out from you not only in Macedonia and Achaia – your faith in God has become known everywhere." 2 Thessalonians 1:7-8

- "First, I thank my God through Jesus Christ for all of you, because your faith is being reported all over the world." – Romans 1:8

II. Learn to pray ceaselessly for brothers and sisters

- "I <u>have not stopped</u> giving thanks for you, remembering you in my prayers. <u>I keep asking</u> that the God of our Lord Jesus Christ, the glorious Father, may give you the Spirit of wisdom and revelation." -- Ephesians 1:16

- "For this reason, since the day we heard about you, <u>we have not stopped praying for you</u>." Colossians 1:9

- "I thank God, whom I serve, as my forefathers did, with a clear conscience, as night and day I <u>constantly remember you in my prayers</u>." – 2 Timothy 1:3

- "<u>We constantly pray for you</u>, that our God may count you worthy of his calling, and that by his power he may fulfill every good purpose of yours and every act prompted by your faith." 2 Thessalonians 1:11

> In groups of 3, **pray** together:
> - Give thanks and pray a blessing for:
>   - **believers** in your life: leaders, peers, disciples, children, family members
>   - **outreach** ministries, evangelism efforts and urban missions. Pray for each other's personal mission fields and opportunities for witness.
> - **Pray for prayer**, so that our prayer is ceaseless, ask God to bless and pour out a spirit of prayer (Zech. 12:10-13:2) on your leaders and on each other. Pray that we might "devote ourselves to prayer and the word" (Acts 6:4), be watchmen (Isaiah 62:7) who pray without ceasing for God's people and mission. Pray for your church to become a "house of prayer for all nations" (Isaiah 56:6-7)

III. Pray for grace and holiness to abound in each believer and church

A. <u>Paul prays that they might be blameless in life</u>

- "May he strengthen your hearts so that <u>you will be blameless and holy</u> in the presence of our God and Father when our Lord Jesus comes with all his holy ones." 1 Thessalonians 3:13

- "He will keep you strong to the end, so that <u>you will be blameless</u> on the day of our Lord Jesus Christ." – 1 Corinthians 1:8

- "We pray this in order that you may live a <u>life worthy of the Lord</u> and <u>may please him in every way</u>: bearing fruit in every good work, growing in the knowledge of God." Colossians 1:10

B. <u>He prays that their love may abound more and more</u>

- "And this is my prayer: that your <u>love may abound more and more</u> in knowledge and depth of insight." – Philippians 1:9

- "And I pray that you, being <u>rooted and established in love</u>, may have power together with all the saints, to grasp how wide and long and high and deep is the love of Christ, and to know this love that surpasses knowledge – that you may be filled to the measure of all the fullness of God." -- Ephesians 3:17-19

C. <u>He prays for them to grow in the Word and in spiritual knowledge</u>

- "And I pray that you, being rooted and established in love, may have power together with all the saints, to grasp how wide and long and high and deep is the love of Christ, and to <u>know this love that surpasses knowledge</u> – that you may be filled to the measure of all the fullness of God." – Ephesians 3:17-19

- "I pray also that the eyes of your heart may be enlightened in order that you may <u>know the hope to which he has called you</u>, the riches of his glorious inheritance in the saints, and his incomparably great power for us who believe." – Ephesians 1:18-19
- "I pray that you may be active in sharing your faith so that you will have a full understanding of every good thing we have in Christ Jesus" Philemon 6

> In groups of 3, **pray** together:
> - Give thanks and pray for grace in spiritual knowledge.
>   - Pray for **fellowship and small groups**, prayer accountability groups, discipleship relationships, etc. to form an umbrella of prayer and care as a defence against Satan and as an advance of the gospel. Pray for those who struggle with addictions.
>   - Pray for the ministries of **teaching and preaching** and those who serve there.

IV. Pray that they may be filled with Christ, his presence and power

A. <u>He prays that they might be filled with Christ himself</u>

- "And this is my prayer: that your love may abound more and more in knowledge and depth of insight, so that you may be able to discern what is best and may be pure and blameless until the day of Christ, <u>filled with the fruit of righteousness</u> that comes through Jesus Christ." – Philippians 1:9-11
- "I pray that out of his glorious riches he may strengthen you with power through his Spirit in your inner being, <u>so that Christ may dwell in your hearts</u> through faith… – that <u>you may be filled to the measure of all the fullness of God</u>." – Ephesians 3:16-19

B. <u>He prays that they may experience God's power</u>

- "We pray this in order that you may live a life worthy of the Lord and may please him in every way: bearing fruit in every good work, growing in the knowledge of God, being <u>strengthened with all power according to his glorious might</u> so that you may have great endurance and patience." – Colossians 1:10-11
- "I pray also that the eyes of your heart may be enlightened in order that you may know the hope to which he has called you, the riches of his glorious inheritance in the saints, and <u>his incomparably great power</u> for us who believe. That power is like the <u>working of his mighty strength</u>, which he exerted in Christ when he raised him from the dead and seated him at his right hand in the heavenly realms." – Ephesians 1:18-20

V. Pray for all the credit to go to Christ

A. <u>He prays that they may glorify God</u>

- "And this is my prayer: that your love may abound more and more in knowledge and depth of insight, so that you may be able to discern what is best and may be pure and blameless until the day of Christ – <u>to the glory and praise of God</u>." – Philippians 1:9-11

> In groups of 3, **pray:**
> - Pray for a fresh filling of the Spirit and for God to deliver us from our idols that rob Him of our worship.
> - Pray for our **worship** ministries to be completely Christ-centric.
> - Close your prayers with a time of short **prayers of praise**, worshiping God.

Martin Luther, (abridgement and paraphrase by Tim Keller) Version 2.0

1. The most important thing in the world

a. The one doctrine which I have supremely at heart, is that of faith in Christ, from whom, through whom, and unto whom all my theological thinking flows back and forth day and night. This rock… which we call the doctrine of justification… was shaken by Satan in paradise, when he persuaded our first parents that they might by their own wisdom and power become like God…. Thereafter the whole world acted like a madman against this faith, inventing innumerable idols and religions with which everyone went his own way, hoping to placate a god or goddess, by his own works; that is, hoping without the aid of Christ and by his own works to redeem himself from evils and sins. All this is sufficiently seen in the practices and records of every culture and nation….

b. The devil our adversary, who continually rages about seeking to devour us is not dead. Likewise our flesh and old man is yet alive. Besides this, all kinds of temptations vex and oppress us on every side, *so that this doctrine can never be taught, urged and repeated enough.* If this doctrine is lost, then is also the whole knowledge of truth, life and salvation lost; if this doctrine flourish, then all good things flourish…

2. Kinds of righteousness

a. Paul expounds the Biblical doctrine with the goal of demonstrating beyond doubt the difference between <u>Christian</u> righteousness and all other kinds of righteousness, for there are many kinds. First, there is political or *civil righteousness* – the nation's public laws – which magistrates and lawyers may defend and teach. Second, there is *cultural righteousness* – the standards of our family and social grouping or class – which parents and schools may teach. Third, there is *ethical righteousness* – the Ten Commandments and law of God – which the church may teach (but only in light of <u>Christian</u> righteousness). [Now it is right to be a good citizen, to be loved and respected by your social group, and to be a morally upright person. So all these may be received without danger]. If we attribute to them no power to satisfy for sin, to please God or to deserve grace… These kinds of righteousness are gifts of God, like all good things we enjoy….

b. Yet there is another, far above the others, which the apostle Paul calls "the righteousness of faith"– Christian righteousness…. God imputes it to us apart from our works – in other words, it is **passive righteousness,** as the others are **active.** For we <u>do</u> nothing for it, and we <u>give</u> nothing for it – we only receive and allow another to work – that is God.

3. The need for Christian righteousness

a. This "passive" righteousness is a mystery that the world cannot understand. Indeed, Christians never completely understand it themselves, and thus do not take advantage of it when they are troubled and tempted. So we have to constantly teach it, repeat it, and work it out in practice. For anyone who does not understand this righteousness or cherish it in the heart and conscience, will continually be buffeted by fears and depression. *Nothing gives peace like this passive righteousness.*

b. For human beings by nature, when they get near either danger or death itself, will of necessity view their own worthiness. We <u>defend</u> ourselves before all threats by recounting our good deeds and moral efforts. But then the remembrance of sins and flaws inevitably comes to mind, and this tears us apart, and we think: "How many errors and sins and wrongs have I done! Please God, let me live so I can fix and amend things." We become obsessed with our <u>active</u> righteousness and are terrified by its imperfections. But the real evil is that we trust our own power to be righteous and will not lift up our eyes to see what Christ has done <u>for</u> us…. So the troubled conscience has no cure for its desperation and feeling of unworthiness unless it takes hold of the forgiveness of sins by <u>grace,</u> offered free of charge in Jesus Christ, which is this passive or Christian righteousness… If I tried to fulfill the law myself, I could not trust in what I had accomplished, neither could it stand up to the judgment of God. So … *I rest only upon the righteousness of Christ… which I do not <u>produce</u> but <u>receive</u>; God the Father freely giving it to us through Jesus Christ."*

4. Law and Grace

a. It is an absolute and unique teaching in all the world, to teach people, through Christ, to live as if there were no Law or Wrath or Punishment. In a sense, they do not exist anymore for the Christian, but only total grace and mercy for Christ's sake. Once you are in Christ, the law is the greatest guide for your life, but until you have Christian righteousness, all the law can do is to show you how sinful and condemned you are. In fact, to those outside of Christian righteousness, the law needs to be expounded in all its force. Why? So that people who think they have the power to be righteous before God will be humbled.

b. Therefore the communicator of the Word of God must be careful when dispensing the knowledge of both law and grace. We must keep the law within his bounds! If you teach that we can be accepted by God through obedience, then Christian righteousness becomes mixed up with earned/moral righteousness in the people's minds. Such a teacher is an ill logician – failing to "rightly divide." On the other hand, if you teach to persons outside of Christ about God's acceptance and love, with no mention of repentance and the cross of Christ, you also confuse and fail to "rightly divide." Rather, he that applies the law and works to the flesh or the old man [the unconverted], and who applies forgiveness of sins and God's mercy to the spirit or the new man [the awakened by the Spirit] does well.

c. For example, when I see a man that is bruised, oppressed with the law, terrified with sin, and thirsting for comfort, it is time to remove out of his sight the law and active righteousness, and that I should set before him by the Gospel the Christian and passive righteousness. Then the man is raised up and realizes the hope of being under grace, not under the law (Romans 6:14)… But upon the man without Christ there must be laid the obligation of works and the law – we *do* have to fulfill the law. This burden must press him down until he put on the new man, by faith in Christ – then he may enjoy the freedom of the spirit of grace. (Nevertheless, no one fully odes this in this life!)

d. Therefore, no one should think we reject the importance of good works or of obeying the Law. When we receive the Christian righteousness, we consequently can live a good life, naturally, out of gratitude. If we try to earn our righteousness by <u>doing</u> many good deeds, we actually do nothing. We neither please God through our works-righteousness <u>nor</u> do we honour the purpose for which the law was given. But if we first receive Christian righteousness, then we can use the law, <u>not</u> for our salvation, but for his honour and glory, and to lovingly show our gratitude.

e. So have we nothing to <u>do</u> to obtain this righteousness? No, *nothing at all!* For this righteousness comes by doing nothing, hearing nothing, knowing nothing, but rather in knowing and believing this only – that Christ has gone to the right hand of the Father, not to become our judge, but to become for us, our wisdom, our righteousness, our holiness, our salvation! Now God sees no sin in us, for in this heavenly righteousness sin has no place. So now we may certainly think: "Although I still sin, I don't despair, because Christ lives, who is both my righteousness and my eternal life." In that righteousness I have no sin, no fear, no guilty conscience, no fear of death. I am indeed a sinner in this life of mine and in my own righteousness, but I have another life, another righteousness above this life, which is in Christ, the Son of God, who knows no sin or death, but is eternal righteousness and eternal life.

5. Living the gospel

a. Now both these things continue while we live here. We are accused, exercised with temptations, oppressed with heaviness and sorrow, and bruised by the law with its demands of active righteousness. These attacks fall upon our "flesh" [– the part of our heart that still seeks to earn our salvation]… Because of this, Paul sets out in this letter of Galatians to teach us, to comfort us, and to keep us constantly aware of this Christian righteousness. For if the truth of being *justified by Christ alone* (not by our works) is lost, then all Christian truths are lost. For there is no middle ground between Christian righteousness and works-righteousness. There is no other alternative to Christian righteousness <u>but</u> works-righteousness; if you do not build your confidence on the work of Christ you must build your confidence on your own work. On this truth and <u>only</u> on this truth the church is built and has its being…

b. *This distinction is easy to utter in words, but in use and experience is very hard.* So you who would be teachers and counselors of others I admonish to exercise yourselves continually in these matters through study, reading, meditation on the Word and prayer – that in the time of trial you will be able to both **inform** and **comfort** both your conscience and others, to bring them from law to grace, from active/works-righteousness to passive/Christ's righteousness. For in times of struggle, the devil will seek to terrify us by using against us our past record, the wrath, and law of God. So if we cannot see the differences between the two kinds of righteousness, and if we do not take hold of Christ by faith, sitting at the right hand of God (Hebrews 7:25) who pleads our case, sinners that we are, to the Father, then we are under the Law, not under grace, and Christ is no Saviour, but a Lawgiver, and is not longer our salvation, but an eternal despair.

c. So learn to speak to one's heart and to the Law. When the law creeps into your conscience, learn to be a cunning logician – learn to use arguments of the gospel against it. Say:

"O law! You would climb up into the kingdom of my conscience, and there reign and condemn me for sin, and would take from me the joy of my heart which I have by faith in Christ, and drive me to desperation, that I might be without hope. You have over-stepped your bounds. Know your place! You are a guide for my behaviour, but you are not Saviour and Lord of my heart. For I am baptized, and through the

Gospel am called to receive righteousness and eternal life... So *trouble me not!* For I will not allow you, so intolerable a tyrant and tormentor, to reign in my heart and conscience – for they are the seat and temple of Christ the Son of God, who is the king of righteousness and peace, and my most sweet saviour and mediator. He shall keep my conscience joyful and quiet in the sound and pure doctrine of the Gospel through the knowledge of this passive and heavenly righteousness.

d. When I have this Christian righteousness reigning in my heart, I descend from heaven as the rain making fruitful the earth. That is to say... I do good works, how and whensoever occasion is offered.... Whoever be that is assuredly persuaded that Christ is his righteousness, does not only cheerfully and gladly work well in his vocation... but submits to all manner of burdens and dangers in his present life, because he knows that this is the will of God, and that this obedience pleases him.

e. This then is the argument of this Epistle, which Paul expounds against the false teachers who had darkened the Galatians' understanding of this righteousness by faith.

APPLICATION QUESTIONS

For Personal Reflection

1. Define passive righteousness and active righteousness in your own words. What does it look like in your own life when you are living in passive righteousness – describe your attitudes, thoughts, actions. What are symptoms that would indicate when you are slipping into active righteousness?

   When I am actively righteous, I...   *When I am passively righteous, I...*

2. What do you find difficult about passive righteousness? Which <u>specific area(s)</u> of your life do you struggle most with active righteousness? Ask God to help you see what would it look like in this area to live in passive righteousness.

   When I am actively righteous, I...   *When I am passively righteous, I...*

For Small Group Discussion

3. What place does the law take in active righteousness versus passive righteousness?

4. What does active and passive righteousness look like applied to <u>prayer</u>?

    Actively righteous prayer   *Passively righteous prayer*

PRAYER PRACTICE:

*   Confess where you tend to live by active righteousness.

*   Write out a prayer, putting the law in its place, using the following prayer as an example. *"O law! You would climb up into the kingdom of my conscience, and there reign and condemn me for sin, and would take from me the joy of my heart which I have by faith in Christ, and drive me to desperation, that I might be without hope. You have over-stepped your bounds. Know your place! You are a guide for my behaviour, but you are not Saviour and Lord of my heart. For I am baptized, and through the Gospel am called to receive righteousness and eternal life… So trouble me not! For I will not allow you, so intolerable a tyrant and tormentor, to reign in my heart and conscience — for they are the seat and temple of Christ the Son of God, who is the king of righteousness and peace, and my most sweet saviour and mediator. He shall keep my conscience joyful and quiet in the sound and pure doctrine of the Gospel through the knowledge of this passive and heavenly righteousness.*

*   Passively receive the righteousness of Christ.

This is a diagnostic tool to use as a "gospel reality check" to guide your spirit in prayer. As you read through the following thoughts that characterize various enemies of gospel transformation, mark the ones that have resonated with you.

Meritorious:
- I do a co-operative work of the Spirit… I also take some of the credit.
- Good deeds are stacked in my favor; bad deeds are stacked against me.

Externalism:
- I'm living a life acceptable to others, but I'm not examining my inner motives.
- My bedrock issues are self-sovereignty and self-righteousness
- Within my heart, I am often characterized by hatred for others or spirit of judgment

Perfectionism:
- Because I'm a child of God, I can't sin anymore.
- Eventually we can live purely

Nihilism:
- I'm as lost as ever.
- My inner life/dialogue is characterized by despair, groveling in sin, no hope for real progress.
- There is a lack of joy in life.

Renovation:
- I can change my own nature. God, please help *me* so *I* can change.
- I am saved by grace. I live by works.
- I live as actively earning my righteousness, rather than passively receiving Christ's righteousness

Pacifism:
- I don't have to do anything. Christ has done everything for me.

APPLICATION QUESTIONS

For Small Group Discussion

5. Which subtle shifts in false thinking/beliefs do you have a tendency to buy into?

6. How does a true gospel perspective address these subtle, but false shifts?

PRAYER PRACTICE:
- Confess and surrender your all your ways that counter Christ's work.
- Confess and receive the work of the Son on the cross on your behalf.
- Praise the Father and ask for a fresh filling of the Spirit to deliver us from our idols that compete with the work of his transformation.

HOMEWORK:

- Pray through Paul's prayers for some of the people on your prayer list.
- Throughout the week, try to be aware to identify any negative thoughts you feel about your prayer life and ask Jesus to speak to it.
- Read through the material for Lesson 5, concentrating on the readings, the personal reflection questions and prayer practice points.

Leaders Discern Calling in Prayer and Mission

GOALS: In this lesson we will...
- ❑ Recognize the role of prayer in maturing our call
- ❑ Understand the gospel riches of our calling
- ❑ Begin to articulate a personal sense of call and mission

Introduction   (See DVD Section 1: Lesson 5)

Pray or be a prey – a prey to fears, to futilities, to ineffectiveness. E. Stanley Jones

We find God's calling at the intersection of three critical life forces:
1. God's Word
2. Life context
3. Prayer.

If God's Word is the general map of life, prayer is where we find the specific path and road to follow on this map. Each of us is called to follow and apply God's word in prayer – in our own specific context.

Apart from prayer, life consists of an endless variety of possibilities and objectives. We wander in aimless uncertainty until we "commit our plans to the Lord, and He will establish them." However, in a life of kingdom prayer we discern the present intent of God's call for our lives. This is prophetic. The path we are to walk is daily illumined in the practice of waiting prayer.

"I cry out to God who fulfils his plans and purpose for me." Psalm 57:2

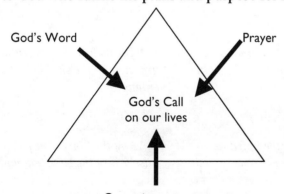

Prayer lights the road ahead of us to move confidently forward. As we wait, prayer turns orange lights into green or orange lights to red, depending on God's plan and purposes.

Christ first calls us to himself, to know, love and follow him. In prayer our true identity as children of God takes deeper root in our hearts and lives.

Are You Living as a Son or Slave?
Adapted from "The Gospel and the Heart" by Timothy Keller

Galatians 4:5-9 tells us:

[4] But when the set time had fully come, God sent his Son, born of a woman, born under the law, [5] to redeem those under the law, that we might receive adoption to sonship. [6] Because you are his sons, God sent the Spirit of his Son into our hearts, the Spirit who calls out, "Abba,[b] Father." [7] So you are no longer a slave, but God's child; and since you are his child, God has made you also an heir. [8] Formerly, when you did not know God, you were slaves to those who by nature are not gods. [9] But now that you know God—or rather are known by God—how is it that you are turning back to those weak and miserable forces[c]? Do you wish to be enslaved by them all over again?

1. When we became Christians, we *"receive the adoption [lit. The sonship]."* Galatians 4:4-5. We became sons of God.

2. Before we were "slaves," but that is true no longer. *"So you are no longer a slave, but a son."* Galatians 4:7

3. Nevertheless, it is possible, even if you are a Christian, to return to some degree into a state of slavery, and to lose our "sonship consciousness." *"Formerly… you were slaves… do you wish to be enslaved… all over again?"* Galatians 4:8-9 (cf. Romans 8:15 *"You did not receive a spirit that makes you a slave again to fear."* i.e. it is possible to fall back into fear/slavery, though we are in fact children of God.

Therefore, the two fundamentally different ways to live are *not* a) as religious or b) as irreligious, but *a) as a slave, full of fear, or b) as a child of God, full of faith working through love*.

There is a two-part "dynamic" to Christian growth. (It is, in a sense, a "combustion cycle." If it is ignited and going in the heart, it results in dynamic character growth.) The two parts are a "negative" and "positive." We see them mentioned in many places.

Colossians 3

v. 1 *Set your hearts on things above, where Christ is seated… who is your life…*	v. 5 *Put to death what belongs to your earthly nature… which is idolatry…*

Hebrews 12

v. 2 *Fixy our eyes on Jesus, the author and perfector of our faith… sat down at the right hand of God…*	v. 1 *Let us throw off everything that hinders and the sin that so easily entangles…*

Romans 8

v. 5 *their minds set on what the Spirit desires…* (v. 14) *those led of the Spirit are sons of God…*	v. 13 *by the Spirit you put to death the misdeeds of the body you will live…*

Galatians 5

v. 25 *Since we live by the Spirit, let us keep in step with the Spirit…*	v. 24 *Those who belong to Christ Jesus have crucified the sinful nature with its passions and desires.*

The "negative" side is *repentance*, to discover the particular idolatries of the heart (Colossians 3:5), our besetting sins (Hebrews 12:1), and uproot them at the motivational level (Romans 8:13). The "positive" side is *faith*, to see ourselves as perfect in Christ (Colossians 3:1), who has done from first to last all that was required for my acceptance (Hebrews 12:2), so that we could be adopted as sons and daughters of God (Romans 8:14). This is the dynamic – a) we uproot the idols of the heart and b) we live out our identity as children of God.

These two elements really are flip sides of each other. As we begin with one, we find that we always pass over into doing the other as well. Each stimulates the other. If either one is de-emphasized, it robs the other also of any power. **How?** *On the one hand,* without a knowledge of our extreme sin and idolatry, the payment of Christ on the cross seems trivial, and the message of it does not electrify or transform. *On the other hand,* without a knowledge of our complete acceptance and adoption through Christ, the message of our sin would so crush us that we would deny or repress it. We would fake that we are righteous, just as the Pharisees did. After a while, you can begin to forget your sinful state and see the world in terms of "good" people and "bad" people. Conservatives fall into this trap often.

But – the more you know his infallible fatherly love, the more you are able to realistically face yourself, your flaws and faults. And the more you see your sin, the more precious and valuable do you find his saving love and grace.

In this project, we will look at how to live as a child of God (the "positive" part of the growth dynamic). Then we will look at how to identify idols (the "negative" part of the growth dynamic).

Sum: What is the difference between a "slave" and a "son"?

Both Galatians 4:1-7 and Romans 8:15-16 contrast slavery with sonship.

Different understanding

Slave – *False definitions – a whole different religion!*
Child – *True definitions*

> **Slave:** "Grace" is God's maintaining <u>your</u> strength and power so to live a better life.
> **Child:** Grace is a transforming power; to be melted by spiritual understandings of gospel truth.

> **Slave:** "Faith is trying hard to do good and be better, establishing your own record (a "righteousness") so God and others will accept you.
> **Child:** Faith is a discipline of remembering and living every moment as an accepted child of God.

> **Slave:** "Obedience" focuses nearly completely on external duties. Examination of attitudes and motivations is too traumatic and is ignored.
> **Child:** Obedience is seeking to please God first in our attitude of love, then in obeying his will. Concentration on principles and attitudes.

Different lifestyle

Slave – *Fear-based life*
Child – *Faith working through love*

Slave: Compulsive obedience. Obeys God and moral codes out of fear of rejection – a compulsive, driven moralism. "Driveness." Unrealistic goals. Often a lot of self-criticism.

Child: Obeys out of joy in your Father and out of gratitude for the certainty of his love. "How can I live so ungratefully to one who will never reject me?"

Slave: Controlled by people. Expectations and opinions of others become the real moral standard. We are controlled by what people think.

Child: Integrity and courage is easier. "The only person whose opinion counts is my Father! Who cares what the rest think?:

Slave: Hiding. Lots of strategies to hide our inner and outer failings from ourselves and one another. Including: gossip, blame-shifting, anger at other races/classes, obsessions, overwork, etc.

Child: Open and transparent. Freedom from having to put up a front. Able to appreciate people who are different and hurting.

Slave: Isolation. Growing feeling that no one understands, that no one cares, no one can be trusted.

Child: Because of openness and transparency, and a lack of self-pity.

Slave: Despair in troubles. Sees difficulties as "pay backs" from God. Result is either guilt (because there's an awareness of moral failure) or bitterness (because there's a feeling of moral accomplishment).

Child: Learns to see discipline as fatherly, loving instruction, preparing us for future tests. Learns lessons and shows patience.

Slave: Begrudging repentance. Admitting failure is destructive of one's very basis for living (that being a sense of moral adequacy). So repentance is galling and is a last resort.

Child: Admitting failure is the basis of a Christian's self-image as an adopted child. Repentance reminds anew of magnitude of his love. Repentance is quick, willing.

B. Turning the corner.

Case study. Here one pastor, John Newton, writes to another pastor who is depressed because of his feeling of guilt over his sins. But the writer points out that he has not ever confessed his __real__ sins, the sins of self-justification:

> *"[You say you feel overwhelmed with guilt and a sense of unworthiness. Well,] you cannot be too aware of the inward and inbred evils you complain of, but you may be (indeed you are) improperly controlled and affected by them. You say it is hard to understand how a holy God could accept such an awful person as yourself. You, then, express not only a low opinion of yourself (which is right!) but also too low an opinion of the person, work and promises of the Redeemer, which is wrong… You complain about sin, but when we examine your complaints, they are so full of self-righteousness, unbelief, pride, and impatience that they are little better than the worst evils you complain of!"*
>
> *~John Newton, to a pastor*

For Personal Reflection, then Small Group Discussion

3. How have you "turned" the corner from the slave-mentality to living as a son or daughter of God?

For Personal Prayer
- Pray if you have not along these lines (you can also personalize it in your journal):

  "Lord, show me the difference between self-justification and real faith. Help me to see the false trusts that keep me feeling like a hired servant with you. Let the cross and your Fatherly love become a living daily reality in my life. Amen."

C. Walking daily as children of God.

Individual sinful acts have sinful motivations. When we ask <u>why</u> we are moved to particular sins, we discover that our sins come because we still seek to find our "justification" (our identity, our sense of worthiness) in other things. Thus, to remember that we are completely loved and righteous in Christ undermines and saps our motives and desire for sin.

<u>Normal activity:</u>	<u>Normal activity:</u>
Going out of your way to help with a project	Going out of your way to help with a project
Slave motivation	*Sonship motivation*
"Do this because, if you succeed, you will know you are not a bum!"	"Do this because Christ was sacrificed for me"
"Do this because then somebody will love you, and you are nobody until somebody does."	"Do this because it will please both my Father and the person I am helping."
Results:	*Results:*
If no gratitude expressed – *anger.*	If no gratitude is expressed – disappointment, but gratitude not the motive
Even if gratitude expressed a sense of being owed – *controlling.*	If gratitude expressed – new, non-controlling relationship possible
If life goes badly, increased *self-pity and bitterness* toward God – "after all, look how good I am to people! How could God treat me like this?"	If life goes badly, trust. "After all, I have already been given more than I deserve. And besides, my Father must have some loving purpose."

Conclusion

Every day, when we face the issues of life, we are to "call out" to God as our Father. That means we are to consciously seek to live as children of God, not as slaves. We are to think out: "Am I acting like a slave or like a child of God here?" Sometimes, if we wait patiently, the Spirit comes "alongside" us (Romans 8:16) and fills us with an awareness of his Fatherly love for us, and acting like a child of God comes naturally. Sometimes our sonship "experience" is low and we have to "gut it out" by faith. Either way, we are being changed into his likeness.

Luther writes: "So learn to speak to one's heart and to the Law. When the Law creeps into your conscience, learn to be a cunning logician – learn to use arguments of the gospel against it. Say: 'Oh law!... trouble me not! For I will not allow you, so intolerable a tyrant and tormentor, to reign in my heat and conscience – for they are the seat and temple of Christ the Son of God, who is the king of righteousness and peace, my most sweet saviour and mediator.' [Then] he shall keep my conscience joyful and quiet in the sound and pure doctrine of the Gospel through the knowledge of this passive and heavenly righteousness." He calls this an effort to keep "this Christian righteousness reigning in my heart."

On the one hand, the gospel changes us because it changes our thinking, bringing it "in line with the truth." Both on the other hand, the gospel changes us because it brings us into actual enjoyment and awareness of the Father. It is not enough to simply know that God accepts you freely in Christ, you must actually experience that love shed in your heart through the work of the Holy Spirit. The Spirit helps us to "call out, 'Abba, Father,'" (Galatians 4:6). Unless we have this experience, we will continue to act as a slave (Galatians 4:7). We therefore must learn to preach the gospel to ourselves (as in Galatians 4:4-5) until it catches fire in our hearts and captures our imagination (as in Galatians 4:6-7).

PRAYER PRACTICE:
- In pairs, pray for each other by name to grow in the grace and reality of our calling as children of God.

William Wilberforce

This account of Wilberforce's life is not so much about prayer (though he is well known to be a man of prayer. He was often heard in the seats of parliament to deeply groan and articulate this prayer "More light Lord! More light Lord!") His life is an example to encourage our quest to live our whole life under God's call.

William Wilberforce (1759-1833) was a British parliamentarian and philanthropist, best known as the leader of the movement that abolished slavery, and arguably the most successful reformer in history. Born in Hull, he attended Cambridge where he became a close friend of William Pitt, the youngest prime minister in British history. His life was turned around by his conversion ("the great change") in 1785, and John Wesley and John Newton encouraged him early in his reforming endeavours.

At one stage in his life, Wilberforce was an active participant in an astonishing sixty-nine different public initiatives, ranging from directly spiritual projects -- he was the founder of the world's first Bible Society – to more secular initiatives, including helping to found the Sierra Leone Colony for freed slaves, the Royal Society for the Prevention of Cruelty to Animals, the Royal Institute of Science, and the National Gallery. His crowning achievements were the abolition of the slave trade in 1807 and of slavery in the British Empire in 1833 – just days before his death. His book, A Practical View of Christianity, was a bestseller for fifty years.

Historian G. M. Trevelyan described abolition as "one of the turning points in the history of the world." Wilberforce's achievements were therefore historic, but they were neither easy nor quick suppression of the slave trade alone took twenty years and full emancipation nearly fifty years. The following readings are a collage of Wilberforce's own words, along with those of his contemporaries and later historians. They underscore what one of his biographers noted -- that a modern person can change modern times, but he or she cannot do it alone.

Wrestling with his Growing Sense of Calling

Wilberforce's first inclination after his conversion to faith in Christ was to leave the world of politics and be ordained as a minister – mistakenly believing, as many do, that spiritual things are higher than secular things. Fortunately, friends counselled him to stay and discover his calling in public life. John Newton and Thomas Scott, for example, were two ministers who wisely persuaded him to serve in Parliament and not become a minister.

Advice from his Friend, Prime Minister William Pitt (the Younger)

The passage below is the advice of his great friend Prime Minister William Pitt (the younger), who had earlier written to him and referred to Wilberforce's "constant call for Something out of the Common Way." His urging here came as a turning point for Wilberforce.

"Wilberforce, why don't you give notice of a motion on the subject of the slave trade? You have already taken great pains to collect evidence, and are therefore entitled to the credit which doing so will insure you. Do not lose time, or the ground may be occupied by another."

--beneath an oak tree on the vale of Keston, May 1787

Wilberforce's Moment of Decision

Wilberforce's decision to take up the cause of abolition was by various events, including Pitt's advice, his own research, and his deep sense of calling.

"So enormous, so dreadful, so irremediable did the Trade's wickedness appear that my own mind was completely made up for Abolition. Let the consequences be what they would, I from this time determined that I would never rest until I had effected its abolition."

--speech to the House of Commons after research into slavery, 1787

Written a few months after the above speech, this famous journal entry represents one of the most audacious statements of life purpose in history. Notice, too, the date, which sets the decision against the backdrop of revolutionary ferment Europe. .

"God Almighty set before me two great objects, the suppression of the Slave Trade and the reformation of manners."

--written in his journal, Sunday, October 28, 1787

From the very first speeches onward, Wilberforce brought to the issue the passion and moral urgency that such a calling inspired.

"Sir, the nature and all the circumstances of the Trade are now laid open to us. We can no longer plead ignorance. We cannot evade it. We may spurn it. We may kick it out of the way. But we cannot turn aside so as to avoid seeing it. For it is brought now so directly before our eyes that this House must decide and must justify to all the world and to its own conscience, the rectitude of the grounds of its decision.... Let not Parliament be the only body that is insensible to the principles of natural justice. Let us make reparation to Africa, as far as we can, by establishing trade upon true commercial principles, and we shall soon find the rectitude of our conduct rewarded by the benefits of a regular and growing commerce."

--conclusion to Wilberforce's first (and unsuccessful) motion against slavery May 1788

For a Leader, Public Responsibility was Christian Responsibility

Wilberforce's journal entry here is in clear and settled contrast to his first inclinations to leave public life.

"My walk, I am sensible, is a public one. My business is in the world; and I must mix in assemblies of men, or quit the post which Providence seems to have assigned me.... My shame is not occasioned by my thinking that I am too studiously diligent in the business of life; on the contrary, I then feel that I am serving God best when from proper motives I am most actively engaged in it."

-- written in his journal, 1788

Recognition of the Daunting Challenges

Championing abolition was a dangerous business. The slave trade occupied a position in the British economy (as a percentage of gross national product) equivalent to that of the defense industry in the United States today. At one stage, Wilberforce was the most vilified man in England. He was even threatened and attacked physically, for example, by slave-trading captains whose reputations and livelihood were menaced by the campaign against slavery.

Letter from John Wesley

The following letter, written in a faltering hand, is one of John Wesley's last messages. The next day, February 25, he sank into a coma and never recovered, dying on March 2. Wilberforce marked the letter "Wesley's last words."

February 24,1791

Dear Sir,

Unless the divine power has raised you to be as *Athanasius contra mundum* [Athanasius against the world], I see not how you can go through your glorious enterprise in opposing that execrable villainy, which is the scandal of religion, of England, and of human nature. Unless God has raised you up for this very thing, you will be worn out by the opposition of men and devils. But if God be for you, who can be against you? Are all of them together stronger than God? O be not weary of well doing! Go on, in the name of God and in the power of his might, till even American slavery (the vilest that ever saw the sun) shall vanish away before it....

That he who has guided you from youth up may continue to strengthen this and all things is the prayer of, dear sir,

Your affectionate servant, John Wesley

In Letters, ed. John Telford (Epworth Press, 1931) VIII, 265.

Letter from John Newton

Newton was a converted slave trader who had become an Anglican rector and renowned hymn writer (including "Amazing Grace"). He had a decisive influence on the young Wilberforce. He urged him not to leave Parliament and encouraged him to take up the championing of abolition, despite its dangers.

Paul's Cray, Kent, July 21, 1796

My very dear Sir,

It is true that you live in the midst of difficulties and snares, and you need a double guard of watchfulness and prayer. But since you know both your need of help, and where to look for it, I may say to you as Darius to Daniel, "Thy God whom thou servest continually is able to preserve and deliver you." Daniel, likewise, was a public man, and in critical circumstances; but he trusted in the Lord, was faithful in his department and therefore, though he had enemies, they could not prevail against him.

Indeed the great point for our comfort in life is to have a well-grounded persuasion that we are, where, all things considered, we ought to be. Then it is no great matter whether we are in public or in private life, in a city or a village, in a palace or a cottage....

I am your very affectionate, and much obliged, John Newton

From The Correspondence of William Wilberforce face, Vol. l, ed. Robert Isaac Wilberforce and Samuel Wilberforce (1840).

The Importance of Community in the Abolition Cause

Partnership, community, and the power of moral influence were critical to the success Wilberforce and his colleagues, who were known as the "Clapham circle" or "the saints." One of their maxims was "Always seek a neighbour before you seek a home." Their conversations were so stimulating and so constant that it was said of them: they were "like a meeting that never adjourned."

People of Character and Integrity

The influence they exercised was again because of the intensity of their passion. The whole group presented to the House of Commons of their day the impressive spectacle of men who put principle before party or profit, "who looked to the facts of the case and not to the wishes of the minister, and who before going into the lobby required to be obliged with a reason instead of with a job."

To advance their causes and to uphold their principles they would support any government, or with equal resolution oppose any government – even though their action might deal a painful blow to their party and their friends.

In consequence the "Saints" gained a unique moral ascendancy over the House of Commons.

> Confidence and respect, and, (what in the House of Commons is their unvarying accompaniment,) power, were gradually, and to a great extent involuntarily, accorded to this group of members. They were not addicted to crotchets, nor to the obtrusive and unseasonable assertion of conscientious scruples. The occasions on which they made proof of independence and impartiality were such as justified, and dignified, their temporary renunciation of party ties. They interfered with decisive effect in the debates on the great scandals of Lord Melville and the Duke of York, and in more than one financial or commercial controversy that deeply concerned the national interests....

From Ernest Marshall Howse, Saints in Politics: The 'Clapham Sect' and the Growth of Freedom. Copyright ® 1952 by University of Toronto Press. Reprinted by permission of HarperCollins Publishers Limited.

Networking before the Age of Networking

The Claphamites lived in great intimacy. They would wander into one another's houses and gardens and always find themselves welcome. There seemed to be a general assumption that a friend could come in at any time. They would also call on one another unexpectedly in the country and expect and receive the same welcome. They liked to spend their holidays with other members of the Sect, often in a series of prolonged visits to one another's houses. The Grants, Thornton, Eliot, and Wilberforce were so close to one another that although each of their houses on Henry Thornton's property had its own garden allotted to it there was no attempt to make any demarcation and they all treated the garden as a form of common property. It was perhaps natural that, living so closely together, the Clapham Sect should marry into one another's families and they did so to an almost incestuous degree. Wilberforce was first cousin to the Thornton and Smith brothers; Stephen married Wilberforce's sister, Gisborne Babington's, Babington Macaulay's, Charles Eliot Venn's. Macaulay, the supply of sisters having been exhausted, married one of Hannah More's pupils. The relationships of the next generation were even more complicated.

Living in such proximity to one's friends was both pleasant and useful. Wilberforce always found "the very prospect [of ret returning to Clapham] mends, fixing and solemnizing my mind." The enthusiasm for one another's good causes with which the group became infected led to the birth of a mass of societies for the relief of every class of unfortunate from Russian sufferers to Irish serving women. Wilberforce has been compared to a Prime Minister of a cabinet of philanthropists, in which each of his ministers held a particular portfolio, Stephen and Macaulay the Slave Trade, Lord Teignmouth the Bible Society, Thornton the Exchequer, Grant India, Macaulay and Hannah More public relations. Milner, Venn, and Simeon were his spiritual consultants, and he looked perhaps more to Babington than anyone else for general advice.

Even if one excludes the contribution made by those who did not live in Clapham, it is safe to say that never in the history of the Church did the inhabitants of a single parish have such an effect on the world. For the Clapham Sect's good works were not limited to England and Africa. They intervened on behalf of the convicts of Australia, the victims of the Napoleonic wars, the Greeks struggling for freedom, the Haitians, the North American Indians, the Hottentots, and the slaves. They distributed bibles and sent out missionaries to every corner of the world. They have been criticized for concentrating so much of their energies on religious campaigns, though it would be unrealistic to expect such religious men to do anything else. But the drive behind their campaigns was so great that their temporal achievements were enough to put any other group to shame. If they had never succeeded in anything else, their share in either of the great victories of Abolition and Emancipation would have guaranteed their place in history.

Robin Furneaux, William Wilberforce (London: Hamish Hamilton 1974), pp. 118-119. Copyright ® 1974 by Robin Furneaux.

Success Came on his Deathbed

On Friday, July 26, 1833, the Bill for the Abolition of Slavery passed its second reading in the House of Commons. It was a Government measure now and its success was assured. Wilberforce lapsed into a coma soon after hearing news of his great success, and died three days later on Monday, July 29, 1833, aged seventy-three. The amount of money cited -- phenomenal in those days -- is the sum with which the planters were to be compensated; it represented about half the market value of their slaves.

"Thank God, that I should have lived to witness a day in which England is willing to give twenty millions sterling for the Abolition of Slavery."

--on hearing news of the success of abolition; 1833

This is the text of the epitaph on Wilberforce's memorial in Westminster Abbey, London.

TO THE MEMORY OF
WILLIAM WILBERFORCE
(born in Hull August 24th 1759, died in London July 29th 1833)

For nearly half a century a member of the House of Commons, and, for six parliaments during that period, one of the two representatives for Yorkshire in an age and country fertile in great and good men, he was among the foremost of those who fixed the character of their times because to high and various talents to warm benevolence, and to universal candour. He added the abiding eloquence of a Christian life.

Eminent as he was in every department of public labour, and a leader in every work of charity, whether to relieve the temporal or the spiritual wants of his fellow men his name will ever be specially identified with those exertions which, by the blessing of God, removed form England the guilt of the African slave trade, and prepared the way for the abolition of slavery in every colony of the empire.

In the prosecution of these objects, he relied, not in vain, on God; but in the process, he was called to endure great obstacles and great opposition: he outlived, however, all enmity: and, in the evening of his days withdrew from public life and public observation to the bosom of his family yet he died not unnoticed or forgotten by his country: the peers and commons of England, with the Lord Chancellor, and the Speaker, at their head, carried him to his fitting place among the mighty dead around, here to repose: till, through the merits of Jesus Christ, his only redeemer and Saviour (whom his life and his writings he had desired to glorify), he shall rise in the resurrection of the just.

APPLICATION QUESTIONS

For Personal Reflection

5. How does Wilberforce's life inspire you?

6. How would you like your life and accomplishments to be summed up?

PRAYER PRACTICE:
- Pray for God to reveal himself and his vision for you.
- Pray for an open and surrendered heart of faith to follow as he leads.

Calling is one way of looking at your whole life:
1.   Given by God.
2.   Forged in prayer and the word.
3.   Discovered in mission and service.

Calling is specific and unique to each of us:
In general we all have the same calling and <u>purpose</u> in life: "to glorify God and enjoy him forever" (Westminster Shorter Catechism). Our <u>mission</u> is to make disciples of all nations. *Calling is forged in the midst of our purpose and mission.* This calling is applied and becomes as unique as each person is.

Calling is comprehensive of our identity in Christ and our service to others:
- Includes *becoming a child of God*: "Called to be saints"
- Includes *who you are*: "I call you by name"
- Includes *what you do*: "Called to be an apostle"
- Includes your *destiny and purpose* in this life: "I will show him what he must suffer for my sake."

Calling is continually in process:
- Includes *assessing your <u>past</u>* of key experiences, moments and relationships that form your life story of God's guiding presence in your life
- Includes *defining your biblical purpose and auditing your <u>current</u> behaviour* in light of God's reason for your existence in the context of his mandates for his people.
- Includes *discovering the <u>future</u>* and identifying / clarifying your personal vision
- Includes *<u>intentionally</u> living, growing and ministering* out of an increasing understanding of the life and ministry God has created you for.

As calling matures it leads:
- to clarity in your life commitments and passions (core values) for what God wants you to do in, through and with you
- to a sense of life purpose
- to a vision or conception of what the things will look like if God brings things to pass in your life
  - Vision often comes in mission chapters
  - Vision is forged in prayer, providence, place and service

Calling leads to purpose, vision, commitments and mission. In turn these help us understand our calling.

Example of a church's purpose: To reclaim a post-Christian country, through reaching its cities

Example of a church/interchurch vision: A church planting movement is established in Canada, having moved from the centers of our cities, and spread across the land.

Example of Core Values/non-negotiable passions: To plant churches that are for the city, for the seeking, for the needy and for the nations

Example of a church mission: In 10 years to plant a city-center church with 3 congregations, and on urban church planting center, with 30 trained leaders of house churches

APPLICATION QUESTIONS

For Group Discussion

11. What is the difference between career and calling?

12. What is the relationship between calling and specific context?

13. How does calling relate to prayer?

DIAGNOSTIC QUESTIONS

For each question, start with personal reflection/prayer, then share your initial thoughts/insights/responses in small groups.

1. What kinds of things move your mind and heart when you pray? For example:
    - *healing the brokeness of souls and bodies*
    - *praying for missionaries/Christian workers/leaders*
    - *praying for those who do not know Christ- near and far*
    - *praising God for his wonders in Creation and Redemption*
    - *praying about your work and workplace*
    - *prayer for your city, country, and its leaders*

    After prayer/reflection write a few sentences about your heart focus in prayer:

2. When you read scripture, or hear scripture read/preached, what parts of scripture, key teachings, commands and instructions, seem most immediate and important to you – "as if God is talking right to me"? Include one or two. For example:
    - *A call to leadership*
    - *Scripture encouragement to teachers/preachers/evangelists*
    - *Passages about loving and caring for others/ social justice*
    - *Teaching on holiness and consecration*
    - *Encouragement to worship, praise and adoration*
    - *Teachings about the importance of your work*
    - *Scripture encouragement to creatively reflect your Maker*
    - *Passages about family life, parenting, marriage*

    After prayer and reflection, write a few sentences about "what God is saying" to you...

3. As you have stepped out in service and ministry and mission, where have you found the greatest fruitfulness/satisfaction? For example:

    - *helping others, especially the needy*
    - *1 on 1 teaching or counseling*
    - *sharing Christ/ discussing Christianity*
    - *listening to the hurting/ encouraging*
    - *praying for the church/others*
    - *sharing the gospel*
    - *public teaching and presentations*
    - *leading or helping lead a small group*
    - *singing or leading in singing*
    - *making peace between brothers*
    - *fixing problems*
    - *helping behind the scenes*
    - *contributing with your work skills at work or outside your workplace*

    After prayer and reflection write a few sentences about your encouragements in ministry/mission:

4. A personal calling statement is your best understanding to date of your unique, personal direction and destiny. It is a holistic statement that integrates what you understand God is calling you to be and to do for his glory. *(See next page for examples)*

    After prayer and reflection, and write a few sentences about who God is leading you to be and what he is leading you to do.

Example calling statements

Example 1: A pastor's/church planter's calling statement:

- I am called to be `in Christ' and `in mission'.

- As a child of God I rest in the unconditional love of my Father in Heaven. Nothing I have done could prevent his love from finding me. Nothing I will do will cause him to lose me or love me any less than he does.

- As a husband I cultivate an open and non-conditional love and friendship with my wife. I encourage her in her gifts and calling.

- Together we pray for and encourage our children, their spouses, our grandchildren in their `in Christ'/ `in mission' calling.

- I partner with her in making our home a ministry center, and our church as a community for our community.

- As a church planter I encourage and train called men and women in the ministry of starting and growing churches – with the aim of restoring the message and ministry of Christ in Canada.

- As a pastor I am called to shepherd the sheep in my care, and to build them up in the teachings and ministry of Christ and in <u>prayer.</u>

Example 2: A wife and mother's calling statement:

- I exist to be loved by God and to love Him more and more with all my heart, soul and mind so that my intimacy with him leads others into an eternal and abundant relationship with him.

- As a child of God, I thrive on a balance of truth and grace found in His Word, and through his people. To keep me on an eternal course, both with who I am becoming and whom I am influencing, I wisely commit to maintain intimate, accountable and life long relationships.

- As a wife and mother, I invest in the lives of my own family, for they have my deepest love and greatest commitment.

- As one called into ministry, I know I have been designed by God to have a deep love for people, and spiritually gifted for evangelism and leadership. Using what He has given me and in his power, my heart's cry is to bring lives from darkness into light, and to deeply disciple those who want to invest in eternity as well. I focus on seeker sensitive and seeker centred relational opportunities within my extended family, community and church relationships.

5. Vision: Calling is eventually expressed in a vision – a picture of what it would look like as God leads you in your calling and mission.

Examples of Vision

I see my family comfortable and open in my presence enjoying healthy relationships that ultimately cultivate our hearts for God in the pain and joys of life. I see time for talking and listening individually and collectively. I see playing and having fun with them. I see mentoring and coaching them with the resources for life that God has blessed us with. I see being available to them emotionally, spiritually, and physically so that they feel our family is a safe place of refuge in the storms of life. I envision a ripple effect that goes far beyond our home. I long to be used in His hands, whatever the cost, to change the course of individuals and entire families for eternity.

I see people whose lives and spirits are enslaved by poverty experiencing the freeing love of Jesus as I use my passion for community development as a way to meet their needs and provide hope through God's redeeming work. I see healthy, safe, Christian communities marked by love, mercy and truth where lost people find hope in Jesus and found people discover their place in God's larger story of redemption..

I see safe, transparent friendships with the people and Christian leaders God brings across my path so that they are encouraged in life and ministry and I not only give but receive the blessings of Christ.

I see myself as a winter tree stripped bare of the last of my fears and resentments. As a tree lives dependent on water, sun, soil and seasons, so I will live in dependence on what God brings into my life. Like a winter tree I will live my life with hands lifted up in silent prayer confidently serving in hiddenness. I see myself praying in every way I know how, while deepening my practice of prayer. I will pray for everyone I know and for governments and rulers. I will pray alone but as part of a praying community, and I will also pray with small groups. I will invite others to walk along side me and learn with me as I step closer to Jesus in my pilgrimage. And finally, I see myself encouraging others through my gifts of listening, discernment, reading and writing to let go of the dead leaves in their lives so that my Church may become a truer house of prayer.

After prayer and reflection, and write a few sentences about the future and how it looks like God is leading you. What will it 'look' like in five years if God leads you in this way?

QUESTIONS

For Small Group Discussion

Share with one another a brief summary of your sense of call, as far as you have discerned it.

1. What did you notice or learn about calling from listening to other people's sense of call?

2. What encouragement can you receive from others' testimonies of calling?

PRAYER PRACTICE:
*   Praise God for each other by name. Pray for each other's growth in the gospel and in calling – as children of God, and as ambassadors for Christ.

HOMEWORK:
*   Continue to pray through your sense of call.
*   Read through the material for Lesson 6, concentrating on the readings, the personal reflection questions and prayer practice points.

Leaders Go Deep in Prayer and Mission

GOALS: In this lesson we will...
- ❑ Pray for our effectiveness as messengers of the gospel in seeking city transformation
- ❑ Explore the potential of prayer as a means to build bridges with seekers
- ❑ Evaluate our conception of the church in relation to the harvest field

Introduction
(See DVD Section I: Lesson 6)

Prayer is "Glycerin"

If the message of the gospel is "nitro," then kingdom prayer is "glycerin" – only when prayer and proclamation are united will there be conversion and spiritual transformation. As John Piper writes, "Prayer is the power that wields the weapon of the Word." Effective prayer leads to fruitful evangelism.

In this lesson we introduce the new concept of prayer evangelism. Prayer evangelism begins with praying for the evangelist. We consider the apostle Paul's prayer life – how he prays for himself and how he asks others to pray for his life and mission. However, by 'prayer evangelism' we also have experienced that prayer is a means of sharing our faith. As we pray for a person by name, we are sure to share the comforts of the gospel. More than this, we have found that spiritual seekers from virtually every background are interested in learning more about prayer. Many are very open to learning how to pray.

Our greatest encouragement at Prayer for the City is going open market with a simple instructional book called *"Journey in Prayer: Learning to Pray the Prayer of Jesus."* It brings prayer instruction to seekers. This has opened all kinds of doors for evangelism. Reviews from seekers have been unusually good. We have given copies to friends, relatives, neighbors.

The compiled testimonies witnessing the power of prayer evangelism convince us that *prayer is a "trojan horse" through which we can bring the gospel into the heart of the secular city and the secular seeker.* You will be encouraged to consider how prayer evangelism can strengthen your witness and advance God's mission in your life and ministry.

In looking at the apostle Paul's prayers for himself, we learn a gospel-centred and kingdom focused way of asking for prayer for ourselves.

Quotes: *E.M. Bounds: To have prayed with will is to have fought well.*
We do not pray that we might do God's work. Prayer is the work.
In missions there is one thing which is utterly indispensable – prayer.

PRAYER PRACTICE:

We will learn how to pray kingdom prayers for ourselves (and other leaders) by praying through Paul's prayers for himself. We will do so in a "concert of prayer" format, alternating back and forth between reading together Scripture and observations about Paul's prayers and immediately praying the Scripture and implications just read.

For each grouping of Paul's prayers listed here:
- *As a large group*, **read together** the verses and observations listed.
- *In small groups of 3*, **pray in response** to the guidelines listed in each grey "prayer box" corresponding to what was just read.

Notice Paul prays for three things:

1. Open doors
2. Boldness
3. Deliverance

Eph. 6:19, 20 ... and for me that words may be given to me that I may open my **mouth boldly** to make known the mystery of the gospel, for which I am an ambassador in chains: that in it I may speak boldly as I should.

Phil. 1:19-22... Through your prayer and the supply of the Spirit of Christ, according to my earnest expectation, that in nothing I shall be ashamed, but that **with all boldness**, as always, so now also Christ will be magnified in my body, whether by life or by death.

Col. 4:2-4 ... Continue earnestly in prayer...praying also for us, that God **would open** to us a door for the word, to speak they mystery of Christ, for which I am also in chains, that I may make it manifest as I ought to speak.

2 Thess 3:1-2 ... Finally brethren, pray for us, that the word of the Lord may have **free course** and be glorified, just as it is with you, and that we may be **delivered** from unreasonable and wicked men; for not all have faith.

Rom 15:31 ... That you strive together with me in your prayer to God for me, that I may be **delivered from** those in Judea who do not believe...

KEY OBSERVATION:

If you want to reach a world, ask prayer for yourself

- Paul does in each of the above requests.
- Not for the lost, but for his own effectiveness.
- This is strategic. He has the promises. He is the instrument. He knows God can change and empower him.
- Effective missionary praying begins with praying for the messenger.
- We may assume that nothing happens in me or through me without this.

I. If you want to win souls, pray for open doors

Col. 4:2-4 Devote yourselves to prayer, being watchful and thankful. And pray for us, too, that God may open a door for our message, so that we may proclaim the mystery of Christ, for which I am in chains. Pray that I may proclaim it clearly, as I should.

a. Assumption #1:
A city town or village or a friend or neighbour is closed until opened through prayer. There must be preparations made before the walls of Jericho fall.

b. Expect great results

1 Cor. 16:9 I will tarry in Ephesus until Pentecost. For a great and **effective door has opened to me,** and there are many adversaries.

2 Cor. 2:12-14 When I came to Troas to preach Christ's gospel, and a **door was opened to me by the Lord**… Now thanks be to God who always leads us in triumph in Christ, and through us diffuses the fragrance of His knowledge in every place.

> **Prayer Practice** in groups of 3:
> - Pray for an **open door** (or open hearts) in a place or with a person you are currently wanting to lead to faith in Christ.

II. Pray for courage to reach those without Christ

Eph. 6:19-20 Pray also for me, that whenever I open my mouth, words may be given me so that I will fearlessly make known the mystery of the gospel, for which I am an ambassador in chains. Pray that I may declare it fearlessly, as I should.

Phil. 1:19-22 Yes, and I will continue to rejoice, for I know that through your prayers and the help given by the Spirit of Jesus Christ, what has happened to me will turn out for my deliverance. I eagerly expect and hope that I will in no way be ashamed, but will have sufficient courage so that now as always Christ will be exalted in my body, whether by life or by death. For to me, to live is Christ and to die is gain. If I am to go on living in the body, this will mean fruitful labor for me. Yet what shall I choose? I do not know!

a. Assumption #2: Without prayer, fear rules our hearts
- Nothing more daunting in the Christian life than evangelism.
- You say you are afraid. You should be. Who isn't. Paul was!

b. Courage comes when we pray
Acts 4:24ff So when they heard that, they raised their voice to God with one accord and said: Lord, you are God… Now Lord, look on their threats and grant to your servants that with all boldness they may speak your word… And when they had prayed, the place where they were assembled together was shaken; **and they were all filled with the Holy Spirit and they spoke the Word of God with boldness.**

"The devil trembles when he sees God's weakest child on his knees." ~Annonymous

> **Prayer Practice** in groups of 3:
> - Confess your fear and pray for **courage** in an area or with a person whom you fear.
> - Ask to be **filled** with God's Spirit and with God's Word.

III.   Pray for deliverance

2 Thes. 3:1-2 Finally, brothers, pray for us that the message of the Lord may spread rapidly and be honored, just as it was with you. And pray that we may be delivered from wicked and evil men, for not everyone has faith.

Rom. 15:31 Pray that I may be rescued from the unbelievers in Judea and that my service in Jerusalem may be acceptable to the saints there.

a.   Assumption #3: There will be opposition to the gospel
- Bring to us the people of your choosing, keep others away.

b.   God will "deliver us from evil"
2 Tim. 4:17-18 But the Lord stood at my side and gave me strength, so that through me the message might be fully proclaimed and all the Gentiles might hear it. And I was delivered from the lion's mouth. The Lord will rescue me from every evil attack and will bring me safely to his heavenly kingdom. To him be glory for ever and ever. Amen.

Prayer Practice in groups of 3:
- **Pray for each other by name** for courage in personal spiritual warfare and for deliverance from evil in ongoing battle.
- **Pray for leaders in your church** for protection and deliverance.

APPLICATION QUESTIONS

For Small Group Discussion

1. Why are Paul's prayers for himself so different than the prayers he prays for the church (see lesson 4)? What do Paul's prayers tell us about him? How does this help you to relate to him?

2. What is the significance of Paul asking prayer for himself? Do you ask others to pray for you? What kinds of prayers do you ask for?

3. What difference will it make as people pray with you in the mission he has called you to?

The Church As Force

Jerry Cook and Stanley C. Baldwin

Do you think of the church as an organized, corporate structure, located in the community at a specific address? Something to which you can direct people? Something identified, visible? Maybe with a steeple and maybe not, but a definitely located entity? That's a partial description of the church-as-field.

In the field concept, the organized church is where the people come to do the work of God. A farmer's field is where he plants his crops and does his work. Just so the field, as it relates to the church, is the arena in which the church does its work. Whatever is to be done by the church is done there.

This concept – that the field is where the work is done – is crucial. You see, Jesus said, "The field is the world" (Matt. 13:38). From that it follows that the work of the church is to be done *in the world*. When we think that the believer's meeting place is where the work is to be done, we have departed from the concept Jesus originally established. Instead of the world being the field, we have made the church the field.

This concept of the church-as-field will determine or at least temper all that the church does. Let's consider how the "field" mentality affects the church in its emphasis, goals, ministry, and motivation. And then we'll consider some of the end results.

The following description may be something of a caricature. It may exaggerate some features. Few churches probably fit the description completely. But I think the description will strike pretty close to home for many.

What does the church-as-the-field emphasize? When we see the church building as the place where the work of God is to be done, we develop the kinds of emphases that will get people into that building. First, we need a great deal of visibility. The church must be prominently located. People must see it and preferably should have to pass it daily enroute to school, work and shopping. After all, how will they ever get there if they don't know where it is? Not only must the church be very obvious, the leaders of the church must take on a very significant PR role. I'm not against public relations, but sometimes PR becomes one of the main things in this concept of the church. Because we have to become visible, the leadership – whether the pastor, the associate, or whoever – must get into the community primarily to bring visibility to the church.

Second, the happenings that take place in this building must be of such a nature that people will be attracted. Program and promotion become very important. A high – powered program and strong promotion, of course, demand a great deal of effort, money and organization. So the church's emphases become visibility, organization, program, and promotion. I'm not saying these are bad. I'm questioning their validity as priorities. These are the main emphases in this concept of the church. We give a great deal of attention to these things, because we see the building as the place where action is.

What goals does the church-as-the-field have? The goals of the church-as-field are defined in terms of numbers in attendance, of budget and of facility. Those things tend to make up our concept of success.

Of course the goals are flexible. If we are not reaching great numbers then we change our success semantics from quantity to quality. We're after a few good men. And we've handled the success problem.

Budget? Obviously, it takes money to run a church. But when this becomes our goal, we have seriously confused means and ends. When we operate the church in order to get money enough to operate the church, we shouldn't be too surprised that people write off the church as something which is opposed to Christ.

Facility is vitally important to the concept of the church-as-field because the only way to increase the field is by enlarging the facility. If you are going to do a great work for God and it's all within the building, then you must have an enormous building.

How does the church-as-field go about accomplishing its ministry? An interesting thing here is that it does not have an adequate description yet of what its ministry is. Its ministry so far is to get people into the building, because that is where the work of God is done.

This work, once the people are gathered, centers around a professional. If people are going to be prayed for then the professional is going to be the person who does it because he has the professional hands. And when there are more heads than his hands can take care of we add another professional. So now we have four hands instead of two. As the field increases we have more heads than four hands can handle, so we add another professional. And then we departmentalize the professional so that we have hands in every area of the members' lives. What we are doing is setting up a rather stringent kind of professional approach to ministry.

The second thing about this kind of ministry is that the arrows all go in. By that I mean the organization is endeavoring to pull people out of the culture into the church. Everything is designed to draw people. We have contests, prizes, and outreach campaigns. I heard of one church that gave away green stamps. At another, the pastor promised to swallow a live goldfish when attendance hit a certain number. Anything, just get them in. Because this is where the action is.

Ministry becomes a positional identity within the organization. That is, if you are going to minister you must be director of something or minister of something or associate something. You will have a title and a position within the organizational structure. As a result, the individual member is easily misled about the meaning of Christian service and is often reduced to a spectator. You see, once he's in the field, unless he wins a position he has little relevance except to help keep the machine going.

He keeps his seat occupied and invites his neighbors, but that's not fulfilling so he becomes a bit confused. Then he either grabs for power or drops out. Or he regresses into a support or nonsupport role of the pastor's program. A lot of pastoral opposition stems from this kind of frustration in people's lives.

What motivates the church-as-field? Basically, the motivation of the church-as-field is to get people in. That is called evangelism. Once you have them in you must keep them in because if you don't the field is going to shrink. So elaborate programs are designed to keep the people. This results in an enormous amount of programming. You had to program to get the people and now you have to program to keep them.

You also must get people serving the church. The reason this is absolutely necessary is that the church is the field. Therefore, if people are to serve the Lord at all, they are going to be doing it within the organization.

Very subtly, an interesting thing happens in our mentality if we are not careful. We begin to exploit people. We're reaching people, not because they are hurting, but because they can help us in our church endeavors. *Just think, if that man with all his money would get saved, what he could do for this church.* Or, *What a good testimony for our church if that notorious sinner was saved here.*

Suddenly the purity of our motives is eroded, and that's a very dangerous thing. It means that at some point we are going to start hurting people. People are going to get chewed up in the machine. At East Hill we pick up pieces of people who have been chewed up in religious machines. We pick them up by the basketful. People who have been hurt, who hate religion, hate the preacher, hate everything to do with the church package. Many of them have a real case.

It's not because anyone wants to hurt people. No pastor is in the ministry to hurt people. I've had pastors come and weep in my office, saying, "I like people. I want to help them. I've spent my life trying to help people, but it seems that at some point they get hurt." Often these pastors have been under such pressure to make the machine hum that they have allowed the people to suffer.

When the church is the field we are also motivated to compete with family, school, television and the world. That is no small task, but we must do it. Why? Because we have to rip people away from other things and get them occupied with the church program.

Now, what are the dangers of this approach to church life? First, the pastoral role is distorted and misdirected. In evangelical churches, the pastor tends to become a superstar. Some men have the ability to carry that role well. Their platform manner magnetizes people. In personal relationships they exude charm and self – confidence. As administrators they rival the top executives in big business. But let's face it. There aren't many of that brand of cat around. True superstars are few and far between. The vast majority of pastors must live in frustration if they work in a situation that demands a super – star.

Under some ecclesiastical systems, the pastor tends to become a puppet instead of a star. He hasn't enough autonomy as a leader to take hold of things and make them happen. He has too many boards between him and what he wants to accomplish. So he becomes a political puppet, compromising everywhere and just trying to keep everybody happy. That's also frustrating.

Whether a pastor becomes a star or a puppet, he is being misdirected. His true role is to be neither of those. Rather he is to be an equipper of the saints.

Even more frightening than what happens to the pastor is what happens to the church. Again the tendency is to go in one of two directions. The end result is usually either mediocrity or subculturization.

Let's trace out how it works. Notice, we're talking end results here. The church-as-field may show absolutely no marks of mediocrity at the beginning. To the contrary, there may be great first – generation excitement. That group of people on whom the church was founded are blessed of God. They are, excited, things are moving, the budget's always met, the building is coming, new people are present every Sunday. Everyone is awake. Hallelujah!

But the second generation is different, and I am not referring to the children of the first generation. I'm talking about the second wave of people who make up a church after it is well established. The building is complete. The income is adequate. The organization is functioning. The church settles into what I call a second – generation compromise. Everyone is quite comfortable now. The church program is going along nicely. The time for personal sacrifice is past. The people sit back to enjoy the fruits of their labors or the labors of the first generation.

The stage is set for third – generation mediocrity. Nothing much is happening anymore. Faces change as people and pastors come and go, but that's about it. Even desperate attempts to shake things up, to get moving again, have little effect. Pastors get discouraged and leave, or settle into mediocrity along with the church. They sort of retire early, so to speak, giving up hope of anything significant happening but sticking with the routine anyhow. It's a living.

God help the poor pastor who ends up with third- generation mediocrity. But frankly, I think that's where most pastors are. That's why they shuffle. They trade this pastorate and its mediocrity for that pastorate and its mediocrity. They get about a year-and-a-half honeymoon out of it and then start looking for another church. Mediocrity is always looking for a way out. Give some release and it may honeymoon with you for awhile. But it always has a way of settling back down if we don't change basic concepts.

The only hope is the rise of a new superstar who can capture the day and move us on to bigger and better things and lead us over the top for Jesus.

If the church-as-field does not end with mediocrity, it will end in subculturization. Or it may be both mediocre and subculturized. A subculture is a separate system within a system. It defines its own lifestyle, has its own speech, and tends to externalize its basic spiritual qualities. It develops its own community. When a church subculturizes, it becomes, as one writer put it, "an island of irrelevance in a sea of despair."

That is, I think, a great danger for the Christian church. I see great segments of the church going in that direction or already there. The tendency always is to establish a community in which there is uniformity. That way we don't have to worry about error or non – predictability creeping in. So the church tends, on the wave of revival, to take the result of that revival and institutionalize it. Years later the institution remains, but the life is long gone.

We tried to go the subculture route at East Hill in the early days. We didn't know any better. We had a close – knit group of about 10 families, and our basic aim was to solve all our own problems, keep our group intact, and add to our little community.

We had visions of establishing a Christian commune. We never were able to pull it off because someone would always come in who didn't look as we did, didn't talk as we talked, and didn't give a hang about our little community. We always had to convert these people to our community concept.

Finally we began to get the message. I was praying one day for the Lord to give me the community and the Lord stopped me. "Never pray for that again," He said. "I am not going to give a community to you. Instead I want you to pray, 'Lord, give me to the community."

This was how I finally awoke to the fact that God didn't want us to be a separate subculture, He wanted us to penetrate every segment of the society in which He had placed us.

Jesus said, "You are the salt of the earth" (Matt. 5:13). Salt, to have any effect at all, must be mixed in with the substance which needs salt. Nobody but a collector sets up saltshakers and admires them. A subcultured church is like a saltshaker on display.

Whether the church-as-field leads to mediocrity on the one hand or to a Christian subculture on the other, the result is the same. The world concludes that religion may be OK for some but it's irrelevant to real life. And Christianity is just another irrelevant religion.

Obviously these are gross generalizations. But these are concepts one must work through to arrive at any adequate definition of the church.

The Church as a Force

The church is people, equipped to serve, meeting needs everywhere in Jesus' name.

What does the church-as-a-force emphasize? In this concept of the church-as-a-force, the field is the world, as Jesus said. That is where the work is to be done. The emphases in the church-as-field model are visibility, organization, program and promotion. The church-as-a-force emphases are worship, training, and fellowship, because *these are the things that produce Spirit- filled people who can meet others' needs in Jesus' name.*

When our people gather on Sundays and on Thursdays, they are not the church at work. To attend services is not to serve the Lord. Services are for what we might call R and R, rest and restoration, and this includes worship and celebration. We get together, we sing, we clap, we praise God, worship, meet one another, talk about Jesus. We don't hear any profanity or dirty stories. It's tremendous. Its unadulterated fun and enjoyment in a pure, clean, loving environment.

When we meet, we read the Bible and the Lord speaks to us in various ways. Brothers and sisters more gifted than we in certain areas minister to us. We thoroughly enjoy it. We're healed. Our lives are changed. We receive tremendous blessings. Why? So that we can gather for a repeat performance on Thursday night because by then we'll need to be pumped up again?

No! The church is rested and restored at meetings so that they can work in the world all week long.

The church is at work right now. People are sitting in board meetings where they are employed. They are driving taxis and trucks and buses. They are meeting in council chambers, in the legislature, in commissioners' offices. They're teaching classes. They're milking cows. They're changing diapers. They are all over the community.

When we get together the next time, we'll share what's been going on. We'll rejoice together over our victories and pray about our needs. Some people are going to be present that were caught in that work of the church out in the world. They are going to begin to understand what Jesus' lifestyle is all about. It's a powerful thing.

We worship, we pray, we fellowship, we learn.

What goals do we set? The church-as-field has goals expressed in numbers, budget, and facility. The church-as-a-force has goals that are personal and individual: We want each member to come to *wholeness,* be *equipped,* and be *released* into the world to minister. Our basic assumption is that the Holy Spirit who fills the pastor can fill every believer to whom the pastor preaches. And each believer is potentially capable of ministering just as surely as the pastor is, though perhaps in a different way.

The role of a pastor is to help Christians start living in the light of the truth. Evangelical Christians tend to have a lot of religion in their hearts, a good bit in their heads, but not much in their feet. And Christianity that doesn't walk around in shoes isn't worth much. It has to walk in shoes, all kinds of shoes – sandals, boots, high heels, and suedes. It has to walk. The role of a pastor is to teach people how to get their Christianity to walk right. If we only teach them how to think Christianity and how to feel it, but not how to walk it, we are failing.

Most church members are content to watch the pastor walk. "Pastor made 435 calls this month." And the poor pastor. He is chewing Rolaids. He's drinking Maalox. His cheeks are sunken. His face has a yellow pallor. And the people come on Sunday mornings and get upset because he doesn't feed them steak. The best he can do is serve a little warmed – over soup. He's been busy.

Do you follow me? It's not my job as pastor to minister to every need in the church. I don't intend to do that. My job is to teach everybody in the church how to minister.

The Bible says that pastors are supposed "to prepare God's people for works of service, so that the body of Christ may be built up" (Eph. 4: 12). Take careful notice of this Scripture for it is foundational to the concept of the church-as-a-force.

Preparing God's people – that's my job, and that's a whole different ball game from doing the ministry myself. The church needs to place its members in a healing environment of love, acceptance and forgiveness. We must bring people to wholeness in such an environment, equip them, and then release them.

What is the ministry of the church-as-a-force? The automatic result of great healing is great outreach. As people come to wholeness, they minister. Other people are touched.

When the church is a force the ministry-by-professionals-only tendency of the church-as-field yields to a ministry by all the believers. Along with this comes an altering, even a dissolution, of the traditional lay-clergy role. That is easy to say but it's hard to do in an established church. People don't know how to let it happen. They don't know how to cope with a pastor who actually expects the people to carry on the ministry. They almost demand that the pastor do the work.

In the church-as-a-force the pastoral leadership is also constantly endeavoring to facilitate the ministry of the members. This means the pastor carefully avoids usurping that ministry. He does not do the work for the people but involves them in doing it themselves.

A man asked me to pray with him about his living situation. He lived in a large apartment complex and felt like Lot in Sodom because of the things going on there. He really wanted to move. Our church could have responded to this situation in a number of different ways. For one, we could have built and operated our own apartments. Financially, we could have handled that with no problem. We had already been approached with that proposal and had property on which to build. But that was not our choice. If we ever did build an apartment house, we would limit the percentage of Christians living in it.

However, I couldn't just say to that man, "No, I'm not going to pray with you. Sit there and tough it out." I said, "Listen, you are not there by accident. Let's begin to work and facilitate some ministry for you. Let's pray. Let's fast, and we'll see what the Lord says to us."

I soon discovered a lot of other people in our church were in similar circumstances. One Sunday night after service we gathered everyone who lived in apartments, a whole roomful of people. I said, "How many of you feel like you want to move?" Many raised their hands. I said, "Why don't we stop asking God for a place to move and start asking Him for a way to infect the place we live? How can we have such a case of Christianity that we become an epidemic?"

They just lit up. The first thing they wanted was for me to appoint a staff member to come and teach a Bible study at their places. I said, "No, I'm not about to do that. That's crazy. Why increase the staff? You live there. How many of you are filled with the Holy Spirit?"

Then they thought I was saying, "Go down by the pool every Sunday morning, set up a pulpit, open the Bible, and say 'hear ye, hear ye!'" I was not saying that at all.

"I'm simply saying to be open for business," I explained. "Now what does that mean to you?"

One fellow decided he should write out his testimony and post it on the bulletin board. He happened to be in charge of an apartment building for 400 adult students of Mt. Hood Community College. He had been a bartender a few months before.

He posted his testimony on the bulletin board, where all the messages are. He attached a note, "If you want to talk about this, see me, manager's apartment." A steady stream of people began coming to him.

Now wouldn't it be foolish to put that man on staff? Or hire someone else as minister or apartment evangelism?

APPLICATION QUESTIONS

For Personal Reflection

13. Which of your attitudes, thinking and actions show evidence that you are church-as-field in some areas of your life?

14. Which of your attitudes, thinking and actions show evidence that you are living a way of life that is church-as-force to the world-as-field?

For Small Group Discussion

15. How have you experienced church-as-field or church-as-force? Evaluate your current church or ministry.

16. How will a priority of kingdom prayer reshape and renew our mentality where church-as-field thinking has taken over?

PRAYER PRACTICE:
- Start by praising the Lord of the harvest.
- Confess and surrender lack of heart/vision/urgency for the world -as-field.
- Cry out for the Lord of the harvest to send you to the world-as-field around you.

1. **Prayer evangelism begins with praying for 'harvest eyes'**

> Matthew 9:³⁵*And Jesus went throughout all the cities and villages, teaching in their synagogues and proclaiming the gospel of the kingdom and healing every disease and every affliction.* ³⁶<u>*When he saw the crowds, he had compassion for them,*</u> *because they were harassed and helpless, like sheep without a shepherd.* ³⁷*Then he said to his disciples, "The harvest is plentiful, but the laborers are few;* ³⁸*therefore pray earnestly to the Lord of the harvest to send out laborers into his harvest."*

APPLICATION QUESTIONS

For Personal Reflection

4. When you look to the field, what is in your heart? (compassion, concern, coldness, fear, apathy, etc)

5. What is the relationship between seeing Jesus and seeing the sheep/the harvest field?

PRAYER PRACTICE:

- Ask the Holy Spirit to show you your heart. Confess coldness of heart.
- Thank Him for any growing burdens for the lost.
- Ask for a fresh vision of Jesus Christ to fill your heart. Ask to be filled with His Spirit and compassion as you are sent out.

<u>Key passage</u> on praying for the lost

> *I urge, then, first of all, that requests, prayers, intercession and thanksgiving be made for everyone—* ²*for kings and all those in authority, that we may live peaceful and quiet lives in all godliness and holiness.* ³*This is good, and pleases God our Savior,* ⁴*who wants all men to be saved and to come to a knowledge of the truth.* ⁵*For there is one God and one mediator between God and men, the man Christ Jesus,* ⁶*who gave himself as a ransom for all men.* I timothy 2

Quote: "The soul winner must be a master of the art of prayer. You cannot bring souls to God if you go not to God yourself. You must get your battle-ax, and your weapons of war, from the armory of sacred communication with Christ. If you are much alone with Jesus, you will catch His Spirit; you will be fired with the flame that burned in His breast, and consumed His life. You will weep with the tears that fell upon Jerusalem when He saw it perishing; and if you cannot speak so eloquently as He did, yet shall there be about what you say somewhat of the same power which in Him thrilled the hearts and awoke the consciences of men." Charles Spurgeon, "The Soul Winner"

Testimony:
The importance of praying for 'appointments' to share the good news:

One church planter reports asking God for 100 appointments to share his faith in his city a six week period. The reason for this unusual request is that it was an international festival time and everyone was trading pins. He purchased 120 lapel pins that represented the gospel in a simple five points. Blue represents hope. (which he explains refers to the hope God puts in the heart of every one of us). Dark Purple represents the darkness in the world and in our own hearts that steals and destroys hope. Red represents the sacrificial love of God. (If the discussion permits he explains the cross as the place of forgiveness and restored hope). Yellow represents the light and freedom of grace for all who accept this message. Green stands for growth, which God gives when the seed of good news is received by faith and planted in the heart.

By the end of six weeks this evangelist reports having given the pin to some 106 people, each time sharing at least the outline of the gospel. About 30 times the conversation was extended. One time he had a one hour discussion with 2 Harley Davidson dealers who wanted to know more about Christianity (because a friend was always trying to share with one of them).

Out of 100 'appointments' not one person gave a hostile or even negative response. In fact more than ½ expressed appreciation. A number entered into deeper discussions. Two Ethiopian Jews enjoyed a long discussion and attended a Bible study that evening.

PRAYER PRACTICE:
- Write a brief prayer for a seeker you know.

- Pray for appointments.

2. **Pray for the messenger (yourself!) the way the apostle Paul prayed for himself**

    See scriptures and exercise above from "Paul's Prayers for Himself"

3. **Prayer evangelism (Prayer as a Bridge/Trojan Horse)**

Prayer is the common language of spirituality – and a bridge to the seeker. Yes, many seekers would like to learn to pray. You might also think of prayer training as a 'Trojan Horse'. Even the most seemingly closed person to Christ will rarely turn down an offer to receive prayer, especially in a time of need or when undergoing difficulty. Through praying with seekers and teaching them to pray, we can introduce them to the riches of Christ and his gospel. We can bring them directly to meet Jesus through prayer.

Prayer Evangelism involves both praying *for* the lost, and praying *with* the lost
- i) Pray for the seeker. Let them know you are praying for them.
- ii) Pray with the seeker… literally 'hands on'
- iii) While sharing the good news, pray with a seeker
- iv) Teach a seeker to pray!

i) Learn to pray for people you are sharing with
There are few more powerful words than when a Christian asks a seeker:
    "Can I pray for you?"
Often a person who might resist a verbal sharing of the gospel will be open to prayer. This is especially true if you have taken time to carefully listen and find out their deeper needs.

Here is one testimony of a veteran church planter who was surprised by a wonderful healing and harvest answer to prayer.:

> *Several years ago, I made my way to an appliance store to pick up some parts for my ailing washing machine. At the conclusion of my purchase, the owner informed me he was closing his business because of his failing health. I expressed sympathy towards him, but as I was leaving felt prompted by the Holy Spirit to pray for him. I turned and spoke with the proprietor that I had a faith in God and had seen people recover after personal prayer. "Can I pray for you", I asked. "If it doesn't take very long", he replied.*
> *After my prayer for his health, recovery and for a personal experience with God, I left. The store did close down the next week and I often thought about what may have happened. Nine months passed and I met Jim Grover who was a new believer in our church one Sunday evening. As he told me his story of meeting a lady from our church who had shared her faith, he too invited Jesus Christ into his life. I was thrilled. He next told me of his "documented" healing. As I probed further into the story, we both began to realize that standing in front of me was the proprietor of the failed business to whom I had prayed with, months earlier. The encounter we had was so brief months earlier, that we had forgotten each other's faces. Who is in your pathway today, that God is wanting you to love on and pray with?*
> > -Harvey Trauter (church planter, director Vision 360 Canada)

For Personal Reflection

7. Recall from your own experience when you were able to pray with someone you were sharing with – even though they might not have been interested in a gospel presentation.

PRAYER PRACTICE:
- Pray for this person now.

ii) Learn to pray with a seeker – Pray the Gospel into them!

You will find it easier to 'pray the gospel into them' than to speak the gospel to them. Let me share a personal experience that I will never forget:

> *Carl, a friend of our family is dying of brain cancer. His head is swollen to twice normal size. He can no longer speck. His family asks me not to talk to him about death or serious things. I ask "Would it be okay for me to pray for Carl?" They reply "of course".*
>
> *At this point I take Carl by the hand and began to pray for him. I pray the gospel into him. I rehearse the promises and invitations of Christ in the gospels. I share in prayer how Jesus lived and died so we can be with him forever. I shared how simple faith brings us into a forever relation with God. I pray for a long time. Two things happen as I am praying:.*
>
> *One, as I pray I feel Carl's hand close tighter and tighter around my fingers. He hears. He understands. He wants me to continue. As I continue to pray tears well up in his eyes. He is crying. I am crying inside too.*
>
> *Second, at the same time his family is grateful and tell me they are glad I came! It is beautiful!*

8. Share a time you were able to 'preach the gospel into someone's heart'

9. Who can you think of whom you would like to pray for in this way?

10. What is their present deep need?

11. What will you pray for them?

PRAYER PRACTICE:
- Pray for this person now.

iii) Offer to teach a seeker(s) to pray.

We have written a pocketbook to teach seekers to pray – *Journey in Prayer: Learning to pray the prayer of Jesus.* Here is what a naturopathic doctor wrote after reading the book.

> *"Thank you for your wonderful book, Journey in Prayer: Learning to pray the prayer of Jesus. I read it upon return from my vacation last week and I found it transformative. I found it both scholarly and practical. Since reading your book, my own prayer practice has become more directed affording me greater mental and emotional clarity and stability. I feel more resilient with a greater sense of spiritual resources and relationship to God, whom I now address as "Father". Thankyou for creating this book which will help many who pray and many for whom I would love to meet up and discuss your book"* -Elizabeth Crosby MD

At the present time of writing, my sister is struggling with cancer. I have been teaching her how to pray the Lord's prayer.. She read our Bible study on prayer, *Seven Days of Prayer with Jesus.* After a period of months she told me 'I call God "My father" every time I pray".

I ask her, "Do you what it means to pray in the Spirit?" She does not. I talk to her about how the Holy Spirit is given to help and strengthen us in prayer and in life. I encourage her to ask to be filled with the Holy Spirit to better pray through her trials. I then ask her "Do you pray in Jesus name?" She does not but wants to know. I tell her about Christ our Mediator and High Priest. He died for us and now lives to pray with and for us. The next time I talk to her she wants me to know "I ask to be filled with the Holy Spirit every day. Now I always pray in Jesus name".

iv) When you begin to make progress in sharing your faith, it is easy to pray with a seeker. It is often well received when you ask the seeker, "Would you like to say a prayer as well." At this point you might ask them to pray after you (which is easier than spontaneous prayer). Of course, this is nothing new. Evangelists have been doing this a long time. Prayer moves a person from theory to practice; from general to personal.

Let me share two examples. The first is personal.

>Ted owns a general store. He has cancer. I have been visiting him for around a year. It begins socially but soon I am able to talk to him about life, death and spiritual things. He is usually open to a conversation. He is always open and thankful when I pray for him in his store.

>At some point, I bring him a bible (an easy translation). I circle many comfort passages in the psalms and gospels. During times of loneliness and pain, he begins to read them. When we meet again, we read some together and I am able to take him deeper into a personal experience of the gospel. He is always happy to have me pray for him. After several conversations I ask, "Would you like to pray with me Ted?" Often he is willing sometimes not. I ask for healing of body and soul. I pray that he will be able to trust Christ and let Christ take him through this journey. He always says "Amen". He offers up simple but sincere prayers. Over time they deepen and gain weight. When we meet I ask how his prayer life is going. It varies, but he is often able to pray.

>During the last days of his life I have the privilege to read, pray, sing hymns, hold his hand, weep with and for him I always ask where he is with Jesus. I tell him I want to meet him in heaven. Ted gives his life to Christ. Being with him on the last day is one of the great privileges of my life.

>When I do the funeral I am able to share this testimony of Ted's suffering and prayer and coming to faith with 60 of his neighbors.

The second example is when a colleague takes prayer training to a little country church and experiences a mini-revival among a group that has pretty much forgotten the gospel:

>In August of 2010 I visited a small congregation in Saskatchewan for the purpose of worshiping God. As I chatted with the people I found out that they had been without a pastor for almost 3 years. I had gone to this small city to help my son get his new business up and running. After the service I asked one lady if I could meet with the elders of the church. I told them that I was there to open a new business in town. One lady said, "Oh, you are here to solicit business!" "Not really," I replied, "I'm also a semi-retired pastor." One of the ladies said, "I think we have just experienced a miracle!"

>Anyway, I suggested that I could preach for them one Sunday in September and if they liked it we could talk. If they didn't, my feelings would not be hurt. They asked me to begin preaching the first Sunday of October.
>What happened after that first Sunday became one of the most amazing experiences I have had in ministry.

>From what I could gather there were about five Christians in this congregation of about 18 people. After several weeks of teaching evangelism and basic Christian doctrine, one man asked me one Sunday, "Do you write out your prayers?" "No, I replied, I enjoy talking to my Father. Would you like to learn how to pray?" I asked the Leadership Team if they would like to do a series on Prayer. There was an overwhelming positive response and we moved ahead. Using the book Seven Days of Prayer with Jesus, I began with the first Petition, "Our Father". (I share this with you because this congregation was a traditional congregation which used the Lord's prayer every Sunday.) I began by teaching them the significance of addressing God as our Father. "Not everyone who talks to God can address Him as Father," I said, "only those who have been drawn into his family. Just like your children, they alone can call you Father or Mother but the neighbor boy or girl down the street does not have that same privilege. Only natural children or adopted children have this priviledge."

>I had spent several weeks on evangelism and now the practical application of the gospel was enjoying a familial relationship with the God of the Universe. "Now," I said, "let's spend some time just talking to God as our Father. Tell him what you really want him to hear. In simple language, with broken hearts and teary eyes, they all prayed to their Heavenly Father. What had happened and what I found so refreshing, was an old concept – the Fatherhood of God, now became a very personal meaningful prayerful experience. In the following week we moved on to the "Hallowed be your name." What

was so amazing about praying this petition was that they had watched Sproul's video on the Holiness of God. Our sense of the Holiness of God and that we could have access to him because of Jesus, was overwhelming. Lives were being changed right before my eyes.

Teaching and preaching evangelism, open and honest preaching of God's Word, the teaching and practicing of prayer ended with a bond that I had not experienced since the first four years of my ministry in the Maritimes.

After eight months with this little struggling congregation, there was a sense of renewal and joy in a new found Saviour. The congregation had almost doubled by the time I left and many people who had been attending for years had come to know Jesus Christ as their personal savior.

For Small Group Discussion

12. Think of a time you have talked with a searching person about prayer. How did they respond? Were you able to take it further?

PRAYER PRACTICE:
- Pray for opportunities to teach someone to pray.

HOMEWORK:
- Use Paul's prayers this week to pray for yourself in your missionfield.
- Read through the material for Lesson 7, concentrating on the readings, the personal reflection questions and prayer practice points.

© Pray for the City: Boot Camp for Urban Mission (info@prayercurrent.com)

Section II
Leaders Build Jesus' House of Prayer

Let's return to the diagram to remind ourselves where we are in the stream of Prayer Bootcamp:

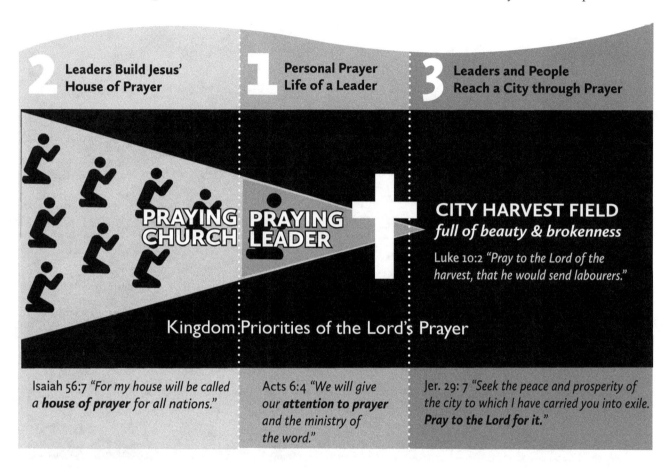

1. We have just completed section one in the center, where we looked at how the **personal prayer life of a leader** begins in the closet in fellowship with Christ. The outcome of this strong personal prayer life, is that they find they become 'active duty' in the fields of harvest.

2. From there we will now dive into section two where we will look at how **leaders lead in prayer** out of that personal prayer life. We will look at the power of leaders praying together with the people.

3. We will conclude later in the third and final section with a look at how God **sends his people out to the city as they pray for it.**

Leaders Build Jesus' House of Prayer

(See DVD Section II introduction)

There are two keys in Prayer for the City training.

1. First, we want to replace 'closed loop' prayer with prayer for the mission and prayer for the city. Closed loop prayer is prayer that is entirely focused to church attendees. We pray for each other – for health, and well being. We pray for our own children and families and sister churches. Closed loop prayer comes from closed door churches.

2. Second, we want to complement prayer that is focused on one's private and inner spiritual life with prayer that is rigorously concerned with the whole church and the whole city. We want to pray for the church in the city.

In order to make these changes leaders will need to train their churches in prayer. Specifically, they will need to train their churches to be houses of prayer which are inwardly faithful and outwardly focused. This is God's design for the church. He wants leaders and people to build a house of prayer for all nations.

Let's look at the Scriptural argument:

I. God is always building a house of prayer.

God promises that his temple will have an open door policy to the nations and that a chorus of prayer and praise shall rise from its midst. This is the intended purpose and destiny of his people!

Isaiah 56: *And foreigners who bind themselves to the LORD...*
7 these I will bring to my holy mountain
   and give them joy in my house of prayer.
   for my house will be called
   a house of prayer for all nations."
8 The Sovereign LORD declares—
   "I will gather still others to them
   besides those already gathered."

By definition, God's temple is a house of prayer or it is not a temple.
In a real sense prayer is a summary for all that we mean by worship.

The ever burning incense within the temple signifies continual prayer:

Exodus 30: 7 *"Aaron must burn fragrant incense on the altar every morning when he tends the lamps. He must burn incense again when he lights the lamps at twilight so incense will burn regularly before the LORD for the generations to come."*

Revlations5:8 *"They were holding golden bowls of incense, which are the prayers of the saints."*

Revelations 8:3 *"The smoke of the incense, together with the prayers of the saints, went up before God from the angel's hand."*

God does mighty works of deliverance in response to prayer;

> Revelations 8:3,4-5 *"4The smoke of the incense, together with the prayers of the saints, went up before God from the angel's hand. 5Then the angel took the censer, filled it with fire from the altar, and hurled it on the earth; and there came peals of thunder, rumblings, flashes of lightning and an earthquake."*

We feel the thunder when God's people are a house of prayer

> Acts 1:14, 2;1-3 *"14They all joined together constantly in prayer,...1When the day of Pentecost came, they were all together in one place. 2Suddenly a sound like the blowing of a violent wind came from heaven and filled the whole house where they were sitting."*

> Acts 4:31 *"After they prayed, the place where they were meeting was shaken. And they were all filled with the Holy Spirit and spoke the word of God boldly."*

> Acts 16:25,26 *"About midnight Paul and Silas were praying and singing hymns to God, and the other prisoners were listening to them. 26Suddenly there was such a violent earthquake that the foundations of the prison were shaken. At once all the prison doors flew open, and everybody's chains came loose."*

II. Jesus is sent by God to purify his temple for prayer.

Jesus comes suddenly to the temple.

He is the promised 'messenger of the covenant'. He comes in storm and 'as a refiners fire' (Malachi 3:1,2). Why does he come? He comes to find if his covenant people have been building a house of prayer!

> Matthew 21: 12 *"Jesus entered the temple area and drove out all who were buying and selling there. He overturned the tables of the money changers and the benches of those selling doves. 13"It is written," he said to them, " 'My house will be called a house of prayer,' but you are making it a 'den of robbers.'"*

The question we must ask: "If Jesus were to come today, would he find a praying people?" Would he find a temple of prayer?

> • Would he commend his covenant people for being a house of prayer for all nations?
> • Would Jesus warn his people to 'strengthen what remains'?
> • Would he cleanse the temple?

III. The house of prayer that Jesus builds

> Acts 1:4-14 *"He gave them this command: "Do not leave Jerusalem, but wait for the gift my Father promised, which you have heard me speak about. ...You will receive power when the Holy Spirit comes on you; and you will be my witnesses to the ends of the earth." When they arrived, they went upstairs... all joined together constantly in prayer, along with the women and Mary the mother of Jesus, and with his brothers.*

Christ's new covenant people are devoted to prayer (leaders and people together)

> Acts 2:42 *"They devoted themselves ...to prayer. 43Everyone was filled with awe, and many wonders and miraculous signs were done by the apostles..."*

Leaders and people, each day in the temple they kept the hour of prayer:

> Acts 2:46,3:1 *"Every day they continued to meet together in the temple courts...One day Peter and John were going up to the temple at the time of prayer—at three in the afternoon."*

Leaders prioritize prayer: Acts 6:4 *"We will devote ourselves to prayer..."*

Leaders and people overcome every obstacle in prayer

Acts 4:23-25,31 *"On their release, Peter and John went back to their own people and reported all that the chief priests and elders had said to them. <u>When they heard this, they raised their voices together in prayer to God.</u> "Sovereign Lord," they said, "you made the heaven and the earth and the sea, and everything in them …<u>after they prayed the place was shaken, they were all filled with the Holy Spirit and spoke the word of God boldly…"</u>*

Christ's mission is advanced through prayer

Acts 12:4,5,10 *"After arresting him, he put him in prison, handing him over to be guarded by four squads of four soldiers each…So Peter was kept in prison, <u>but the church was earnestly praying</u> to God for him…**they came to the gates of the city. <u>It opened for them by itself."</u>***

Christ's power come as his people pray

Acts 4:31-34 *"…after they <u>prayed the place was shaken,</u> they were all filled with the Holy Spirit and spoke the word of God boldly All the believers were one in heart and mind. No one claimed that any of his possessions was his own, but they shared everything they had. With <u>great power</u> the apostles continued to testify to the resurrection of the Lord Jesus, and much grace was upon them all. There were no needy persons among them.*

It is Christ's desire and intent: we are a temple of the Holy Spirit, we are becoming a house of prayer for all nations.

Jesus' Priority to Build a House of Prayer

GOALS: In this lesson we will...
- ❑ Evaluate our view and priority of prayer and mission
- ❑ Evaluate the degree of "mission vs. maintenance" present in our lives and ministries
- ❑ Evaluate the health and progress of prayer in our churches

Introduction   (See DVD Section II: Lesson 7)

Prayer is key to avoiding the maintenance cycle
After a brief surge of prayer and mission all too often a church subsides into a mode of maintenance.

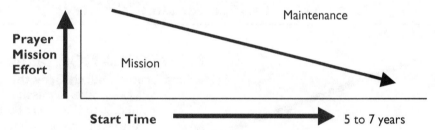

Our initial passion is to start and grow churches that are "city soluble" – seven day a week communities which challenge and serve our city. Within a few years, church plants often drift into "Sunday morning" Christianity where all efforts and resources are focused on achieving a one hour dramatic experience.

To counter this decline and reverse the momentum we need to launch our churches with concerted kingdom prayer. We will study and apply the New Testament sequence of mission with integrity. We will discover the power of connecting the gospel to our prayers and our prayers to the mission of Christ.

Return to kingdom prayer is the critical means that renews us in Christ and his mission.

A Praying Great Commission Leader/Church		**A Prayerless Maintenance Driven Leader/Church**
Loves its community	⟷	Fears its community
Opening gates	⟷	Building walls
Tired, but loving it	⟷	Fatigue/Frustration
Fellowship in ministry	⟷	Fighting over details, personalities
Growth in grace/converts	⟷	Numerical plateau or decline
Good teaching with focus on harvest	⟷	Poor outreach, focus on teaching only
Prayer for lost and harvest workers	⟷	Prayer focus on health of members
Focus on resources for harvest	⟷	Focus on buildings and schools

What we are trying to achieve is starting churches and ministries that avoid the typical path of maintenance. Such a mission or ministry begins with a clear focus and most of its initial efforts on mission. Time can lead to a mere "survival faith." What can stem the tide of maintenance and renew the mission?
Prayer – an ongoing focus and priority on missional prayer.

Life Cycle of a Maintenance Ministry

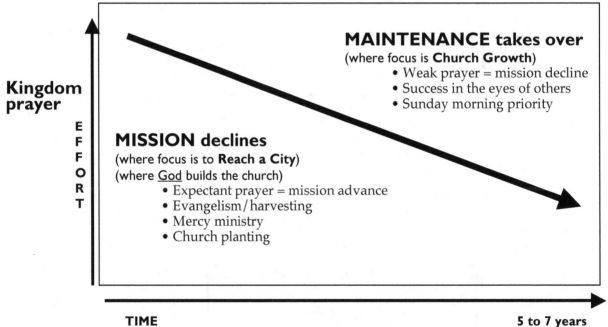

Kingdom prayer

EFFORT

MAINTENANCE takes over
(where focus is **Church Growth**)
• Weak prayer = mission decline
• Success in the eyes of others
• Sunday morning priority

MISSION declines
(where focus is to **Reach a City**)
(where <u>God</u> builds the church)
• Expectant prayer = mission advance
• Evangelism/harvesting
• Mercy ministry
• Church planting

TIME   **5 to 7 years**

By God's grace, through kingdom prayer, we come to know his vision for our city. He inserts us into the artery and nerve centres of our community. We become shelter for the seeking and exploited. He raises leaders to go before us as they follow Christ into his mission. He provides resources needed to follow him.

APPLICATION QUESTIONS

For Personal Reflection

1. In what ways are you missional in your attitudes, thinking and actions?

2. In what ways are you maintenance – oriented in your attitudes, thinking and actions?

For Small Group Discussion

3. What evidences can you see that demonstrate that your church/ministry cultures are missional?

4. What evidences can you see that demonstrate that your church/ministry cultures are maintenance – oriented?

5. What drives us into maintenance mode? How might a continual priority and commitment to kingdom prayer in your church/ministry affect how missional or maintenance – oriented it is?

PRAYER PRACTICE:
- Praise the Lord of the harvest and his redeeming work.
- Thank him for evidence and growth seen in being missional.
- Confess and surrender maintenance – oriented attitudes, thinking and actions.
- Cry out for a spirit of expectant prayer and outward missional focus and advance.

This study indicates prayer as the first priority in a clear sequence.

Prayer and the Sequence of New Testament Mission

John Smed

The Place of Prayer in New Testament Mission

In order to plant and grow a church with integrity, a church planter, pastor or leader must apply to the biblical means of growth as found in Acts. Develop concerted prayer (1:14, 2:1), practice bold evangelism (2:41, 4:3 – 4), evidence a radical commitment to community (2:42 – 47), exercise church discipline (5:13 – 14), develop shared leadership (6:1 – 7), nurture lay evangelism (8:4), and champion church planting (9:31). These means accompany the explosive and joyous expansion of the early church.

There is also integrity of sequence in the early church narrative. Study of the text reveals that the order is as significant as the events themselves. The history in Acts is not presented randomly by Luke. He is conscious of giving the church a pattern for future mission activity. He presents a chronology with a purpose. It is somewhat like a combination lock – numbers mean little apart from the sequence (leave out a number, or change the order, and nothing happens). Integrity in mission requires that the sequence be followed in the order presented in Acts.

I   The New Testament Sequence

1. <u>New Testament mission advance consists of five 'stages' in chronological sequence.</u>
    First is the outpouring of Christ's power in the context of 'waiting' prayer (Acts 1:8,14, 2:1 – 4).
    Second is conversion growth through the preaching of Christ's person and work (Acts 2:36 – 41).

    Third is community formation, notably from the harvest of new converts (Acts 2:41 – 47).
    Fourth is mobilization through leadership selection and lay deployment (Acts 6:1 – 8, 8:4).
    Fifth is multiplication through extensive church planting (Acts 9:31).

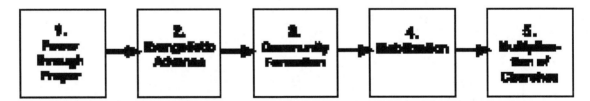

It is important to note that each stage is essential and each builds upon the previous. No stage can be eliminated and the order cannot be altered if the Spirit's plan is to be fulfilled. For example, without power through prayer, there can be no effective harvest. Without conversion growth, community formation and church planting will be an unreal shadow of the early church.

This identifies a weakness in much present mission endeavor. <u>An inadequate prayer base and an even weaker launch into evangelism results in slow growth anemic churches.</u> If churches are growing rapidly, it is often through response to advertising and programs, resulting in transfer and not conversion growth. It is not uncommon for churches to add a hundred or more attendees without a single conversion.

2.   The five stages build on each other and each is continually repeated in the history of vital churches. We note this in the Acts history. Following the first Pentecost – harvest – community sequence in chapters one and two – culminating in the community formation of Acts 2:42 – 47 – the key events in this history are repeated in chapter 4:31-33

The cycle of prayer, a baptism of power, and community formation after Pentecost is repeated in this 'second' Pentecost:

Thus an expanded representation of the five stages looks like this:

Prayer and Empowering (2:1 – 4) . . . Prayer and Empowering (4:31) . . . .
"All were filled…"   *"After they prayed…they were all filled with the Holy Spirit"*

Proclamation and Harvest (2:40 – 41) . . . Proclamation and Harvest (4:33) . . . .
"Those who accepted his message [were] 3000" "With great power the apostles testified to the resurrection.

Community Formation (2:42 – 47) . . . Community Formation (4:32) . . . .
"Every day they continued to meet together…" "All the believers were one in heart and mind…"

Mobilization (6:1 – 4, 8:4) . . . Mobilization (ch. 10ff.)
"Those scattered preached the word [everywhere]" "Those scattered…began to preach to Greeks also…."

Church Multiplication (9:31 to end of Acts)
"The church throughout Judea, Galilee and Samaria grew in numbers."

This repeated pattern serves to notify the church of all ages – these world changing events are not one time or temporary — they are to be continuously repeated throughout the on – going expansion of the church. Renewed empowerment by the Holy Spirit is to be continuous in the church![1]

Consider most any church today and you will find that the Acts' history has been neglected. In fact, the time when the sequence is followed is more the exception than the rule. There is only one approach that has biblical warrant. Whatever the implications, we must return to the New Testament pattern. It is a matter of integrity.

In doing so, there will be practical consequences for church planters and church leaders. For example, in our haste to generate offerings for a new mission we may hasten to community formation (stage 3), and leadership selection (stage 4). It is easy to neglect the priority of prayer and evangelism.

We may be tempted to agree with the ideal, and then dismiss it as impractical or too expensive. Can it be that honoring Christ in these matters is not possible today? Is it possible that following scripture would result in failure to carry out the great commission? We believe the issue is deeper. The issue is our own courage and integrity.

To turn resolutely to God on these matters, we must first consider who it is that initiates and empowers this order of church planting.

---

[1] The inaugural outpouring of the Spirit creates ripples throughout the world as the Spirit continues to come in power. Pentecost is the epicentre; but the earthquake gives forth further after – shocks. Those rumbles continue through the ages. Pentecost itself is not repeated; but a theology of the Spirit which did not give rise to prayer for his coming in power would not be a theology of *ruach*! (Sinclair Ferguson, *The Holy Spirit*, IVP, 1996, p. 91.)

II   Jesus Christ as the Lord of Mission

Prayer is essential to starting and growing churches. Why? Because Jesus initiates and renews the process of church mission with the words of the great commission. He declares his Lordship of the harvest: **"All authority in heaven and earth has been given to me. Go therefore!"** As the captain of our faith, he sets the agenda: we are to **"make disciples of all nations"** by teaching Christ and baptizing new converts. By promising his presence: **"I will be with you to the end of the age,"** he declares that he will accompany his witnesses. As our apostle and high priest, he goes before us. He takes the first hit. He takes it at the cross. He makes the decisive breach in the enemy ranks, and now he bids us follow. He sheds first blood – his! – and invites us to mix our blood with his on the field of his battle. There is <u>no cost</u> for salvation, but a dear price will be exacted of his followers.

<u>Christ sets the agenda and sequence for the disciples</u>. In prayer, they are to "wait for the gift my father promised." On doing so they "shall receive power when the Holy Spirit has come upon you, and you shall be witnesses to Me in Jerusalem, and in all Judea and Samaria, and to the end of the earth" (Acts 4:1 – 5). They are to wait in prayer before they witness. They are to witness before they harvest. It is a matter of obedience. It is a matter of integrity. It is essential for success.

They do wait in prayer (Acts 1:14, 2:1). They receive power and witness with great effect (2:41). This reveals that Jesus' words here are more than command. They are promise. Within 7 to 9 years after Pentecost we see his initial promise confirmed with the extensive penetration of three countries with church multiplication:

The churches throughout all Judea, Galilee, and Samara had peace and were edified. And walking in the fear of the Lord and in the comfort of the Holy Spirit they were multiplied. (9:31)

New Testament believers follow the sequence. They wait in prayer; witness, form community, mobilize, and multiply according to his command and promise. <u>The Lord Jesus directs the entire process and guarantees the outcome</u>. He will do the same for his people today. We only need to follow him as he has called us to in his word.

The completed sequence for New Testament mission includes the work and word of the harvest Lord:

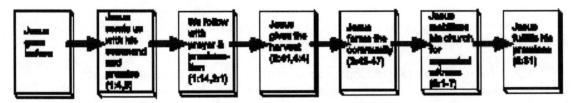

How encouraging! He goes before us. He bids us follow. He directs, inspires and empowers us for the mission. His promise guarantees the outcome. We are made ready and willing to turn with renewed hope to the great adventure and high calling of filling this world with his message and ministry.

III   The Five Stages In Historical Order

In considering the five stages of apostolic mission, we can outline the biblical history, provide implications for planting and growing churches today, and include practical suggestions on how to follow this pattern.

1.   **<u>The first priority is empowerment through waiting prayer.</u>**

We must emphasize <u>waiting</u> when it comes to Christ empowering his people for this mission. The disciples are to "wait for the Promise of the Father, which you have heard from me, for John baptized with water, but you shall be baptized with the Holy Spirit not many days from now." It is, of course, a matter of simple obedience to wait. Even more, it is absolutely necessary to wait for the Holy Spirit's endowment before proceeding. The battle will be hard – pitched and to the death. As the seven sons of Sceva found out (Acts 19:14) – the enemy's power is great. Malice, treachery, and murder will be our lot; as with the leader so with follower. Advance will only be possible with supernatural resource. Every advance will be met by a counter attack; every reformation by a counter – reformation. The disciples must wait. They do wait. They are not idle. They are involved in importunate prayer:

These all continued with one accord in prayer and supplication, with the women and Mary the mother of Jesus, and with his brothers ....Now when the day of Pentecost had fully come, they were all with one accord in one place...(Acts 1:14, 2:1)

<u>This promise and this obedience issues into the most widespread manifestation of the Holy Spirit in the history of humanity:</u>

And suddenly there came a sound from heaven, as of a rushing mighty wind, and it filled the whole house where they were sitting....(Acts 2:1 – 4)

Far from a once – for – all event, this empowering from God is to be repeated until Christ's work through the church is accomplished:

So when they heard that, they raised their voice with one accord and said; "Lord, You are God....And when they had prayed, the place where they were assembled together was shaken; and they were all filled with the Holy Spirit, and they spoke the work of God with boldness. (Acts 4:23 – 31)

The application of this narrative is straightforward. <u>We must pray</u>. <u>We must wait</u>. We must continue to pray and wait until the Lord gives both power and wisdom to enter into the battle. Out of ignorance, or a perception of necessity, or a simple lack of integrity, many church mission endeavors have failed from the start because they fail at this point. Our only hope is to begin here; to begin with prayer and to be stubborn in our resolve to wait for power on high.

Application – Keeping the Sequence:

1) Each church planter / mission leader should recruit prayer partners (usually 50) to pray daily for this project until a local prayer base is established. The same applies to a pastor seeking to renew a church.

2) Each church planter / pastor / leader should spend at least one day each month in fasting and prayer for the work. From the start he should bring others in. Prayer walks and prayer strategy should focus on gaining a prophetic understanding of the target community along with seeking to discern God's heart and plan for the community. Boldness for witness is the driving force of this prayer. No major actions or decisions should be made unless bathed in prayer.

3) From the day a nucleus form in a new church, or a new mission endeavor is launched, missional prayer groups and prayer training need to start.

2. **The second stage in planting and growing churches is evangelistic harvest.** After being baptized with the Holy Spirit, New Testament believers go forth to a harvest of three thousand and then two thousand souls. Listening to Christ, they wait. Waiting, they receive. Receiving, they harvest. How few today are willing to hold out for the blessing!

This stage is characterized by two related forms of harvest – discovery and deliverance. Men and women's hearts and minds are opened by the preaching of Christ crucified. They discover Christ and see for the first time:

Now when they heard this, they were cut to the heart, and said to Peter and the rest of the apostles, "Men and brethren what shall we do?" (Acts 2:37)

Luke also describes an array of healings and exorcisms. This promises for us that a great deliverance from very real forms of sin and slavery will accompany the Spirit's advance:

Then fear came upon every soul, and many wonders and signs were done through the apostles. (Acts 2:43)

Application – Keeping the Sequence:

1) In starting and renewing churches we must recruit and send out men who have a proven track record in evangelism and an undying determination to "pray for broke." Perhaps our greatest need is here, as well as our greatest failing. Too few are faithful in evangelism. Sending bodies and church leader boards are too eager to support a good teacher or a good manager. If we fail here, we fail before we start.

2) The prayerful establishment of *outreach ministries* for business people, on campus, and in the community is a priority. As well, from the beginning the 'lost of the lost' – the poor, the handicapped, the addicted, and the demon – oppressed must find hope and shelter in our midst. Christ shows the way – he was a "friend of sinners." In the New Testament history there is no separation between evangelism and mercy / social justice. The two always go together. To divide these is to divide Christ.

3. **The third stage in Christ's pattern for mission is community formation**. This is the time we discover if we have followed Christ in stages one and two. Our hearts thrill with joy and burn with envy at the description of the first community of Christ in Acts 2:42 – 47, and Acts 4:32 – 25:

Those who gladly received the word were baptized . . . . and they continued steadfastly in the apostles' doctrine, and fellowship, in the breaking of bread and in prayers . . . . Now all who believed were together, and had all things in common . . . . breaking bread from house to house, they ate their food with gladness and simplicity of heart, praising God and having favor of all the people. And the Lord added to the church daily those who were being saved.

It is impossible to argue against it: the health and the excitement of the New Testament church is directly proportional to the abundance of new converts. <u>A vital community forms spontaneously out of the fertile soil of evangelism.</u>

What a redeemed community is born here! Radical witness. Overall devotion to prayer. Amazing deliverance. Radiant joy. Selfless and sacrificial giving. This is the fruit of newly regenerated hearts. Simply contrast this scene with the average church. We must admit with tears that our churches seem mundane in comparison. Little faith and little expectancy results in a small harvest and a strategy burdened church. When God works people declare his wonder. When he is silent, discussions center on philosophy of ministry, networking, goals and objectives.

Application – Keeping the Sequence:

1) <u>New Testament community arises spontaneously from conversion growth</u>. In one sense nothing can be done to 'start' a worshipping community. It simply happens as a result of stage one and two (prayer and evangelism). Conversely, nothing can be done to stop a community from forming as a result of people being saved. We must be ready to hold out and hold on until we see the earnest of the Holy Spirit in this. We can never be assured of Christ's blessing unless we use Christ's methods, and honor the sequence he has set before us.

2) In the new church plant, if evangelism is moving ahead, community formation, including formal worship services, should begin. However, it is better to wait than start too soon.

    At launch time, the church should have a balanced mixture of gathering Christians, new converts and seekers. Ideally this could be no more than one half mature Christians, and the others new converts and seekers.

    Prayer and outreach must remain a firm priority. Otherwise, finding a facility, purchasing equipment and arranging worship services become the priority.

3) For a growing church seeking to establish new principles and priorities, care needs to be taken to expand time spent on harvest ministries. For example each pastor and mission leader should ensure they schedule several hours in personal evangelism each week. In terms of staff and leadership selection priority should always be given to those who pray and to gatherers. It is much easier to manage growth than to get growth.

4. **The fourth stage in New Testament mission is leader selection and mission mobilization.**

Several critical events occur simultaneously when the church prays and chooses its first leaders (Acts 6:1 – 7). Notice that growth momentum and attendant problems requires leadership selection:

Now in those days, when the number of disciples was multiplying, there arose a dispute (6:1)

Wisely, the apostles choose to both expand the leadership base and involve the people in selecting them. They pray a blessing on these leaders. The results are outstanding! Seven Grecian Jews are selected. This is to the credit of the Hebrew Jews. These men become outstanding ministers with Stephen and Philip leading the way. Stephen becomes the first martyr. There is an added result to this persecution: "Those who were scattered went everywhere preaching the word" (8:4). Philip becomes the first evangelist to the Samaritans and beyond to the Ethiopian eunuch (Acts 8:5, 26ff). As a result "a great many of the priests were obedient to the faith" (6:7).

The church is mobilized as never before. An explosive advance of the proclamation ministry of the apostles takes place here. Through the attendant persecution of Stephen and the church, <u>the apostolic witness goes democratic and international</u>.

Now those who had been scattered by the persecution in connection with Stephen traveled as far as Phoenicia, Cyprus and Antioch, telling the message only to Jews. Some of them, however, men from Cyprus and Cyrene, went to Antioch and began to speak to Greeks also, telling them the good news about the Lord Jesus. The Lord's hand was with them, and a great number of people believed and turned to the Lord. (Acts 11:19 – 21)

Application – Keeping the Sequence:

1) <u>"Organization" and leadership selection needs clearly to be defined in terms of mission first and church government second</u>. The key issue is expanding the apostolic witness, not simply the control and order of the church. We should have 'mobilization services' rather than organizational services. Leaders need to be trained in prayer, servant and word ministry as well as governance and doctrine. Like Stephen and Philip (and Jesus!), all leaders are to be "servant/witnesses." Sheep always follow their shepherds. Candidates for church leadership must be faithful prayer for the lost and sharing Christ.

5. **The fifth stage in New Testament mission is church multiplication:**

Acts 9:31 should be read as a summary and celebratory culmination of the preceding narrative of the first four stages:

Then the churches throughout all Judea, Galilee, and Samaria had peace and were edified. And walking in the fear of the Lord, and in the comfort of the Holy Spirit, they were multiplied.

This is the completion of phase one of Christ's strategy to reach a world. Prayer receives empowerment; boldness issues forth in reaping; reaping unites God's people in dying sacrifice and resurrection joy; the saints are mobilized throughout several countries. Church multiplication completes the pattern he establishes for our work.

Notice that there has been extensive penetration of the gospel and new congregations formed 'throughout all Judea, Galilee, and Samaria'. Whole countries are reached!

There is hope and promise for us here. If we hold steadfast to the Lord's pattern for planting and growing his church, we will taste of the same banquet of joy.

Application – Keeping the Sequence:

1) Plan for church multiplication to follow the first four stages of planting and growing churches. This involves the realization that a healthy biblical church is self – reproducing.

2) From the beginning of every church plant, and as soon as possible for the renewing church should have a church planting intern on staff who is praying and preparing to launch the first daughter church. Ideally, a new intern can be brought on board every few years to perpetuate the process locally, regionally and internationally. (It helps smaller churches if the interns raise missionary support). It is not impossible . Our little church in Vancouver trained and sent out four church planters and three pastors in the first ten years.

3) Budgets should reflect the intent to plant other churches. Revolving funds and partnership funds can be established to fund interns and actual launching of new works.

4) Transplants from the mother church to a daughter church should consist of harvest pray – ers and harvest workers.

Needless to say, our people will have to be trained in prayer and in mission in order to understand these things. *Serious resistance* can be anticipated from those who are ignorant of the New Testament pattern, or its implications for the local church.

Summary and Conclusions

The five stages of New Testament mission as presented in the book of Acts are successive, yet as the new church grows, each element is in continuous dynamic relation with and feeds the others. We notice that prayer always fuels evangelism; evangelism in turn necessitates prayer. Community formation issues from both prayer and evangelism, and at the same time the new community is 'devoted to prayer', and grows evangelistically (2:47).

In the mobilization stage, prayer, evangelism, and community dynamics influence and are also the result of effective mobilization (leadership selection). Notice how the community of believers share in and rejoice in the outcomes of selection, and how a 'great many' are added to the faith (6:1 – 7). A similar encouraging epilogue accompanies the fifth stage as the church grows in 'the comfort of the Holy Spirit, and were multiplied' (9:31).

The church thus progresses through the five stages by adding on, not leaving behind, the prior elements. At the same time, the earlier stages are expanded and strengthened as the church advances. *How wonderful is God's plan. How important to lay a right foundation by following the plan!*

It is not too dramatic to use the illustration of a star to explain how the New Testament strategy works. Think of stage one, prayer and empowerment, as the nuclear core which fuels all the heat and light which emanates from the star. As long as the core generates power, heat and light result. If it begins to cool, the process slows down, and can even reverse itself, imploding into a super gravitational black hole, from which even light cannot escape. This aptly describes the difference between a praying evangelizing church, and one that has lost its core of power and prayer.

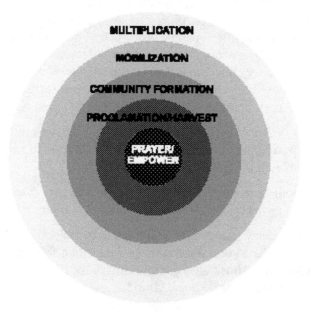

Conclusion:

The New Testament sequence has seldom been implemented. We need to ask, 'Why?'. The pattern is simple and the process of implementation is not complicated.

That we do not follow the history of Acts is partly due to ignorance. Church planters and mission leaders have not been instructed or trained regarding the New Testament pattern. In the final analysis, however, our problem is a failure of integrity. Too often we allow fear and unbelief to influence our entire approach to growing and planting churches. We go with little prayer. We send men who are not committed to personal evangelism. We build core groups and found community on the infertile soil of non – evangelizing Christians. We select leaders with no reference to the harvest and then train them in doctrine and governance. We allow church planting to be the voluntary task of a few churches. With few exceptions, minimal conversions and barren churches are the result.

We must humbly confess – we define our goals and objectives in categories **where success can be achieved with or without a manifest work of God's Spirit.** In order to guarantee that quotas are met, we simply bypass the uncertain element of God's working.

> [The church] is not in control of the mission. Another is in control, and his fresh works will repeatedly surprise the church, compelling it to stop talking and to listen. Because the Spirit himself is sovereign over the mission, the church can only be the attentive servant. The sober truth is the Spirit himself is the witness who goes before the church in its missionary journey . . . . The church is witness insofar as it follows obediently where the Spirit leads.
> – *Lesslie Newbigin,* The Open Secret

The road to integrity involves revised approaches. The road to integrity for many of us requires repentance. The road to integrity begins in prayer. We need to seek God for forgiveness first, and then, with renewed hearts, for the courage, resolve and wisdom to apply the priority of prayer according to the New Testament sequence of mission.

APPLICATION QUESTIONS

For Personal Reflection

6. As Christ dwells in each of us, we are a "mini – church." <u>Evaluate yourself</u> in these priorities. Place and X on the continuum.

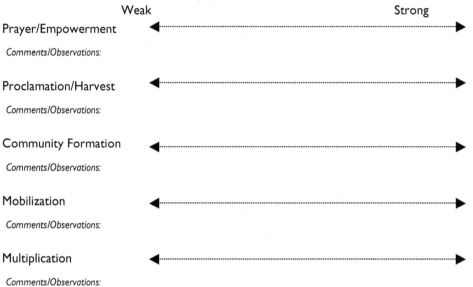

Weak   Strong

Prayer/Empowerment

Comments/Observations:

Proclamation/Harvest

Comments/Observations:

Community Formation

Comments/Observations:

Mobilization

Comments/Observations:

Multiplication

Comments/Observations:

Summarize your observations and evaluation:

7. <u>Evaluate your church/ministry</u> (corporate) in the priorities of the 5 stages. Draw an X on the line.

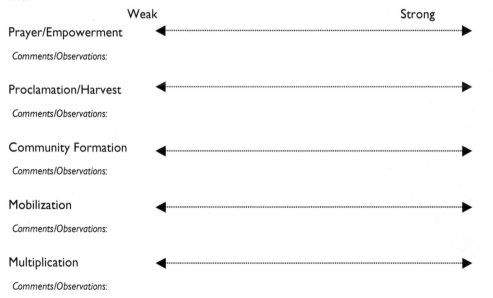

Weak   Strong

Prayer/Empowerment

Comments/Observations:

Proclamation/Harvest

Comments/Observations:

Community Formation

Comments/Observations:

Mobilization

Comments/Observations:

Multiplication

Comments/Observations:

Summarize your observations and evaluation:

For Small Group Discussion

8. Why is the sequence so important? What is the result of going out of sequence?

9. Why do we fear waiting in prayer?

10. Where is the balance in your church/ministry in the five stages? How is your progress in "waiting prayer"? What does waiting mean or what does it look like for your church in its present season?

11. How can we keep prayer a priority in the latter four stages?

PRAYER PRACTICE:
- How do these evaluations and observations guide you to pray?
- Start your prayer time by worshiping God and wait on his Spirit to lead you in prayer.
- Confess and surrender prayerlessness and the things that keep you from waiting in prayer..
- Cry out for a spirit of expectant prayer and for the Lord of the harvest to impart to you his heart for redemption.

Evaluate your church or ministry using the sample evidences listed below.

	No Pulse		Holding		Soaring
	1	2	3	4	5
1. Our leader meetings are as much about prayer as about planning	1	2	3	4	5
2. Our leaders prioritize prayer for our mission to our community as well as for our congregation's needs	1	2	3	4	5
3. Small group meetings are a balance of prayer and bible study and fellowship	1	2	3	4	5
4. In our church we have regular days and extended times of prayer	1	2	3	4	5
5. Our corporate prayer times (public worship) are balanced: Christ centered, concerned with holiness, and with mission	1	2	3	4	5
6. We coach/train small group leaders in kingdom prayer	1	2	3	4	5
7. There is a real sense of spiritual warfare as we pray together	1	2	3	4	5
8. Mission and evangelistic growth can be traced to our prayer times	1	2	3	4	5
9. Our leaders are men and women of gospel-driven prayer	1	2	3	4	5
10. Our ministries and outreaches are empowered by consistent/concerted prayer	1	2	3	4	5
11. We conduct regular kingdom prayer training workshops	1	2	3	4	5
12. We pray with urgency and habit for the lost, straying, and missing in action that God has brought through our doors	1	2	3	4	5
13. We are constantly building one on one prayer partnerships	1	2	3	4	5
14. There is and increasing cry for social justice in our prayer life together	1	2	3	4	5
15. Our prayer times contain a balance of kingdom priorities: worship, mission, confession & pastoral care	1	2	3	4	5

APPLICATION QUESTIONS

For Small Group Discussion

12. Summarize strengths and encouragements to praise God for.

13. What other evidences of growth in corporate prayer do you see in your church/ministry?

14. Summarize weaknesses to confess, surrender and trust God to address.

15. What are your specific challenges to growing as a "house of prayer"? How can these be addressed – practically and more importantly in prayer?

16. Begin to brainstorm ideas to foster growth in corporate kingdom prayer.

PRAYER PRACTICE:
- Praise God for encouragements and evidences seen of growth in corporate prayer.
- Confess and surrender weaknesses.
- Ask the Spirit to pour out a spirit of grace and supplication.

HOMEWORK:
- In light of your corporate prayer evaluation, begin praying about how God may move your group to address the feedback and insights surfaced by the evaluations.
- Read through the material for Lesson 8, concentrating on the readings, the personal reflection questions and prayer practice points.

The Power of Praying Together for Renewal & Revival

GOALS: In this lesson we will...
- ❑ Explore the role of prayer in historical examples of revival
- ❑ Evaluate the degree of "gatheredness" and "sentness" in our lives and ministries
- ❑ Evaluate and plan toward the progress of prayer in our churches and ministries

Introduction

(See DVD Section II: Lesson 8A)

Prayer is warp and woof. Think of a weaving loom. The tapestry of prayer is anchored in the vertical strands of our relationship with God. The cloth is tied together by the horizontal strands of our relationships with each other. The tapestry gains its strength colour and texture with our prayers for one another. When we look up to God in prayer we worship him and receive his grace. At the same time the substance of prayer is richly horizontal as we pray for our brothers, sisters and neighbors with the passion and grace given to us by the Father.

If prayer is only vertical, it will lack the unifying presence of others. If only horizontal it will lose its gospel anchors. It follows that prayer finds it power and purpose not only in individual prayer but in united prayer. The vertical and horizontal dimensions in prayer are woven together in our common thanks and intercession.

What we cannot obtain by solitary prayer we may by social because when our individual strength fails, their union and accord are effectual. ~Chrysoston

The Power of United Prayer

Andrew Murray

Murray captures the heart and soul of united prayer. This discipline is a sweet dimension of our prayer life. And the synergy of united prayer promises answers of power and blessing.

"Again I say unto you, that if two of you shall agree on earth as touching any thing that they shall ask, it shall be done for them of my Father which is in heaven. For where two or three are gathered together in my name, there am I in the midst of them" (Matthew 18:19-20).

One of the first lessons of our Lord in His school of prayer was not to pray visibly. Go into your closet and be alone with the Father. When He has taught us that the meaning of prayer is personal, individual contact with God, He gives us a second lesson: You also need public, united prayer. He gives us a very special promise for the united prayer of two or three who agree in what they ask. As a tree has its root hidden in the ground and its stem growing up into the sunlight, so prayer needs secrecy in which the soul meets God alone and public fellowship with those who find their common meeting place in the Name of Jesus.

The reason why this must be so is plain. The bond that unites a man with his fellow-men is no less real and close than that which unites him to God: He is one with them. Grace renews not only our relationship with God, but our relationships with our fellow human beings, too. We not only learn to say "My Father." It would be unnatural for the children of a family to always meet their father separately, never expressing their desires or their love jointly. Believers are not only members of one family, but of one Body. Just as each member of the Body depends on the other, the extent to which the Spirit can dwell in the Body depends on the union and cooperation of everyone. Christians cannot reach the full blessing God is ready to bestow through His Spirit until they seek and receive it in fellowship with each other. It was to the hundred and twenty praying together in total agreement under the same roof that the Spirit came from the throne of the glorified Lord in the same way; it is in the union and fellowship of believers that the Spirit can manifest His full power.

The elements of true, united prayer are given to us in these words of our Lord. *The first element is agreement as to the thing asked.* It isn't enough to generally consent to agree with anything another may ask. The object prayed for must be some special thing, a matter of distinct, united desire. The agreement must be, as in all prayer, in spirit and in truth. In such agreement exactly what we are asking for becomes very clear. We find out whether we can confidently ask for it according to God's will, and whether we are ready to believe that we have received it.

The second element is the gathering in the Name of Jesus. Later, we will learn much more about the necessity and the power of the Name of Jesus in prayer. Here our Lord teaches us that His Name must be the center and the bond of the union that makes them one, just as a home contains and unites all who are in it. "The Name of the Lord is a strong tower: the righteous runneth into it, and is safe" (Proverbs 18: 10). That Name is such a reality to those who understand and believe in it, that to meet within it is to have Him present. Jesus is powerfully attracted by the love and unity of His disciples: "Where two or three are gathered in my Name, there am I in the midst of them" (Matthew 18:20). The presence of Jesus, alive in the fellowship of His loving, praying disciples, gives united prayer its power.

The third element is the sure answer: "It shall be done for them of my Father." Although a prayer meeting for maintaining religious fellowship, or for our own edification, may have its use, this was not the Savior's reason for recommending it. He meant it as a means of securing special answer to prayer. A prayer meeting without recognized answer to prayer ought to be the exception to the rule. When we feel too weak to exercise the faith necessary to attain a distinct desire, we ought to seek strength in the help of others. In the unity of faith, love, and the Spirit, the power of the Name and the presence of Jesus acts more freely, and the answer comes more surely. The evidence that there has been true, united prayer is the fruit – the answer, the receiving of the thing for which we have asked. "I say unto you, it shall be done for them of my Father which is in heaven."

What an extraordinary privilege united prayer is! What a potential power it has! Who can say what blessing might be gained if the believing husband and wife knew they were joined together in the Name of Jesus to experience His presence and power in united prayer (I Peter 3); if friends were aware of the mighty help two or three praying in concert could give each other; if in every prayer meeting the coming together in the Name, the faith in His presence, and the expectation of the answer stood in the foreground; if in every church united, effective prayer were regarded as one of the chief purposes for which they are banded together; if in the universal Church the coming of the Kingdom and of the King Himself were really a matter of unceasing, united crying to God!

The Apostle Paul had great faith in the power of united prayer. To the Romans he writes, "I beseech you, brethren, by the love of the Spirit, that ye strive together with me in your prayer to God for me" (Romans 15:30). He expects in answer to be delivered from his enemies and to prosper in his work. To the Corinthians he declares, "God will still deliver us, ye also helping together on our behalf by your supplications" (2 Corinthians 1:11). He expects their prayer to have a real share in his deliverance. To the Ephesians he writes, "With all prayer and supplication, praying at all seasons in the Spirit for all the saints and on my behalf, that utterance may be given unto me" (Ephesians 6:18-19). He makes the power and success in his ministry dependent on their prayers. With the Philippians he expects that his trials will become his salvation and increase the progress of the gospel, through your supplications and the supply of the Spirit of Jesus Christ" (Philippians 1:19). When telling the Colossians to continue praying constantly, he adds, "Withal praying for us too, that God may open unto us a door for the word" (Colossians 4:3). And to the Thessalonians he writes, "Finally, brethren, pray for us, that the word of the Lord may run and be glorified, and that we may be delivered from unreasonable men" (2 Thessalonians 3: 1-2).

It is quite evident that Paul perceived himself as the member of a Body whose sympathy and cooperation he depended on. He counted on the prayers of these churches to gain for him what otherwise might not be given. The prayers of the Church were to him as real a factor in the work of the Kingdom as the power of God.

Who can say what power a church could develop and exercise if it would assume the work of praying day and night for the coming of the Kingdom, for God's power, or for the salvation of souls? Most churches think their members gather simply to take care of and edify each other. They don't know that God rules the world by the prayers of His saints, that prayer is the power by which Satan is conquered, and that through prayer the Church on earth has access to the powers of the heavenly world. They do not remember that Jesus has, by His promise, made every assembly in His Name a gate to heaven, where His presence is to be felt, and His power experienced by the Father fulfilling their desires. We cannot sufficiently thank God for the blessed week of united prayer, with which Christendom, in our days, opens every year. It is of unspeakable value as proof of our unity and our faith in the power of united prayer, as a training school for the enlargement of our hearts to take in all the needs of the Church, and as a help to united persevering prayer. But it has been a special blessing as a stimulus to continued union in prayer in the smaller circles. When God's people realize what it means to meet as one in the Name of Jesus, with His presence in the midst of a Body united in the Holy Spirit, they will boldly claim the promise that the Father will do what they agree to request.

Lord, teach us to pray.

Blessed Lord! You ask so earnestly for the unity of Your people. Teach us how to encourage our unity with Your precious promise regarding united prayer. Show us how to join together in love and desire, so that Your presence is in our faith in the Father's answer.

O Father! We pray for those smaller circles of people who meet together so that they may become one. Remove all selfishness and self-interest, all narrowness of heart and estrangement that hinders their unity. Cast out the spirit of the world and the flesh through which Your promise loses all its power. Let the thought of Your presence and the Father's favor draw us all nearer to each other. Grant especially, blessed Lord, that Your Church may believe that it is by the power of unified prayer that she can bind and loose in heaven, cast out Satan, save souls, remove mountains, and hasten the coming of the Kingdom. And grant, good Lord, that my prayer circle may indeed pray with the power through which Your Name and Word are glorified. Amen.

APPLICATION QUESTIONS

For Personal Reflection

1. "Evidence that there's been true, united prayer is the fruit." How much priority do answers to prayer take in your own prayer life?

2. How have you experienced prayer to help in building community? Are there any current areas of disunity that can be committed to prayer?

3. Explain how you are dependent on the prayers of others. Can you identify specific people who are "guarding your back" in prayer?

PRAYER PRACTICE:
- Start by recalling and thanking God for specific answers to prayer you have seen in the past.
- Thank God for any unity you are experiencing. Bring before him any struggles with disunity.
- Thank God and pray for those who are praying for you. If you currently do not have others praying for you, ask the Spirit to reveal people you can approach for prayer down the road.

New York City Prayer Meeting

1857 Prayer Revival in America

Sometimes it is during the days of hopelessness and despair that revival comes.
So it was in the middle of the nineteenth century. In the United States, it was a spiritual, political, and economic low point. Many people had become disillusioned with spiritual things because of preachers who had repeatedly and falsely predicted the end of the world in the 1840's. Agitation over the slavery issue had bred much political unrest, and civil war seemed imminent. A financial panic hit in 1857. Banks failed, railroads were bankrupt, factories closed, unemployment increased. Many Christians realized the need for prayer in such dire situations, and prayer meetings began to spread around the country.

This account of revival in America provides an astonishing example of the genesis and rapid explosion of united prayer before and during revival. From very small and humble beginnings to more than ten thousand meeting to pray each day, a river of genuine repentance and sincere conversions accompanied this. This phenomenon spread from city to city.

Ferment from Fulton street

A quiet, zealous forty-six-year-old businessman in New York was appointed on July 1,1857, as a missionary in downtown New York at the Dutch Church. A few months later Jeremiah Lamphier felt led by God to start a noon-time weekly prayer meeting in which business people could meet for prayer. Anyone could attend, for a few minutes or for the entire hour. Prayers were to be comparatively brief. Lamphier rented a hall on Fulton Street in New York City and advertised its availability for prayer meetings.

The first day, September 23, 1857, <u>Lamphier prayed alone for half an hour</u>. By the end of the hour, six men from at least four denominational backgrounds joined him. Two days later the Bank of Philadelphia failed. The next Wednesday there were twenty. On October there were nearly forty. The meeting was so blessed that they decided to pray together daily. On October 10 the stock market crashed. The financial panic triggered a religious awakening, and people flocked to the prayer meetings. One week later there were over one hundred present, including many unsaved who were convicted by the Holy Spirit of their sin. Within six months 10,000 people were gathering daily for prayer in New York City alone.

Within one month pastors who had attended the noon prayer meetings in Fulton Street started morning prayer meetings in their own churches. Soon the places where the meeting were held were overcrowded. Men and women, young and old of all denominations met and prayed together without distinctions. The meetings abounded with love for Christ, love for fellow Christians, love for prayer, and love of witnessing. Those in attendance felt an awesome sense of God's presence. They prayed for specific people, expected answers, and obtained answers.

The three rooms at the Fulton Street Church were filled beyond capacity, and hundreds had to go to other places. By early February a nearby Methodist Church was opened, and it immediately overflowed. The balconies were filled with ladies. By March 19 a theater opened for prayer, and half an hour before it was time to begin, people were turned away. Hundreds stood outside in the streets because they could not get inside. By the end of March over six thousand people met daily in prayer gatherings in New York City. Many churches added evening services for prayer. Soon there were 150 united prayer meetings each day across Manhattan and Brooklyn.

The movement explodes

Within three months similar meetings had sprung up across America with other cities experiencing a renewed interest in prayer. Noon prayer meetings sprang up all across America in Boston, Baltimore, Washington, D.C., Richmond, Charleston, Savannah, Mobile, New Orleans, Vicksburg, Memphis, St. Louis, Pittsburgh, Cincinnati, Chicago, and in a multitude of other cities, towns, and in rural areas. Thousands began praying in these services and in their own homes. In Chicago, the Metropolitan Theater was filled every day with 2000 people assembling for prayer. Five prayer meetings took place daily in Washington, D.C. Five thousand or so attended daily services in the Academy of Music Hall. In Louisville, several thousand came to the Masonic Temple for prayer each morning. Two thousand assembled for daily prayer in Cleveland, and the St. Louis churches were filled for months at a time. Meetings began in February in Philadelphia, with Jayne's Hall soon becoming overfilled; they removed partitions and added space for six thousand people to attend daily meetings. Meetings were held at noon each day in public halls, concert halls, fire stations, houses, and tents. The newly formed Y.M.C.A. also played an important role in holding prayer meetings and spreading the revival throughout the country.

In New York, gospel tracts were distributed to those in attendance, with instructions that they pray over the tracts and then give them to someone God brought to mind. Newspapers began to report on the meetings and the unusual spirit of prayer that was evident. In February, 1858, Gordon Bennett of the *New York Herald* gave extensive coverage to the prayer meeting revival. Not to be outdone, the *New York Tribune* devoted an entire issue in April, 1858 to news of the revival. News of the revival quickly travelled westward by telegraph. This was the first revival in which the media played an important role in spreading the revival.

By the end of the fourth month, prayer fervor burned intensely across the nation. It was an awesome but glorious demonstration of the sovereign working of the Holy Spirit and the eager obedience of God's people.

America had entered a new period of faith and prayer. Educated and uneducated, rich and poor, business leaders and common workmen – all prayed, believed, and received answers to prayer. Even the president of the United States, Franklin Pierce, attended many of the noon prayer meetings.

Prayer fervor everywhere

Unlike earlier awakenings in history, prayer was the main instrument of this revival. This was not a revival of powerful preaching. This was a movement of earnest, powerful, prevailing prayer.

The prayer meetings were organized in the cities by lay people and were interdenominational. Tents were often set up as places where people could gather for prayer, introducing a custom followed by later revivalists. The meetings themselves were very informal – any person might pray, exhort, lead in a song, or give a word of testimony, with a five minute limit placed on each speaker. In spite of the less structured nature of the prayer meetings, they lacked the extreme emotionalism which some had criticized in earlier revivals.

All people wanted was a place to pray. Sinners would come and ask for prayer. Someone would individually pray for them, and in minutes the newly saved person was rejoicing in Christ. Prayers would be asked by name for unconverted friends and loved ones from all over the country. In a day or two, testimonies would be given of how the prayers had already been answered. In some towns, nearly the entire population became saved.

Six months previous to Lamphier's prayer meeting boom, few would have gathered for a prayer service. But now a spirit of prayer occupied the land, as though the church had suddenly discovered its real power. The majority of the churches in most denominations experienced a new dimension of prayer. The *Presbyterian Magazine* reported that as of May there had been fifty thousand converts of the revival. In February, a New York Methodist magazine reported a total of eight thousand conversions in Methodist meetings in one week. The Louisville daily paper reported seventeen thousand Baptist conversions in three weeks during the month of March. And according to a June statement, the conversion figures stood at 96,216--and still counting. All but two of the youth in one high school were saved. A similar event took place in Toledo, Ohio. These are just brief examples of what was happening constantly all across the nation.

<u>The accounts of the prayer meetings during those revival years describe how the people would quietly gather at the place of prayer promptly at the appointed hour.</u> Whoever was leader for the meeting—a layman or a minister— arose and announced a hymn. They sang one or two verses with great joy, the leader prayed briefly, and then turned the service over to the members. Any person was free to speak or pray for no longer than five minutes. If the person took more than that time, a small bell was rung and it was someone else's turn.

Requests for prayer, often coming from distant places, were spoken or read. Often sinners arose and requested prayer for themselves. Members gave testimonies of answers to prayer, and the people praised the Lord. Brief exhortations on prayer or revival were allowed but limited to five minutes. Many testified of revival progress in various locations. Promptly at the closing of the hour the leader rose and pronounced the benediction, and the people quietly left the building. Occasionally someone might stay behind to pray with a spiritual seeker.

The Invisible Cloud of God's Presence

A canopy of holy and awesome revival influence — in reality the presence of the Holy Spirit —seemed to hang like an invisible cloud over many parts of the United States, especially over the eastern seaboard. At times this cloud of God's presence even seemed to extend out to sea. Those on ships approaching the east coast at times felt a solemn, holy influence, even one hundred miles away, without even knowing what was happening in America. Revival began aboard many ships. Ship after ship arrived with the same story: both passengers and crew were suddenly convicted of sin and turned to Christ before they reached the American coast.

Reports came in of hundreds being converted in prayer meetings, private homes, workshops, and fields. Often the doors of businesses held signs reading, "Closed, will reopen at the close of the prayer meeting."

For months multitudes of churches opened every evening for prayer, and some of them had from three to five services of prayer each day. All were filled. The services consisted of simple prayer, confession, exhortation, and singing. But it was "so earnest, so solemn, the silence... the singing. ..so over-powering" that the meetings were unforgettable. A canvas tent was erected for outdoor meetings, and it immediately filled with people. In four months' time, a total of 150,000 people attended the ministry in the tent, with many conversions. Philadelphia churches reported five thousand converts.

The Presbyterians in Northern Ireland heard of the awakening in Philadelphia and sent fraternal delegates. These delegates returned to their homeland and reported what they had seen, and the revival broke out in Ireland, spreading across the British Isles.

Revival in the Army

Because of the bitter tensions of the Civil War and the slavery issue, for a time it seemed that the southern states would not be as powerfully influenced by the revival as the northern ones had been. Others dispute this assumption. An unusually powerful revival broke out among the southern troops stationed around Richmond, Virginia, in the autumn of 1861. It began in the hospitals among the wounded men and then spread into the camps as these men returned to active duty. Prayer meetings were organized and hundreds converted. The movement spread rapidly throughout the army, reaching the troops of Tennessee and Arkansas.

Revival was encouraged by Generals Robert E. Lee and Thomas J. "Stonewall" Jackson, who were well known as devout Christians. By the mid-summer of 1863 the revival had spread through all the Confederate armies, and thousands of men had been converted. Chaplains and lay missionaries went out among the troops, preaching and distributing tracts and dealing personally with hungry hearts. By the end of the war at least 150,000 soldiers had been converted, and more than a third of all of the southern troops had become praying men. The revival among the southern troops was primarily a revival of prayer, as the earlier revival in the North had been. While the best estimates are that 6.6 percent of the entire population of the United States was converted during the revival, the percentage among the southern troops was 21 percent. The North really did not win the war—prayer and a mighty revival did!

America's good gift
This was the first revival beginning in America with a worldwide impact. Even ships coming into British ports told of the revival in America. Ireland soon began to experience a prayer meeting revival as well, with crowds becoming so large they had to meet in the open air.

Thirst for the Spirit in Scotland
When Andrew Bonar heard of the work in Ireland, he increased his prayer for a revival in Scotland. In his diary of July 3, 1859, he wrote, "Again this night in sorrow of heart over the terrible carelessness, indifference, deadness of this 'valley of dry bones.' O my God, come over to Scotland and help us!"

Within two months Andrew Bonar found himself in the midst of revival in Scotland. On September 10th he wrote in his diary, "This has been a remarkable week: every day I have heard of some soul saved among us..." All classes became interested in salvation, backsliders returned, conversions increased, and Christians desired a deeper instruction in spiritual truths. Families established daily devotions, and entire communities underwent a noticeable change in morals.

Similar changes were noted as revival spread to Wales, England, and beyond. There was an absence of great names connected with the revival; lay people in prayer were the prime instruments used by God in awakening the people. The preaching, which had often become too intellectual and lifeless, now concentrated on the gospel truths of Christ and His cross.

The results of the revival of 1859 in the areas of evangelism, missions, and social action continued for decades. Many who became Christian leaders during the second half of the nineteenth century were greatly affected by the revival-- such as D.L. Moody, William Booth, C.H. Spurgeon, and A.B. Simpson. As James Buchanan of Scotland summarized, it was a time when "new spiritual life was imparted to the dead, and new spiritual health imparted to the living."

On Corporate Prayer For Revival

Jonathan Edwards

A Humble Attempt to Promote the Agreement and Union of God's People Throughout the World in Extraordinary Prayer For a Revival Of Religion And The Advancement Of God's Kingdom On Earth, According To Scriptural Promises And Prophecies Of The Last Time.

The Future Glorious State of Christ's Church

'This is what the LORD Almighty says: 'Many peoples and the inhabitants of many cities will yet come, and the inhabitants of one city will go to another and say, 'Let us go at once to entreat the LORD and seek the LORD Almighty. I myself am going.' And many peoples and powerful nations will come to Jerusalem to seek the LORD Almighty and to entreat him'(Zech. 8:20-22).

In this chapter Zechariah prophecies of the future, glorious advancement of the Church. It is evident there is more intended than was ever fulfilled in the Jewish nation during Old Testament times. Here are plain prophecies describing things that were never fulfilled before the coming of Messiah, particularly what is said in the two last verses in the chapter where Zechariah speaks of 'many people and strong nations worshiping and seeking the true God,' and of so great an addition of Gentiles to the Church that the majority of visible worshipers consist of Gentiles, outnumbering the Jews ten to one.

Nothing ever happened, from the time of Zechariah to the coming of Christ, to fulfill this prophecy. It's fulfillment can only be in the calling of the Gentiles during and following apostolic times, or in the future, glorious enlargement of God's Church in the end times, so often foretold by Old Testament prophets, particularly by Zechariah. It is most likely that the Spirit of God speaks here of the greatest revival and the most glorious advancement of the Church on earth, the blessings of which will benefit the Jewish nation.

Indeed, there is great agreement on this point, between this prophecy of Zechariah, and other prophecies concerning the Church's latter day glory. Consider Isaiah 60:2-4,

'See, darkness covers the earth and thick darkness is over the peoples, but the Lord rises upon you and his glory appears over you. Nations will come to your light, and kings to the brightness of your dawn. Lift up your eyes and look about you: All assemble and come to you; your sons come from afar, and your daughters are carried on the arm.'

Without doubt, this entire chapter foretells the most glorious state of the God's Church on earth, as does Isaiah 66:8, Micah 4:1-3 and Isaiah 2:1-4:

'In the last days the mountain of the LORD'S temple will be established as chief among the mountains; it will be raised above the hills, and peoples will stream to it.'

'Many nations will come and say, 'Come, let us go up to the mountain of the LORD, to the house of the God of Jacob. He will teach us his ways, so that we may walk in his paths.' '

'The law will go out from Zion, the word of the LORD from Jerusalem. He will judge between many peoples and will settle disputes for strong nations far and wide. They will beat their swords into plowshares and their spears into pruning hooks. Nation will not take up sword against nation, nor will they train for war anymore.'

Nothing whatsoever has happened to fulfill these prophecies. Moreover, since the prophecy in my text (Zech. 8:20-22) and the following verse agrees with them, there is reason to think it addresses the same times. Indeed, there is remarkable agreement in the description given throughout this chapter with the representations of those times elsewhere in the prophetic books.

We find it common in the prophecies of the Old Testament that when the prophets are speaking of the favors and blessings of God on the Jews, attending or following their return from the Babylonian captivity, the Spirit of God takes the opportunity from there to speak of the incomparably greater blessings on the Church, that will attend and follow her deliverance from the spiritual Babylon, of which those were a type.

The Power of Prayer

In Zechariah 8:20-22 we have an account of how this future advancement of the Church should occur. It would come to fruition as multitudes from different towns resolve to unite in extraordinary prayer, seeking God until He manifests Himself and grants the fruits of his presence. We may observe several things in particular:

1. The good which shall be brought by prayer: God Himself

Scripture says, 'They shall go to pray before the Lord, and to seek the Lord of Hosts.' The good that they seek for is 'The Lord of Hosts,' Himself. If 'seeking God' means no more than seeking the favor or mercy of God then 'praying before the Lord,' and 'seeking the Lord of Hosts' must be looked upon as synonymous. However, 'seeking the Lord' is commonly used to mean something far more than seeking something from God. Surely it implies that God Himself is what is desired and sought after.

Thus, the Psalmist desired God, thirsted after Him and sought after Him:

'O God, thou art my God; early will I seek thee. My flesh longeth for thee, in a dry and thirsty land, where no water is, to see thy power and thy glory, so as I have seen thee in the sanctuary ... My soul followeth hard after thee ... Whom have I in heaven by thee? And there is none upon earth that I desire besides thee.'

The Psalmist earnestly pursued after God; his soul thirsted after Him, he stretched forth his hands unto Him. All of God's saints have this in common: they are those that seek God. 'This is the generation of them that seek Him.' 'Your heart shall live that seek God,' etc.

If this be the true sense of this phrase 'seeking the Lord of Hosts,' then we must understand that God who had withdrawn Himself, or, as it were, hid Himself, would return to His Church, granting the fruits of His presence and communion with His people, which He so often promised, and for which His Church had so long waited.

The prophets occasionally represent God as being withdrawn and hiding Himself: 'Verily thou art a God that hideth thyself, O God of Israel, the Savior. I hid me, and was wroth.' The prophets then go on to represent God's people seeking Him, searching and waiting for and calling after Him. When God answers their prayers and restores and advances His people, according to His promise, then He is said to come and say, 'Here am I' and to show Himself, and they are said to find Him and see Him plainly.

'Then you will call, and the Lord will answer; you will cry for help, and he will say: Here am I'

'The Sovereign Lord will wipe away the tears from all faces; he will remove the disgrace of his people from all the earth. In that day they will say, 'Surely this is our God; we trusted in him, and he saved us. This is the Lord, we trusted in him; let us rejoice and be glad in his salvation.' We wait for you; your name and renown are the desire of our hearts.' (Isa. 58:9; Isa. 45:17,19; Isa. 25:8-9)

2. We may observe who it is that will be united in seeking the Lord

'The inhabitants of many cities ... yea, many people and strong nations.' Many people from all over the world will unite to seek the Lord.

From the the prophecy, it seems reasonable to assume that this will be fulfilled in the following manner: First, God's people will be given a spirit of prayer, inspiring them to come together and pray in an extraordinary manner, that He would help his Church, show mercy to mankind in general, pour out his Spirit, revive His work, and advance His kingdom in the world as He promised.

Moreover, such prayer would gradually spread and increase more and more, ushering in a revival of religion. This would be characterized by greater worship and service of God among believers. Others will be awakened to their need for God, motivating them to earnestly cry out to God for mercy. They will be led to join with God's people in that extraordinary seeking and serving of God which they see around them. In this way the revival will grow until the awakening reaches whole nations and those in the highest positions of influence. The Church will grow to be ten times larger than it was before. Indeed, at length, all the nations of the world will be converted unto God.

3. Next, we can observe the manner in which they agree to pray

'Let us go speedily to pray,' or, as it says in the margin: let us go continually. Literally translated this means, 'let us go in going.' The Hebrew language often doubles words for emphasis (e.g., the holy of holies signifies that which is most holy). Such doubling of words also denotes the certainty of an event coming to pass. For example, when God said to Abraham, 'in multiplying, I will multiply thy seed,' God implies that He would certainly multiply his seed, and multiply it exceedingly.

4. Finally, this prophecy gives us a picture of this union in prayer being an inviting and happy thing

We sense God's pleasure, and the results prove tremendously successful. From the whole of this prophecy we may infer that it is well pleasing to God for many people, in different parts of the world, to voluntarily come into a visible union to pray in an extraordinary way for those great outpourings of the Holy Spirit which shall advance the Kingdom of our Lord Jesus Christ that God has so often promised shall be in the latter ages of the world.

An Example From History

Let me relate a brief history of what has happened in Scotland:

In October of 1744, a number of ministers in Scotland, considering the state of God's Church, and mankind in general, believed that God was calling those concerned for the welfare of the Church to unite in extraordinary prayer. They knew God was the Creator and source of all blessings and benefits in the Church so they earnestly prayed that He would appear in His glory, and strengthen the Church, and manifest His compassion to the world of mankind by an abundant outpouring of His Holy Spirit. They desired a true revival in all parts of Christendom, and to see nations delivered from their great and many calamities, and to bless them with the unspeakable benefits of the Kingdom of our glorious Redeemer, and to fill the whole earth with His glory.

These ministers consulted with one another on this subject and concluded that they were obliged to begin such prayer and attempt to persuade others to do the same. After seeking God for direction, they determined that for the next two years they would set apart some time on Saturday evenings and Sunday mornings every week for prayer as one's other duties would allow. More importantly, it was decided that the first Tuesday of each quarter (beginning with the first Tuesday of November) would be time to be spent in prayer. People were to pray for either the entire day or part of the day, as they found themselves disposed, or as circumstances allowed. They would meet in either private prayer groups or in public meetings, whichever was found to be most convenient.

It was determined that none should make any promises or feel under strict obligation to observe every one of these days without fail; for these days were not holy or established by sacred authority. However, to prevent negligence, and the temptation to make excuses for trivial reasons, it was proposed that if those who resolve to pray cannot take part on the agreed upon day, they would use the next available day for the purpose of prayer.

The primary reason for this cooperation in prayer was to maintain, among the people of God, that necessity of prayer for the coming of Christ's Kingdom, which Christ directed his followers to do. We are, unfortunately, too little inclined to pray because of our laziness and immaturity, or because of the distraction of our own worldly, private affairs. We have prayed at times, but without special seasons for prayer, we are, likely, to neglect it either partially or totally. But when we set aside certain times for prayer, resolving to fulfill this commission unless extraordinarily hindered, we are less likely to neglect it.

It was thought that two years would be a sufficient trial period, after which time would be given to evaluate fruitfulness of the endeavor. It was not known but thought best to allow some time to make some adjustments if necessary. The time period, though short, was thought sufficient to judge its fruitfulness. Those involved would have the opportunity to communicate their thoughts, and perhaps improve, on this manner of prayer.

Great success seems to have met their labors for great numbers in Scotland and England, and even some in North America joined with them. As to Scotland, many people in the four chief cities, Edinburgh, Glasgow, Aberdeen, and Dundee joined. There were also many country towns and congregations in various other areas that participated. A Mr. Robe, of Kilsyth, stated that 'There were then above thirty societies of young people there, newly erected, some of which consisted of upwards of thirty members.'

The two years ended last November. Just prior to this, a number of ministers in Scotland agreed on a letter, to be printed and sent abroad to their brethren, proposing to them, and requesting of them, to join with them in continuing this concert of prayer, and in the endeavors to promote it. Almost five hundred copies of this letter were sent over to New England, with instructions to distribute them to the Massachusetts-Bay area, Connecticut, New Hampshire, Rhode Island, New York, New Jersey, Pennsylvania, Maryland, Virginia, Carolina and Georgia. Most were sent to a congregational minister in Boston along with a letter from twelve ministers in Scotland. Other copies were sent to other ministers in Boston, and some to a minister in Connecticut.

The proposal, dated August 26, 1746, opens with an explanation of the purpose and times for the concerts of prayer, and an entreaty to the ministers to communicate their opinions after the two year period had completed.

The ministers then go on to assure their Bostonian brethren that the concerts are not to be seen as binding; men are not expected to set apart days from secular affairs, or 'fix on any part of ... precise days, whether it be convenient or not.' Nor are they to be seen as 'absolute promises, but as friendly, harmonious resolutions, with liberty to alter circumstances as shall be found expedient.' Because of such liberty these prayer times cannot be judged to infringe upon those 'religious times' appointed by men.

The Boston ministers are to understand that these prayer concerts are not restricted to any particular denomination, but is extended to all who have 'at heart the interest of vital Christianity, and the power of godliness; and who, however differing about other things, are convinced of the importance of fervent prayer ...'

It was proposed that the prayer should extend for seven more years and the ministers agreed to this. However there was concern that zeal for spreading news of the concert would wane because of the length proposed. Nevertheless, it was agreed that the first period of time (two years) was too short.

Those ministers in Boston said of this proposal: 'The motion seems to come from above, and to be wonderfully spreading in Scotland, England, Wales, Ireland and North America.'

APPLICATION QUESTIONS

For Personal Reflection

4. Evaluate the typical themes of your prayer life. How much of your prayers seek God himself? How much of your prayers seek the advancement of his church?

5. How would a greater focus on God's glory make a difference in your prayer life?

For Small Group Discussion

6. What practical prayer principles can we learn from these examples from Murray, New York City and Scotland?

7. Jonathan Edwards speaks of *a spirit of extraordinary prayer poured out that primarily seeks God and church advance, uniting many cities, spreading worship and service, visible, voluntary, continually, pleasurable and happy.* Have you experienced this before? How does our current corporate prayer life reflect this?

PRAYER PRACTICE:
- Start with worship and praise of our glorious Father.
- Ask for a spirit of prayer and supplication and heart for church advance.
- Cry out for revival!

In Matthew 5:13-16, Jesus uses two key images to teach us about who we are as the church:

> *"You are the salt of the earth. But if the salt loses its saltiness, how can it be made salty again? It is no longer good for anything, except to be thrown out and trampled by men.*

> *"You are the light of the world. A city on a hill cannot be hidden. Neither do people light a lamp and put it under a bowl. Instead they put it on its stand, and it gives light to everyone in the house. In the same way, let your light shine before men, that they may see your good deeds and praise your Father in heaven.*

The image of salt reflects the widespread nature of the church as disciples are sent as agents of God's grace and truth into the harvest field.

The image of light reflects the gathered nature of the church as the strength of our love for and unity with one another emanates into strong witness to a dark world.

It is not uncommon to debate and compare the relative importance of fellowship and mission. But it is not a matter of *"either* one *or* the other." *Both* are required to work in tandem for a thriving fruitful faith and mission.

APPLICATION QUESTIONS

For Personal Reflection

8. Evaluate how "gathered" you currently are with other believers.

9. Evaluate how "sent" you are. What different "mission fields" or areas of influence is Jesus sending you to currently?

10. Are there any imbalances that need to be addressed? If so, what two concrete actions can you take to move toward a healthier balance?

For Small Group Discussion

11. What is the relationship between the gathered and sent nature of God's people?

12. How does the gospel give us confidence to pursue both dynamics without reservation?

13. Evaluate your church/ministry's degree of "gatheredness" in fellowship and care.

14. Evaluate your church/ministry's degree of "sentness" in mission to the surrounding community.

15. Are there any imbalances that need to be addressed? If so, what are different ways you can move toward a healthier balance?

PRAYER PRACTICE:
- Pray for a strong sense of "kingdom gatheredness" in your church and in your relationships and fellowship with other believers that would send you outward.
- Pray for God to send you to the people and fields of his choosing.
- Pray that the gospel would advance because of a strong and healthy dynamic of gatheredness *and* sentness in your life and church.

Here are some ideas to get you started in thinking about ways to incorporate more prayer into the corporate prayer life of your church.

1. *Train your people with equal priority in prayer and the Word. Start with your leaders.* Encourage and equip them to grow in gospel and kingdom-centred prayer through prayer training. Pray in ministry teams – with and for each other. Work with them in how they are leading their teams and ministries – how are they soliciting prayer and supporting others in prayer?

2. *Keep the 50:50 ratio of prayer:work in your ministries and meetings.* Keep the ball rolling with short prayers interspersed throughout your meetings – rather than one solid block of prayer, and not just at the start and end.

3. *Use the Lord's Prayer priorities in other avenues of prayer in the church* including in worship services, planning meetings, small group and ministry meetings.

4. *Turn small groups into prayer cells* to strengthen the mission of your church.

5. *Pray for the church in the city in your worship services:* Have kingdom-centred prayers lead the congregation in gospel-centred prayer as a model to others. Have them pray for the ministries of your church and for other churches and ministries reaching out to the city.

6. *Have regular "Days of Prayer"* especially at major crises and crossroads. (See Lesson 12)

7. *Regular prayer walks around the church neighbourhood* will grow members in harvest heart and eyes for your church's mission field.

8. *Send out regular prayer communications* with passion and power. Remember to send thanksgiving and answers to prayer also.

9. *Bring it home!* Continue praying together in families, starting with your own.

10. *Pray for your flock by conducting prayer visitation* with congregants to simply pray for them. "We want to come to pray for you" is the announced reason for your visit. The stage is set for ministry of a very rich kind. Nothing gets our attention more than answered prayer, and nothing witnesses more to those who are being drawn into God's church than seeing prayers met with power. Since taking steps to deliberately reach out to the congregation of Grace Vancouver Church by forming a healing prayer team, we have seen a marked increase in prayer needs being met. In our first few months of deliberate prayer visitation and intercessory prayer meetings, two people from our church who had been looking for work for over a year immediately received job opportunities after we prayed for them. Marriage problems, sickness, anxiety, and a host of other needs have been met with real deliverance. Some may have not seen immediate delivery, but the pastoral act of going to someone's home and simply praying for them creates a shepherd/ member bond that cannot be underestimated.

For Discussion with Your Leaders

In light of your corporate prayer evaluations from the previous lesson, pray and plan together with your leaders a "Prayer Priority Plan" to address the feedback and insight surfaced from the evaluation. How will you add more prayer to the church life? How does God want to grow you in prayer?

HOMEWORK:
- Pray about who you may ask to join with you in praying and planning towards more prayer in your church/ministry.
- Read through the material for Lesson 9, concentrating on the readings, the personal reflection questions and prayer practice points.

Reaching a World through Prayer

GOALS: In this lesson we will…
- ❑ Pray for our leaders using Scripture
- ❑ Explore the connection between revival and prayer
- ❑ Practice a model of prayer for personal revival connected to personal evangelism

Introduction

(See DVD Section II: Lesson 9)

When leaders and people pray together, there are often signs of revival:

> On their release, Peter and John went back to their own people and reported all that the chief priests and the elders had said to them. [24] When they heard this, **they raised their voices together in prayer to God**…. [31] After they prayed, the place where they were meeting was shaken. And they were all filled with the Holy Spirit and spoke the word of God boldly.

> With great power the apostles continued to testify to the resurrection of the Lord Jesus. And God's grace was so powerfully at work in them all [34] that there were no needy persons among them. Acts 11:23ff.

In a similar way, the church experiences great power and deliverance when God's people pray for their leaders. When Peter is thrown in prison by Herod we read:

> Peter was kept in prison, but the church was earnestly praying to God for him.(Acts 12:5)

As the people pray – not only is Peter is set free from chains and prison guards by an angel, we thrill to read that God opens the iron doors of the city so the gospel mission can increase.:

> [10] They passed the first and second guards and came to the iron gate leading to the city. **It opened for them by itself,**

Throughout his ordeal, Peter has been surrounded by the prayers of God's people. They have been praying all night!

> He went to the house of Mary the mother of John, also called Mark, where many people had gathered and were praying

The epitaph of this prayer narrative concludes with a simple grand phrase:

> 24 But the word of God continued to spread and flourish.

In this lesson we will look at how we can pray for your leaders (which is also how you can ask for prayer as a leader). We will also look at a simple pattern that keeps our prayer partnerships focused on the gospel and mission – where we pray for personal renewal that leads to God using us as agents of transformation and revival around us. Revival and prayer go together. They always have. When leaders and people pray, God has already begun to revive the church. When God's people pray for their leaders, God answers by sending his agents of power to open the gates of the city – and the hearts of men and women – for effective gospel proclamation.

> *Lift up your heads, ye gates of brass!*
> *Ye bars of Iron! yield;*
> *And let the King of Glory pass,--*
> *The Cross is in the field.*

- **Pray for each leader to be prepared for the spiritual battle:**
  "For our struggle is not against flesh and blood, but against the rulers, the powers, against the world forces of this darkness…" Ephesians 6:12

- **Pray that each leader would have a single heart for God's glory:**
  "Jesus, lifting up his eyes to heaven, said 'Father, the hour has come; glorify Your Son, that the Son may glorify You…'" John 17:1

- **Pray for each leader to have a blameless character:**
  "An elder, then, must be above reproach, the husband of one wife, temperate, prudent, respectable, hospitable, able to teach…" 1 Timothy 3:2

- **Pray for each leader's protection and health for the family**

- **Ask for each leader to faithfully live and preach God's Word:**
  "preach the Word; be ready in season and out of season…" 2 Timothy 4:1,2

- **Ask that each leader would preach the gospel with power and simplicity:**
  "we preach Christ crucified, to the Jews a stumbling block and to Gentiles foolishness; but to those who are the called… Christ the power of God and the wisdom of God…" 1 Corinthians 1:23,24

- **Ask that each leader would have open doors for effective evangelistic ministry:**
  "that God will open up for us a door for the Word, so that we may speak forth the mystery of Christ…" Colossians 4:3

- **Pray for each leader to minister in grace and sincerity:**
  "He who is a true minister of God preaches that he would wish to have hung up in the sunlight or who has the sunlight shining right through him." C.H. Spurgeon

- **Ask for each leader to have energy and wisdom to cope with the weight of responsibilities of leading the church:** "there is the daily pressure on me of concern for all the churches. Who is weak without my being weak? Who is led into sin without my intense concern?" 1 Corinthians 11:28,29

- **Pray for the flock under their care (your congregation!)**
  - For increasing holiness and blamelessness in life
    - Colossians 3:1-11
    - 1 Thessalonians 4:3-7
  - For growth in love and unity among the congregation
    - John 13:34,35
    - John 15:12-17
    - John 17:9-11
  - That we may be filled with the Holy Spirit's power
    - Ephesians 5:18
    - Colossians 1:28,29
  - That we may glorify God
    - 2 Thessalonians 1:9
    - Philippians 1:11
    - Ephesians 1, 3:21

APPLICATION QUESTIONS

For Small Group Discussion

1. Why is it important to pray for your leaders? How are you currently praying for your leaders?

2. Why is it important for you as a leader to be asking for prayer in seeking to fulfill your call?

3. How dependent are you on others' prayers for you?

PRAYER PRACTICE:

- Take some time to pray for your leaders, using these Scriptures as a pattern for prayer.
- Pray for your own humility and courage to ask others for prayer as a leader. Pray for God to raise up a team of people who can support you in prayer.
- (In class small group prayer time), pray for each other by name – as we all lead and influence in various areas, including our families, colleagues, friends, neighbours, ministries, etc.

Quotes on Prayer and Revival

If my people, who are called by my name, will humble themselves and pray and seek my face and turn from their wicked ways, then will I hear from heaven and will forgive their sin and will heal their land. 2 Chronicles 7:14

These quotes speak of the connection between prayer and revival. In the judgment of these godly and noted Christians, kingdom prayer precedes, accomplishes and prolongs revival.

- "There has never been a spiritual awakening in any country or locality that did not begin in united prayer." *A.T. Pierson*

- "There is a lot of praying *about* revival, but that will not bring it about. Jesus did not pray about things, He brought them about by prayer." *Armin Gess*

- "There have been revivals without much preaching; but there has never been a mighty revival without mighty prayer." *R.A. Tory*

- "Every new Pentecost has had its preparatory period of supplication." *A.T. Pierson*

- "If prayer is a fireplace, and people set themselves to praying, then the fire can't be far behind." *Anonymous*

- "To be a Christian without prayer is no more possible than to be alive without breathing." *Martin Luther*

- "After studying prayer and spiritual awakenings for 60 years I've reached this conclusion – whenever God is ready to do something new with His people, He always sets them praying." *Dr. J. Edwin Orr*

- "William Carey and a small praying band in Kettering, England, prayed mightily for nearly eight years before mighty revival came. William Wilberforce was used of God to bring moral and spiritual awakening to England. He had the backing of a group in his church that convenanted together to pray three hours a day." *Wesley Duewel*

- "When people sense the Lord is near, they also want to talk with Him. Revival and prayer always go together." *David Mains*

- "Here is a tremendous truth, God's very revelation on the subject of church revival: Like priest, like people. The congregation seldom rises above the level of the minister. If he is a man of faith and love, the congregation will become that way. If he is a man of prayer, he will build a praying people." *Armin Gesswein*

- "When prayers and strong pleas for revival are made to God both day and night; when the children of God find they can no longer tolerate the absence of revival blessings; when extraordinary seeking of an extraordinary outpouring becomes extraordinarily earnest; and when the burden of prayer for revival becomes almost unbearable, then let praying hearts take courage, for the Spirit of God who is the spirit of revival has brought His people to this place for a purpose." *Richard Owen Roberts*

APPLICATION QUESTIONS

For Personal Reflection

4. Which of the above quotes inspires you most? Challenges you most?

PRAYER PRACTICE:
- Why not write out your own prayer for revival – and pray it as you do!

How to Pray for Revival in the Church and City

John Smed

Revival and prayer go together.

The Epicenter of Revival is identified for us by Luke:

> *Acts 1:8,14, 2:1,3:6,41… 1Wait for the promise…You shall receive power…13When they arrived, they went upstairs to the room where they were staying…14They all joined together constantly in prayer, along with the women and Mary the mother of Jesus, and with his brothers. When the day of Pentecost came, they were all together in one place. ..36 he pleaded with them, "Save yourselves from this corrupt generation." **41Those who accepted his message were baptized, and about three thousand were added to their number that day.***

We need also to pay very close attention to the after shock!

> *Acts 4:4,23:…many who heard the message believed, and the number of men grew to about five thousand… On their release, Peter and John went back to their own people and reported all that the chief priests and elders had said to them. **24When they heard this, they raised their voices together in prayer to God… 31After they prayed,** the place where they were meeting was shaken. And they were all filled with the Holy Spirit and spoke the word of God boldly. **32**All the believers were one in heart and mind. No one claimed that any of his possessions was his own, but they shared everything they had.*

Notice and ponder: The Pentecost experience of chapter 2 is repeated in chapter 4:31ff. It is a repeatable experience. Indeed the intensity and extent increases!

What is the eventual result?

A harvest of newborn believers and an exponential increase in new churches.

> *Acts 9:31…Churches multiplied throughout Jerusalem, Judea and Samaria…growing in grace and fear of the Lord….*

We can find extraordinary examples of prayer and revival in history.

1727: Wednesday 13 August - Herrnhut, Germany (Zinzendorf's reflections)

No one present could tell exactly what happened to the Moravians on Wednesday morning, 13 August 1727 at the specially called Communion service. The glory of the Lord came upon them so powerfully that they hardly knew if they had been on earth or in heaven. Count Nicholas Zinzendorf, the young leader of that community, gave this account many years later:

'We needed to come to the Communion with a sense of the loving nearness of the Saviour. This was the great comfort which has made this day a generation ago to be a festival, because on this day twentyseven years ago the Congregation of Herrnhut, assembled for communion (at the Berthelsdorf church) were all dissatisfied with themselves. They had quit judging each other because they had become convinced, each one, of his lack of worth in the sight of God and each felt himself at this Communion to be in view of the noble countenance of the Saviour. ...

'This firm confidence changed them in a single moment into a happy people which they are to this day, and into their happiness they have since led many thousands of others through the memory and help which the heavenly grace once given to themselves, so many thousand times confirmed to them since then' (Greenfield 1927:15).

Zinzendorf described it as 'a sense of the nearness of Christ' given to everyone present, and also to others of their community who were working elsewhere at the time. The congregation was young. Zinzendorf, the human leader, at 27, was about the average age of the group.

Their missionary zeal began with the outpouring of the Holy Spirit. Count Zinzendorf observed: 'The Saviour permitted to come upon us a Spirit of whom we had hitherto not had any experience or knowledge. ... Hitherto we had been the leaders and helpers. Now the Holy Spirit himself took full control of everything and everybody' (Greenfield 1927:21).

Prayer precedes Pentecost. The disgruntled community at Herrnhut early in 1727 was deeply divided and critical of one another. Heated controversies threatened to disrupt the community. The majority were from the ancient Moravian Church of the Brethren. Other believers attracted to Herrnhut included Lutherans, Reformed, and Anabaptists. They argued about predestination, holiness, and baptism.

At Herrnhut, Zinzendorf visited all the adult members of the deeply divided community. He drew up a covenant calling upon them 'to seek out and emphasise the points in which they agreed' rather than stressing their differences. On 12 May 1727 they all signed an agreement to dedicate their lives, as he dedicated his, to the service of the Lord Jesus Christ.

On 22 July many of the community covenanted together on their own accord to meet often to pour out their hearts in prayer and hymns.

On 5 August the Count spent the whole night in prayer with about twelve or fourteen others following a large meeting for prayer at midnight where great emotion prevailed.

On Wednesday, 13 August, the Holy Spirit was poured out on them all. Their prayers were answered in ways far beyond anyone's expectations. Many of them decided to set aside certain times for continued earnest prayer.

On 26 August, twentyfour men and twentyfour women covenanted together to continue praying in intervals of one hour each, day and night, each hour allocated by lots to different people.

On 27 August, this new regulation began. Others joined the intercessors and the number involved increased to seventy seven. They all carefully observed the hour which had been appointed for them. The intercessors had a weekly meeting where prayer needs were given to them.

The children, also touched powerfully by God, began a similar plan among themselves. Those who heard their infant supplications were deeply moved. The children's prayers and supplications had a powerful effect on the whole community.

That astonishing prayer meeting beginning in 1727 lasted one hundred years. It was unique. Known as the Hourly Intercession, it involved relays of men and women in prayer without ceasing made to God. That prayer also led to action, especially evangelism. More than 100 missionaries left that village community in the next twenty-five years, all constantly supported in prayer.

I. **The 6 R's of Revival and What Revival Looks Like Today** Zech. 8:3-23

1. God **returns** in power and joy to his people

2. God's people **respond by returning** to him

3. The Savior **removes** guilt shame and judgement

4. God **reforms** our lives – in heart and actions

5. He **revives** our worship of Christ

6. God **restores** our mission and purpose- to make a praying people

God returns in power to renew the city

Zechariah 8:3 This is what the LORD says: "I will return to Zion and dwell in Jerusalem. Then Jerusalem will be called the City of Truth, and the mountain of the LORD Almighty will be called the Holy Mountain."

4 This is what the LORD Almighty says: "Once again men and women of ripe old age will sit in the streets of Jerusalem, each with cane in hand because of his age. 5 The city streets will be filled with boys and girls playing there."

God's people respond by returning ton him.

... 7 This is what the LORD Almighty says: "I will save my people from the countries of the east and the west. 8 I will bring them back to live in Jerusalem; they will be my people, and I will be faithful and righteous to them as their God."

The Savior removes guilt shame and judgement

13 As you have been an object of cursing among the nations, O Judah and Israel, so will I save you, and you will be a blessing. Do not be afraid, but let your hands be strong."...

God reforms our lives- in heart and actions:

16 These are the things you are to do: Speak the truth to each other, and render true and sound judgment in your courts; 17 do not plot evil against your neighbor, and do not love to swear falsely. I hate all this," declares the LORD.

God revives our worship of Christ

18 Again the word of the LORD Almighty came to me. 19 This is what the LORD Almighty says: "The fasts of the fourth, fifth, seventh and tenth months will become joyful and glad occasions and happy festivals for Judah. Therefore love truth and peace."

God restores our mission purpose and prayer- to make a praying people.

20 This is what the LORD Almighty says: "Many peoples and the inhabitants of many cities will yet come, 21 and the inhabitants of one city will go to another and say, 'Let us go at once to entreat the LORD and seek the LORD Almighty. I myself am going.' 22 And many peoples and powerful nations will come to Jerusalem to seek the LORD Almighty and to entreat him."

23 This is what the LORD Almighty says: "In those days ten men from all languages and nations will take firm hold of one Jew by the hem of his robe and say, 'Let us go with you, because we have heard that God is with you.' "

1. When revival is real, the Lord returns in power and joy to dwell among his people (3-5)

i) To the exiles God promises pervasive urban joy

> *Zechariah 8: 3. This is what the LORD says: "I will return to Zion and dwell in Jerusalem. Then Jerusalem will be called the City of Truth, and the mountain of the LORD Almighty will be called the Holy Mountain." 4 This is what the LORD Almighty says: "Once again men and women of ripe old age will sit in the streets of Jerusalem, each with cane in hand because of his age. 5 The city streets will be filled with boys and girls playing there."*

This is repeated in history again and again and again!

> *Zinzendorf described it as 'a sense of the nearness of Christ' given to everyone present, and also to others of their community who were working elsewhere at the time…Their missionary zeal began with the outpouring of the Holy Spirit. Count Zinzendorf observed: 'The Saviour permitted to come upon us a Spirit of whom we had hitherto not had any experience or knowledge. … Hitherto we had been the leaders and helpers. Now the Holy Spirit himself took full control of everything and everybody' (Greenfield 1927:21).*

2. Next: God's people return to him in response

> *Zechariah 8: 7,8 This is what the LORD Almighty says: "I will save my people from the countries of the east and the west. 8 I will bring them back to live in Jerusalem; they will be my people, and I will be faithful and righteous to them as their God."*

Note the order is important!... This is how sovereign grace works…God is always the initiator of revival.

3. God Removes our sin shame and judgment 13,14

> *Zechariah 8:13 As you have been an object of cursing among the nations, O Judah and Israel, so will I save you, and you will be a blessing. Do not be afraid, but let your hands be strong." 14 This is what the LORD Almighty says: "Just as I had determined to bring disaster upon you and showed no pity when your fathers angered me," says the LORD Almighty*

4. Revival = God reforms our heart and our actions 16,17

iWe see this is the intent of God when he restores the exiles:

> *Zechariah 8: 16 These are the things you are to do: Speak the truth to each other, and render true and sound judgment in your courts; 17 do not plot evil against your neighbor, and do not love to swear falsely. I hate all this," declares the LORD.*

A wonderful example of God reforming hearts in history:

1735 January - New England, America (Jonathan Edwards)

Jonathan Edwards, the preacher and scholar who later became a President of Princeton University, was a prominent leader in a revival movement

Edwards wrote that 'a great and earnest concern about the great things of religion and the eternal world, became universal in all parts of the town, and among persons of all degrees and all ages; the noise among the dry bones waxed louder nd louder; all other talk but about spiritual and eternal things, was soon thrown by.

'The minds of people were wonderfully taken off from the world; it was treated among us as a thing of very little consequence. They seemed to follow their worldly business more as a part of their duty, than from any disposition they had to it.

'It was then a dreadful thing amongst us to lie out of Christ, in danger every part of dropping into hell; and what persons' minds were intent upon was, to escape for their lives, and to fly from the wrath to come. All would eagerly lay hold of opportunities for their souls, and were wont very often to meet together in private houses for religious purposes; and such meetings, when appointed, were wont greatly to be thronged.

'And the work of conversion was carried on in a most astonishing manner, and increased more and more. Souls did, as it were, come by flocks to Jesus Christ. From day to day, for many months together, might be seen evident instances of sinners brought out of darkness into marvellous light.

Edwards described these characteristics of the revival:

'(a) An extraordinary sense of the awful majesty, greatness and *holiness of God*, so as sometimes to overwhelm soul and body, a sense of the piercing, all seeing eye of God so as to sometimes take away bodily strength; and an extraordinary view of the infinite terribleness of the *wrath of God*, together with a sense of the ineffable misery of sinners exposed to this wrath, and

'(b) Especially longing after these two things; to be *more perfect in humility and adoration*. The flesh and the heart seem often to cry out, lying low before God and adoring him with greater love and humility. ... The person felt a great delight in singing praises to God and Jesus Christ, and longing that this present life may be as it were one continued song of praise to God. ... Together with living by faith to a great degree, there was a constant and extraordinary distrust of our own strength and wisdom; a great dependence on God for his help ... and being restrained from the most horrid sins' (Pratney 1994:92-93).

i) Example from history:

1859 Monday 14 March - Ulster, Ireland (James McQuilkin)

Revival swept Great Britain also, including the Ulster revival of 1859.During September 1857, the same month the Fulton Street meetings began, James McQuilkin commenced a weekly prayer meeting in a village schoolhouse near Kells with three other young Irishmen. This is generally seen as the start of the Ulster revival. The first conversions in answer to their prayer came in December 1857. Through 1858 innumerable prayer meetings started, and revival was a common theme of preachers.On 14 March 1859 James McQuilkin and his praying friends organised a great prayer meeting at the Ahoghill Presbyterian Church. Such a large crowd gathered that the building was cleared in case the galleries collapsed. Outside in the chilling rain as a layman preached with great power hundreds knelt in repentance. This was the first of many movements of mass conviction of sin.

The revival 1859 brought 100,000 converts into the churches of Ireland.

1904 A century ago Wales experienced the last National Religious Revival, a revival that brought in an extra **100,000 new converts** according to the estimates of the time, and a movement **that quickly spread to the 4 corners of the World**. Yet that great move of the Spirit had very small beginnings. Beginnings that didn't always involve the great preachers of the day – erudite and educated as they were, but instead included, for instance a young teenager from New Quay, Cardigan – Florrie Evans – who in a youth meeting in **February 1904** declared publicly that she loved the Lord Jesus with all her heart. With these words the Spirit seemed to fall on the meeting and the fire quickly spread to other young people in the Cardiganshire area.

The Welsh Revival was the farthest reaching of the movements of the general Awakening, for it affected the whole of the Evangelical cause in India, Korea and China, renewed revival in Japan and South Africa, and sent a wave of awakening over Africa, Latin America, and the South Seas.

*Revival historian Edwin Orr observed: 'The early twentieth century Evangelical Awakening was a worldwide movement. It did not begin with the phenomenal Welsh Revival of 1904-05. **<u>Rather its sources were in the springs of little prayer meetings</u>** which seemed to arise spontaneously all over the world, combining into streams of expectation which became a river of blessing in which the Welsh Revival became the greatest cataract. ...*

APPLICATION QUESTIONS

For Small Group Discussion

5. What is the relationship between revival and reform?

6. What might revival look like in our world today? Imagine and describe the practical effects of the fruit of the gospel in your world. How would prayer have its due place?

PRAYER PRACTICE:
• Respond in prayer by crying out for revival!

Prayer and evangelism are two of those things in life that simply don't happen if we do not intentionally incorporate them into our lives. Meeting in prayer accountability teams is one way to develop these priorities in your life and in the lives of others. The following questions are designed to help you reflect on how God is working in and around you, and spur you to see how God is growing you as a gospel-centred Christian in your world.

1. <u>CHRIST IN YOU</u>: How are you growing in the gospel?
   (How is it being revealed to you? How are you "preaching it" to yourself?)

"See to it, brothers and sisters, that none of you has a sinful, unbelieving heart that turns away from the living God. But encourage one another daily, as long as it is called Today, so that none of you may be hardened by sin's deceitfulness." Hebrews 3:12-13

Remember, the path of maturity in Christian life is in many ways just a journey whereby o increasingly "gets the *Gospel*." We need to continually rely on the Holy Spirit to reveal Chris more fully, and we need to actively and intentionally remind and "preach" it to ourselves of this over and over again.

If we are not experiencing God's grace personally or if we are not growing in the Gospel *ourselves*, we have nothing to witness of and share afresh with others around us. We need to *preach* the Gospel to ourselves and have God give us a fresh revelation of the Gospel precisely because the lie is holed up in our heart and must be preached out!

Even when we are spiritually feeling strong, we must still preach the gospel to ourselves then – for we know the enemy will attempt to strike when we are in tune with God and being used by Him for His work.

In either case, the recognition that our own salvation is supernaturally based solidly in Christ's finished work leads us to pray with grace for God's supernatural transformation in the lives of those we pray for.

2. <u>CHRIST AROUND YOU</u>: How are you praying for your "focus group"?
   (Who does God want you to focus your prayers and witness/evangelism towards?)

"Then Agrippa said to Paul, "Do you think that in such a short time you can persuade me to be a Christian?" Paul replied, "Short time or long—I pray God that not only you but all who are listening to me today may become what I am, except for these chains." Acts 26:28-29

Recognizing that God is the real missionary in evangelism—and thus prayer is the real work, reaching people with the gospel begins and continues by praying for them. The Holy Spirit must go before us in our witness. As we align with God's heart through prayer, He changes our hearts towards others, and we grow in confidence and trust in Him to change their hearts.

Your focus group consists of a small group of people that you are specifically concentrating your efforts in prayer and evangelism. Generally speaking, these are people for whom you feel a burden. They are those that you are praying for consistently for opportunities and boldness to love with Christ's love (see question #3). People in your focus group are not yet Christians, but they are people that you are praying would see the light of Christ. This could include people in your workplace, family, household, neighbourhood, circle of friends, current or former business associates, seekers in your church…Keep it limited to two to four people to encourage a more concentrated and specific focus in prayer and witness. Pray and ask God to show you who to include in your focus for any given season.

3. <u>CHRIST THROUGH YOU</u>: **What opportunities have you been given to be an intentional witness in deed and word** (so people experience grace and come to Christ)?

"Let us consider how we may spur one another on toward love and good deeds. Let us not give up meeting together, as some are in the habit of doing, but let us encourage one another – and all the more as we see the Day approaching." Hebrews 10:25

(-) Are there obstacles in my life that obscure Christ? Are there any areas that God is showing you need the gospel to break through in giving you grace and freedom from sin or weakness that negatively influences your witness for Christ?

(+) Deeds of love and hospitality: How can I show Christ's love in a practical way to those in my focus group? Pray for ideas and, most important, opportunities and open doors. Follow through with love and intentionality.

As you pray for people, God will give you His heart for them. He will answer the prayers He lays on your heart. As you pray for open doors as Paul did (Col. 4:3) you should find that this is one request that God is eager to answer.

Now connect regularly with other Christians to share and pray.

Times with your prayer partner(s) are for encouragement, accountability and prayer. The point is not to plow through the questions for the sake of completing them all. God desires to renew you in the grace of being His child.

Now multiply yourselves.

Christ sends his disciples out two by two. Spiritual multiplication is the heart of Jesus' strategy in reaching the world.

After meeting for some time regularly, you will hopefully find things progressing towards adding a new person to your group, to become a group of three. When a fourth is added some time later, pray in a group of four until ready to split off into twos again.

Pray for wisdom and ask God to surface the people who might be added to the group next. God desires to use your prayer and sharing times to impart a missional focus to each person in the group. As even one excitedly shares answers to prayer and opportunities for witness that God grants them, it serves to spur the others on in continuing to pray and watch for opportunities with their own focus groups.

PRAYER PRACTICE:
- Practice using these 3 key questions to guide your reflection/sharing and prayer time:
    - *On your own at home,* try these questions to guide your reflections/prayers in a journal.
    - *With a partner in class,* try sharing and praying with a partner through these questions.

DEBRIEF & APPLICATION QUESTIONS For Group Discussion

1. Discuss your experience. What help/hindrance did the questions provide?

2. Who can you share this with? In what contexts can you see using these guiding questions?

HOMEWORK:
- Pray for your leaders this week using the Scriptures outlined in this lesson.
- Pray about who you might approach as a potential prayer partner.
- Try using the Missional Prayer Partnership questions in your own devotional time this week.
- Read through the material for Lesson 10, concentrating on the readings, the personal reflection questions and prayer practice points.

We have included "A Burning and Shining Light" as an appendix to this week's lesson. Although not easy reading it is very important for our focus on prayer for city. University of Ottawa history professor David Lyle Jeffrey traces the progress of gospel prayer, preaching and works of mercy and justice over a hundred years period – illustrating the advance of the gospel from evangelism to church renewal to complete societal renovation.

Jeffrey details the account of England during the great awakening. In many people's minds, this revival constitutes the greatest example of religious and cultural renewal in western history. Here we read historical examples of the centrality of prayer, proclamation and justice and mercy. Jeffrey reveals the convergence of prayer, proclamation, and mercy in the complex phenomenon of revival. The weighty conclusion of this essay focuses on the hidden lives of prayer. Jeffrey gives proper acknowledgement to prayer as the source and continuance of true revival.

A Burning and Shining Light

Excerpts from David Lyle Jeffrey

Established Authority and the "Rule of Reason"

Enlightenment England was tolerant of stark economic contrasts and locking political contradictions, and it cultivated genteel hypocrisy. This was the so-called age of reasoning and what were considered to be rational models from a classical past now furnished patterns for the regulation of nature and human nature alike. This was a culture as suspicious of personal inspiration as it was evasive of candid passions... Any claim to individual spiritual experiences, any pretense to vision, or any excess of zeal ("enthusiasm") was eschewed as rational and vulgar – even socially dangerous. The definition of religious extravagance was codified by the Enlightenment philosopher John Locke, "Reason," he said, "must be our last judge and guide in everything."

In fact, reason was the ultimate guide and judge in almost nothing, even where most laboriously invoked, to rationalize its failure. Yet the notion that it had somehow eclipsed faith, as science eclipsed superstition, had already helped bring about a massive decline in national religious life. Nationalism had reinforced the moderationism of the Established Church, which for political as well as spiritual reasons became highly intolerant of any form of visible spirituality. After the collapse of the monarchy with Charles II in 1660, the Church became effectively a department of state. Both Puritans on the left and Catholics and Anglo-Catholics on the right were driven out of the Church with vindictive ferocity.

First, there were laws making it effectively illegal for anyone to receive communion except in an Anglican church. These were followed by a political revision of the Book of Common Prayer which made loyalty to the monarchy an article of faith and Christian obedience (1662); then came the Act of Uniformity in the same year, making it unlawful to seek any reform of the constitution of church or state, and requiring all clergy to take an oath of allegiance to these terms. Nearly two thousand rectors and vicars refused, and were ejected from their pastorates without compensation. Many eminent pastors and scholars, including Richard Baxter, Isaac Watts (father of the hymn writer), both grandfathers of the Wesleys, and lay teachers such as John Bunyan were among those disenfranchised, and often imprisoned, to a total of one-fifth of the English clergy. Worse, those driven out were, as the Anglican historian J. R. Green observes, "the most learned" of the clergy, who "from the time of the Reformation had played the most active and popular part in the life of the Church."

Denied their churches, these people began to meet in homes. The enraged state party immediately instituted the Conventicle Act (1664) which "punished with fine, imprisonment and transportation [i.e., to penal colonies abroad] all persons who met in greater numbers than five." When the determined pastors organized groups of five and worked around the clock to serve them, the fury of the government expressed itself in the Five Mile Act (1665), which provided a penalty of more than one year's salary and six months in jail for any who so much as approached within five mites of any town, borough, or parish in which they had previously taught or preached.

But the authorities were not finished. Prodded by a king and royal party notorious for unprecedented licentiousness and corruption (John Wesley wrote of Charles II that "Bloody Mary was a lamb, a mere dove, in comparison of him"), the Puritans, Baptists, Presbyterians, Independents, Quakers, and any Anglicans who would not swear absolute allegiance were, with Catholics, systematically excluded from the universities, denied any form of public employment and driven out of "polite society."....

....

Another element of the muddiness of the time was moral, gross carnality on a scale that even today makes appalling reading for most of us. From the reign of Charles II, whose mistresses, illegitimate children, court orgies, and wholesale and predatory debauchery indeed recalled Roman times, down through the middle of the eighteenth century, the private behavior of much of upper-class English society was luridly carnal and politically corrupt. In many of its privileged devotees, such a life created all the usual diseases of dissipation, and behind the elegant veneer of official society lay much dry rot – social, psychological, and spiritual. On great country estates, magnificent palaces in the Augustan (new Roman) style were built at fabulous cost. Here, in fresco-painted halls supported by marble columns and adorned with neoclassical art treasures, the wealthy wined, dined, caroused, and idled their lives away. Their quest for innovative entertainment produced grotesque excess: Lord Francis Dashwood (who with Benjamin Franklin revised the Book of Common Prayer for American Episcopal use), for example, presided over one of many "Hell Fire Clubs." He had underground caves and grottoes beneath his palace at West Wyckham in which he held satanic orgies by torchlight; participants attired as medieval monks debauched young girls brought in for the occasion dressed as nuns.

Nor did this sort of behavior go without the tacit approval and even participation of the Established clergy. Many of them had an abundance of idle time on their hands. Lesser scions of noble families held "pluralities" – the earnings of several parishes at once without serving in any, except through hired deputies who were paid starvation wages. Better placed members of the privileged classes could expect bishoprics, at about two hundred times the salary of a parish priest, which were given out as part of the system of political patronage. Few of these men were true shepherds; most were indolent and many entirely dissolute. Bishops often kept grand houses in London, in which they hosted a constant round of parties for the social elite. Hannah More, who knew many of the least worldly of these prelates, offers in a letter to one of her sisters an insight into one of the more polite gatherings of her clerical acquaintances:

> On Monday I was at a very great assembly at the Bishop of St. Asaph's. Conceive to yourself one hundred and fifty or two hundred people met together, dressed in the extremity of fashion; painted as red as bacchanals; poisoning the air with perfumes; treading on each other's gowns; making the crowd the blame; not one in ten ably to get a chair; protesting they are engaged

to ten other places; and lamenting the fatigue they are not obliged to endure; ten or a dozen card tables crammed with dowagers of quality, grave ecclesiastics and yellow admirals; and you have an idea of disassembly. I never go to these things when I can possibly avoid it, and stay when there as few minutes as I can.

...

The practical result of the expulsion of genuine spiritual leadership from the Church and of the nearly complete corruption of its administrative hierarchy was a wholesale neglect of spiritual life at the parish level. H.C.G. Moule, bishop of Durham in the early part of our century, reflects concerning this time:

> The churches in London and the large cities continued to be all but empty. . . Addison (the hymn writer) pronounced it to be an unquestionable truth that there was less appearance of religion in England than in any neighbouring state, whether Protestant or Catholic. And Montesquieu declared that "there was no religion in England – that the subject if mentioned in society excited nothing but laughter."

When, with the rise of the evangelical movement, some of these churches began to be filled, the official hierarchy expressed predictable alarm, fueled by almost paranoid speculation concerning the possible consequences.

Those in authority looked for every possible weapon by which to repress any popular threat to their dominance. One of the best which lay to hand seemed to be the rule of reason, with its classical standards of "taste" and 'judgment''. This they aimed at the "enthusiasm" of the new converts to evangelicalism, as though they thought themselves learned philosophers defending the state against an invasion of insane barbarians. Typical was Archbishop Drummond of York, who on coming to investigate an evangelical Anglican priest at Helmsley in 1760 and listening to his sermon, accosted him afterward in the street, shouting, "If you go on preaching such stuff you will drive all your parish mad! Were you to inculcate the morality of Socrates, it would do more good than canting about the new birth." "Madness" was thus the charge most often levied against any sort of serious and outspoken Christianity, and it is certain that many were locked up in insane asylums for life simply for preaching or declaring their faith openly. "Reason" became at once the arch enemy of visible faith and the shiboleth of a dead religion.

"On Monday morning many of the slaves had got out of irons, and were attempting to break up the gratings; and the seamen not daring to go down the hold to clear our pumps, we were obliged, for the preservation of our lives, to kill fifty of the ringleaders and stoutest of them. It is impossible to describe the misery the poor slaves underwent, having had no fresh water for five days."

Poverty and Misrule

Within the shadow of polite society and yet untouched by the myth of reason, London seethed with other life – the miserable existence of the ordinary poor. From a variety of economic causes, the cities had been growing; the capital itself more than doubled in Wesley's lifetime. Many, coming in hope from rural poverty, looked for respectable work in vain.

Adequate housing could not be built fast enough, nor was there sufficient purchasing power among those who most needed the shelter. Deteriorated tenements in rat-infested districts were operated by slum lords and ruled by an often vicious underworld. Prostitution, gambling, "gaming" establishments offering the systematic torture of animals as entertainment, pickpocketing and more serious felonies, and a prodigious traffic's alcohol were among the most evident preoccupations of the urban poor.

The disease of alcoholism was endemic. Hogarth's engraving entitled "Gin Lane" offers all too realistic a portrait of the depredation wrought upon the urban populace especially by the huge trade in spirits. It was perhaps, as W. E. H. Lecky called it, "the *master curse* of English life." England had always been a beer drinking country; in 1688, with a population of slightly more than five million, the national consumption was more than twelve and a half million barrels, or about 90 gallons for every man, woman, and child. But gin was something far more serious. In 1750, the consumption of gin – poorly distilled and often virtually poisonous – was eleven million gallons. Some idea of the total debilitation wrought by this plague may be imagined in terms of simple items of record: in this same year, of 2,000 houses in the St. Giles, Holburn, district of London, 506 – one quarter – were gin shops. Even in Westminster every eighth house had been turned into a gin outlet. Henry Fielding, the novelist and magistrate, reckoned in alarm that gin was "the principal sustenance (if it may be called) of 100,000 people" in London.

Within the rising merchant class, loansharking, smuggling, embezzlement, stock frauds, and investment in the gin trade were among the activities which helped to reinforce and maintain social evils in all classes. The worst of these evils was the slave trade, in which abomination England became the undisputed international leader after 1713, and from which it thereafter derived fabulous wealth. This cruel degradation of human life in which people were treated more viciously than most Western societies now tolerate treatment of animals, created a hell on earth more grotesque in its brutality than can be described here in detail. Suffice it to say that by 1750 British ships were carrying off nearly fifty thousand slaves each year to British plantations abroad with about a third of that number perishing of cruelty and starvation enroute or in their first year in the Americas. Concerning a slave ship such as the one on which John Newton served, the Annual Register for 1762 records this first-hand report:.

On Friday the men slaves being very sullen and unruly, having had no sustenance of any kind for forty-eight hours except a dram, we put one half of the strongest of them in irons. On Saturday and Sunday all hands, night and day, could scarce keep the ship clear, and were constantly under arms. On Monday morning many of the slaves had got out of irons, and were attempting to break up the gratings; and the seamen not daring to go down the hold to clear our pumps, we were obliged, for the preservation of our lives, to kill fifty of the ringleaders and stoutest of them. It is impossible to describe the misery the poor slaves underwent, having had no fresh water for five days. Their dismal cries and shrieks, and most frightful looks, added a great deal to our misfortune; four of them were found dead, and one drowned herself in the hold.[1]

This "legitimate business" grew so rapidly within the next three decades that in the years between 1783 and 1796 alone, while William Wilberforce was rallying support in his spiritual warfare against the political and business forces which practiced it, more than eight hundred thousand slaves were transported from Africa to the New World plantations – most of them in British ships.[2] And it is unfortunate, but necessary to report, that not all of the evangelical leaders were free of involvement in this terrible traffic. George Whitefield purchased and owned slaves, as did Lady Selina, countess of Huntington, even as Wesley and others of their number were crying out in the name of Christ for abolition.[3]

Rome indeed. If the evangelical reformers of this period denounced social evils in what now seem to us extreme terms, we must remember that the England of their day was for them as Rome itself was for St. Jerome or St. Augustine – a den of iniquity so vast and so rationalized in its habits and appetites that only a call to radical purity could make clarity of the confusion. Rather, they saw virtually the whole order of society, despite its reigning myths, as under a tyrannous depravity. It became central to their calling to proclaim it so. This fearless denunciation of social mores as much as the doctrine of the new birth aroused the furious opposition they met from landed gentry and state church hierarchy alike.

When an open air preacher like George Whitefield could gather thirty thousand of the London poor for a sermon in Kensington Common, and comparable numbers at Moorfields (1742), there were of course reasons for the Establishment to fear the winds of revolution might be building for a storm. But what the Establishment could not see was that the maverick evangelist and his colleagues were only the most visible manifestations of a profoundly spiritual revolution, the scope and consequences of which would not be fully known for years to come. For all across the British Isles, in America, in every class and corner of society a mysterious wind was beginning to blow, softly but surely.

"Huntingdon is quite a mother to the poor; she visits them and prays with them in their sickness; and they leave their children to her for a legacy when they die, and she takes care of them. I was really astonished at the traces of religion I discovered in her . . . and cannot but glorify God for her. More cheerfulness I never saw intermingled with devotions."

Revival and Reform

Selena Shirley was soon soon to be wife to Earl Hastings, Lord Huntingdon. Since about nine years of age, she has been quietly but intensely praying for a deepening of her spiritual life, and for a good man to be her husband. Both prayers are about to be answered, but in the context of an unexpected call to a tumultuous public responsibility. The life of Lady Selina, countess of Huntingdon (1707-1791) was coextensive with the eighteenth-century revival movement and is an exemplary witness to the evident provision of the Holy Spirit for the work he was about to do.

From 1742, Lady Huntingdon frequently invited Charles and John Wesley as well as others among their followers to visit her home at Donnington Park and to preach to members of the aristocracy she had assembled there for that purpose. During this same period she commenced her acquaintance with Isaac Watts, who was the permanent houseguest of her friend. Shortly after the death of her two sons by smallpox, in 1744, she met and became fast friends also with Philip Doddridge, another clergyman of the Dissenting tradition to whom she regularly turned for spiritual counsel until Doddridge's death a few years later.

After her husband's death in 1746, Lady Huntingdon devoted herself utterly to support of the growing revival. She did this in a variety of ways, not least of which was to contribution of more than a hundred thousand pounds in her lifetime to support lay preachers, ordained pastors, schools, and a seminary college at Trevecca in Wales and to alleviate the suffering of the needy poor. In a time when many parishes paid an annual salary of forty pounds, this was a prodigious sum. But it is also clear that she provided for many years invaluable political protection for many of the evangelical leaders and less well known pastoral servants of the movement. This she achieved by exercising one of the rights so often abused by members of her class – purchasing advowsons and appointing evangelical clergymen to them – and by extension of another – the peer's right to appointment of private Anglican chaplains. Among the most notable of those under her protection were George Whitefiled, Howell Harris, John Fletcher, John Berridge, Henry Venn, William Romaine, Augustus Toplady, Martin Madan, and Thomas Haweis. But the list is long, as is that of the more than forty chapels she founded and built all over England and Wales.

<u>Above all, she was a prayer warrior, supporting every aspect of the work of the Spirit in her time which she could identify</u>. Much of this, as Doddridge suggests in a letter to his wife, remained of course hidden from public view:

> Huntingdon is quite a mother to the poor; she visits them and prays with them in their sickness; and they leave their children to her for a legacy when they die, and she takes care of them. I was really astonished at the traces of religion I discovered in her . . . and cannot but glorify God for her. More cheerfulness I never saw intermingled with devotions.

Yet, while not herself a writer or evangelist, she was a central figure among those raised up to specific responsibility in the revival, and it is not difficult to see in retrospect how crucial was her role. As her chief biographer puts it, "wherever she was called by the providence of God she was acknowledged as a 'burning and shining light'"– the singular praise which occurs again and again in the tributes paid in that century to persons of acknowledged spiritual leadership.

Fruits of the Gospel

A historical perspective nevertheless affords us some understanding of the unfolding of the eighteenth century revival.

From the very first the Oxford Methodist students had been actively involved in prison ministry and charity instruction for poor children as part of their spiritual exercise. When first Whitefield and then the Wesleys took to itinerant preaching, they extended their concern to orphans, the illiterate poor, and the desperate condition of inmates in mental hospitals as well. While Whitefield's Georgia orphanage seems to have been a dubious project, or the concern he shared with the Wesleys for improving the condition of those whom the Establishment were content to ignore was a foremost part of his evangelical witness. John Wesley, for his part, translated and edited a "Christian Library" of fifty books, mostly classics of spirituality, to provide for the education of his unschooled followers. The enormous proceeds of these works and his other publications, in turn, he entirely gave away to aid poor lay preachers and their families, charity schools, prisoners, and other missions of mercy so that he died, by deliberate design, virtually penniless.

The prison ministry alone was remarkable. Into the intolerable, vermin-ridden darkness of prisons such as London's infamous Newgate – as well as its namesake in Bristol – Methodists went to preach to inmates and their jailors and to bring food, blankets, medicine, and clothing they had collected. The conditions they met were unspeakable, with torture and starvation commonplace and jailors growing rich from the public exhibition of famous prisoners (especially just before their execution), from the gin trade, and from prostitution (often forced). The inmates might be pickpockets, murderers, or simply persons unable to pay their debts; all met with the same treatment. The lot of political prisoners was not much better. In 1759, Wesley went to a prison near Bristol to visit a company of French prisoners of the Seven Years' War:

> About eleven hundred of them, we are informed, were confined in that little place, without anything to lie on but a little dirty straw, or anything to cover them but a few foul, thin rags, either by day or night, so that they died like rotten sheep. I was much affected, and preached in the evening on (Exodus 23:9) "Thou shalt not oppress a stranger; for ye know the heart of a stranger, seeing ye were strangers in the land of Egypt." Eighteen pounds were contributed immediately, which were made up to 24 pounds the next day. With this we bought linen and woollen cloth, which were made up into shirts, waistcoats and breeches. Some dozens of stockings were added; all which were carefully distributed, where there was the greatest want. Presently after, the Corporation of Bristol sent a large quantity of mattresses and blankets. And it was not long before contributions were set on foot at London, and in various parts of the Kingdom.[4]

Often the bishops denied Methodist preachers entrance to the prisons and asylums; as Wesley quipped caustically: "We are forbidden to go to Newgate, for fear of making them [the inmates] wicked, and to Bedlam for fear of driving them mad."[5] But they persisted wherever they could, and with remarkable results. In 1761, Wesley wrote a letter to the *London Chronicle* describing a remarkable transformation of Bristol's Newgate. It was now clean and neat, with "no fighting and brawling"; there was an unprecedented system of equitable arbitration for prisoners; drunkenness, prostitution, and abuse had been eliminated. Women prisoners had been separated from the men. Tools and materials were provided to allow for productive employment, and payment was made to prisoners from profits and goods sold. There were regular church services, Bibles had been distributed, and free medical services were available. The keeper or warden who brought all these reforms into effect was a Mr. Dagge, an early convert of the Methodists' preaching in his own prison.

Methodist preachers, many of whose names have not survived and many of whom were not ordained Anglican clergy but simply lay preachers, continued in this ministry wherever they could gain access to prisons.

They gave spiritual counsel to those condemned to execution, and as Hogarth's famous engraving illustrates, they regularly accompanied them through leering mobs of spectators to the scaffold, encouraging them to repentance or to hope in their newly found justification in Christ.

John Fletcher is typical of the preachers' unflagging dedication in these matters. Very ill and in convalescence in Switzerland for the tuberculosis which was soon to claim his life, he went to minister to prisoners and took the occasion to preach to "2000 people in a jail yard, where they were come to see a poor murderer two days before his execution." "I was a little abused by the bailiff," he adds in characteristic understatement, "and [was] refused the liberty of attending the poor man to the scaffold where he was to be broken on the wheel. I hope he died penitent."

Apparently many did, in England and elsewhere, accompanied to their last by "despised Methodists," who often suffered the pelting of filth and other humiliations for living out their faithfulness to the gospel.

Conditions in institutions for the mentally ill – effectively another species of degrading prison – were, if anything, more despicable. To begin with, as even the fate of Christopher Smart suggests, persons could be committed indefinitely without substantive justification. Then, especially if they were too poor to afford the expense of private institutions and were clapped into the ironically named Bedlam (from Bethlehem), they could be chained till death on filthy straw mats, beset by rats at night and the prodding and jests of paying sideshow minded visitors by day. Cowper, in a compounding of ironies, used to visit Bedlam for these cruel purposes with classmates from Westminster School, and it was a regular Sunday diversion of the wealthy effete, such as the ladies depicted in the last engraving of Hogarth's series entitled "The Rake's Progress"; even notable politicians such as Bolingbroke and literary men like Johnson participated in this horrible diversion. Yet here too to the Methodists and other evangelicals brought light, ministering to individuals and by their persistence both directly and indirectly through the political process they did much to mitigate the evils which were being practiced. And it was the force of evangelical influence that caused charitable institutions such as Magdalene House, a hospice for prostitutes and abused female children, to be founded.

> These then are some of the visible "fruits of the Spirit" which characterized revival in the age of Wesley. Beyond the huge crowds at Whitefield's open air sermons or the more than one hundred thousand followers of Wesley organized into societies for fellowship, study and worship all over England, these practical outworkings of faith, and others like them, including the abolition of the slave trade, give irrefragable evidence that something miraculous was being accomplished. The revival, which historian J. R. Green has said, "changed . . . the whole tone of English society. . .The [Anglican] Church was restored to new life and activity. Religion carried to the hearts of the people a fresh spirit of moral zeal, while it purified our literature and our manners. A new philanthropy reformed our prisons, infused clemency and wisdom into our penal laws, abolished the slave-trade, and gave the first impulse to popular education."[6]

What we see in the principal biographies of the period is, in effect, only the tip of an iceberg, while very little of its base snow visible. But this is just where a study of spirituality makes its contribution.

The Missionary Tradition

The Methodist Synthesis

When people from a Protestant tradition think of spiritual vocation, they usually think in terms of a call to active ministry. The scriptural model they have in mind is that afforded by the prophets, and it envisions above all a work of preaching, teaching, and visible activism. Wesley, traveling by horseback or carriage a quarter of a million miles to preach more than forty-five thousand times in his lifetime, talked about "the world as his parish."[1] Like the prophets of Israel he had no parish priesthood, but ranged all over the British Isles in his preaching of repentance and renewal, like the judges of Israel he organized reform. Whitefield was still more singular, perhaps, in his dedication to mass evangelism – preaching over eighteen thousand sermons to much larger audiences – but he too had projects of reform. Both were concerned, in a Pauline way, with mission outreach; each involved themselves in raising support and volunteers.

For John Wesley, as he said many times in his life, there was "no Christianity which was not social Christianity." Charles puts the point succinctly in one of his hymns for use "After Worship":

Actions He more than words requires,
Actions with right intention done,
Good works the fruit of good desires,
Obedience to His will alone,
Pure hope which seeks the things above,
Practical faith, and real love.

For Wesley, successful missionary outreach in fact is always built upon a foundation of rich meditative spirituality. He said to his coworkers:

> It cannot be that the people should grow in grace unless they give themselves to reading. A reading people will always be a knowing people. A people who talk much will know little. Press this upon them with your might, and you will soon see the fruit of your labours.

His own education, which so largely involved absorption in spiritual writers rather than traditional theologians, provided the model.

Contemplation of Christ crucified and adoration of the cross were central elements of Wesley's spiritual experience. This emphasis was reinforced by the Moravians, whose hymns and teaching often stressed the physical suffering of Christ. Wesley translated some of these hymns (although often modifying their extreme intensity of focus upon the cross), the best known of which is Count Zinzendorf's "Jesus, thy Blood and Righteousness."

Though the emphasis in his own life's work and teaching grew to be overwhelmingly mission-oriented, he retained his interest in a deep spirituality of the inner life because he believed that without it an evangelistic

"A continual desire is a continual prayer – that is, in a low sense of the word; for there is a far higher sense, such a close uninterrupted communion with him."

enterprise would soon wither and die of exhaustion. This was the reason for his extraordinary commitment to spiritual reading among his followers, and to their development of the contemplative's ardent pursuit of a life of prayer:

> A continual desire is a continual prayer – that is, in a low sense of the word; for there is a far higher sense, such a close uninterrupted communion with him.[7]

In the hymns of Charles – always regarded by the Wesleys as an intrinsic part of their teaching and evangelizing – these elements of their spirituality are faithfully reflected.

Among those of the active tradition in eighteenth-century spirituality none was perhaps more "outward" than George Whitefield. We might expect this from a man who could draw twenty to thirty thousand people for an outdoor sermon. Prototype of the modern mass evangelist, he was first and foremost a preacher; everything else came well behind. He built no organization comparable to Wesleyan, and beyond some of his sermons, journal entries, and a few letters he has left us only a small literary legacy. But as we shall see, no one aroused more wrath against the spirit of the revival than this man, and during the early years none had so large an impact for the revival upon public consciousness.

Whitefield possessed superb rhetorical skills. Atheists like Lord Bolingbroke and Lord Chesterfield, who came to hear him only to scoff and who rejected his message, nevertheless congratulated him sincerely for a mastery of Ciceronian rhetoric which they could only envy. He had dramatic training and dramatic skills, and above all an amazing sense of stage presence. As we see in some of what follows, he could control unruly crowds, even mobs like those at Moorfields, where hecklers hurled excrement and exposed themselves naked from trees in an attempt to divert the audience.

Though never on Wesley's scale, Whitefield was also committed to practical works of mercy. He regularly employed his sermons not only for a call to repentance and spiritual renewal but also as an opportunity to raise money for various missionary projects. John Newton tells a remarkable story of how Whitefield once collected six hundred pounds at a single Sermon for the inhabitants of an obscure village in Germany that had been burned down – hardly the sort of cause which Londoners might normally be expected to become excited about. After the sermon, Whitefield apparently said, "We shall sing a hymn, during which those who do not choose to give their mite on this awful occasion may sneak off." No one stirred. Whitehead then descended from the pulpit, ordered all doors but one to be barred, and stood there holding the collection plate himself as the congregation squeezed past one by one.[8]

> *"Religion does not consist in doing great things, for which few of us have frequent opportunities, but in doing the little necessary things of daily occurrence with a cheerful spirit, as to the Lord."*

....

This impetus in the latter part of the century, which seems far removed from quiet Christianity, clearly owed much to the vital connection between revival and reform forged by the Wesleys and their followers. Among the evangelical Anglicans, this emphasis was characterized by a practical direction toward the life of ordinary lay Christians. Newton indicates this workaday application to ordinary life in many of his letters to laypeople; one of them, to a married couple in his congregation, includes the following lines:

> At the best, if a contemplative life is more quiet, an active life is more honorable and useful. We have no right to live to ourselves. I do not think our Lord blamed Martha for providing a dinner for himself and his twelve apostles, but I suppose she was too solicitous to have things set off very nicely, and perhaps lost her temper. Methinks I see her breaking in upon him, with her face red with heat and passion, to huff her sister. This was her fault. Had she sent the dinner in quietly and with a smiling face, I believe he would not have rebuked her for being busy in the kitchen, while he was in the parlour. We like to have our own will; but submission to his is the great point. Religion does not consist in doing great things, for which few of us have frequent opportunities, but in doing the little necessary things of daily occurrence with a cheerful spirit, as to the Lord.[9]

Yet there were some whose opportunities allowed them to do great things, and one of the most eminent evangelical Anglican laypersons of any period, of course, was Newton's friend and parishioner William Wilberforce. That Newton, having been in his youth corrupted by the slave trade, should now be a source of pastoral encouragement to the likeable and hardworking young member of Parliament who more than anyone was to bring about an end to this abomination, now seems a perfection of divine logic.

Wilberforce, influenced in his conversion by Philip Doddridge's *Rise and Progress*, well illustrates the affection and respect evangelical Anglicans felt toward the Independents and Puritans, but he followed no particular theological controversy of his time with interest.[69] He was simply a person of the renew birth" who found himself in a political arena where practical opportunities for translation of the gospel were many. He had a distinct sense of calling, a vocation of spiritual life in the active world, and it placed him at the leadership of the abolition movement. Yet, as his writings declare, he was also an exemplary Christian of the inner life and built his life of active service upon the basis which he describes in his literary work of spiritual reflection, *Real Christianity*. For many decades this work was considered to be a kind of manifesto of evangelical Christianity. In his life's work of reform and organization for evangelism, including some of the formative planning for British foreign missions, Wilberforce shows himself to have been deeply sustained from within in his pursuit of the "real" mission-oriented and active spirituality he championed.

An old American evangelist once wondered aloud "how can there be a deep revival in a shallow generation?" The men and women in this book have something to teach us about that – and it is clear that their answer involved neither condescension to shallowness nor imitation of it. For them, mature Christian spirituality can only grow from a mature Christian mind and such a mind can only come to be when it has first hid itself in the mind of Christ.

The history of English spirituality in the eighteenth century can be seen in one way as a movement from inner to outer life, from the narrow confines of dwindling independent churches and student Holy Clubs outward boldly into the turbulence of society and the needy world, but also from a necessary deep inwardness of personal spirituality to the pressures of active commitment to missionary enterprise

> *"Somewhere, we may suppose, sometime before all these remarkable events of revival began, there was one – or dozens, or hundreds, but perhaps just one – person praying."*

at home and abroad. It can also be seen as a rich tapestry of interconnections which tie together faithful Christians of Anglo-catholic, conjuror, Independent Dissenter, and Established Church communities into one seamless web of spiritual ministry to their culture. This tapestry is wider as well as more intricate than these pages can show and contains many gems of spiritual patterning even the specialized historian will not be able to discern. Yet from quite another point of view, some of these – hidden lives of prayer – may have been most central of all to the grand design.

Somewhere, we may suppose, sometime before all these remarkable events of revival began, there was one – or dozens, or hundreds, but perhaps just one – person praying.

Far from the maddling crowd of London, perhaps in a little cottage somewhere in the hills of southern Wales, it is the break of a new day, and spring sunlight spills through the window and across the shoulders of someone rebuilding a fire from the cold night's embers. She is kneeling on the stones of her hearth, kneeling as she prays each morning, to ask that God by his spirit will bring revival to her country and its people. And as she rises to commence with love and joy to serve her god in the ordinary round of a quiet life, she is singing an old hymn. Perhaps it will be this very morning that a lifelong faithfulness of intercession will begin to be gathered in the hand of the Master Weaver toward the base of his own great loom, a thread of purest gold, burning and shining, reflecting and revealing his matchless light.

APPLICATION QUESTIONS

For Personal Reflection

1. Which inspires you most from this historical account of revival?

2. What challenges you most?

3. How does this fuel your vision for revival? How does this move you to pray?

PRAYER PRACTICE:
- Respond in prayer by crying out for revival!

[1] J. Wesley Bready, *England: Before and After Wesley* (London: Hodder & Stoughton, 1938), p. 101.

[2] Wilberforce suggested in his *Twelve Propositions* (1789) a more conservative figure of "about thirty-eight thousand" per year.

[3] Arnold Dallimore, *George Whitefield: The Life and Times of the Great Evangelist of the Eighteenth Century Revival,* 2 vols. (Westchester, Ill.: Cornerstone, 1970; 1980), vol. 2, pp. 219, 368-69.

[4] John Wesley, *Journal,* ed. Nehemiah Curnock (London: Epworth, 1938), entry for October 15, 1759.

[5] *Journal,* February 22, 1750.

[6] J.R. Green, *A Short History of the English People* (London, 1877-89), vol. 3, p. 736.

[7] *Letters,* vol. 5, p. 283. Cf. Gordon S. Wakefield, *Methodist Devotion: the Spiritual Life in the Methodist Tradition 1791-1945* (London: Epworth, 1966), pp. 25-32.

[8] A.C.H. Seymour, *The Life and Times of Selina, Countess of Huntingdon,* 2 vols. (London: Painter, 1844), vol. I, p. 42.

[9] This letter, to a Mr. And Mrs. Coffin, "On Serving in the Ordinary Duties of life," may be compared to his letter entitled "God's Will and Our Ambitions"

Section III
Leaders Reach a City through Prayer

Let's return to the diagram to remind ourselves where we are in the stream of Prayer Bootcamp:

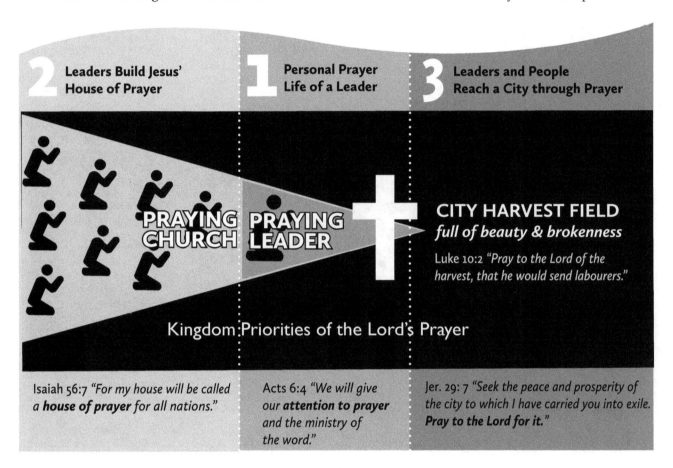

1. We started in the centre in section one looking at how the **personal prayer life of a leader** begins in the closet in fellowship with Christ. The outcome of this strong personal prayer life, is that they find they become 'active duty' in the fields of harvest.

2. From there we explored in section two the power of leaders **praying together with the church.**

3. We will end now looking at the third and final section the outcome when the first two realities are happening – where the result of praying leaders who lead **praying churches follow Jesus into the harvest field.** How beautiful when God sends his people out to love and serve the city as answers to their own prayers!

I f you join us for worship at Grace Vancouver Church, you will come to a time in the service called "Prayer for the Church in the City." This prayer will not be brief. It is a time of rich reflection and passionate plea. We contemplate the place and purpose of the church in the city. We ask God to keep us separate from the city – in its independence from God. We also pray that God will empower us and send us to be 'city-soluble'. Like salt, we cry out to penetrate the city with justice and good works. Like light, we pray for courage to announce the good news of Jesus coming.

We pray for the city and the church in the city,

> *I have posted watchmen on your walls, Jerusalem; they will never be silent day or night.*
> *You who call on the LORD, give yourselves no rest, and give him no rest till he establishes Jerusalem*
> *and makes her the praise of the earth.*
> Isaiah 62

Even in exile, God's people pray for the city – for God to care for it. God will hear this prayer and bless the city with prosperity and order. Notice that the fate and future of God's people is tied to the well being of the city.

> *Seek the peace and prosperity of the city to which I have carried you into exile. Pray to the*
> *LORD for it, because if it prospers, you too will prosper."*
> Jeremiah 29:7

We are always to pray for the leaders and authority structure of the city we live in:

> *I urge, then, first of all, that petitions, prayers, intercession and thanksgiving be made for all people— 2 for*
> *kings and all those in authority, that we may live peaceful and quiet lives in all godliness and holiness. 3 This is*
> *good, and pleases God our Savior, 4 who wants all people to be saved and to come to a knowledge of the truth.*
> 1 Timothy 2:1ff

Notice again that the fate of the city and the future of the church is tied together. We might say the intertwined destiny of church and city is contained in our prayers. On the one hand, the outcome of our prayer will be peace and safety so we can worship God; "that we might live peaceable and godly lives."

> *On the other hand, the full answer comes when God fulfills his saving purposes in the lives of our neighbors*
> *and friends; This is good, and pleases God our Savior, 4 who wants all people to be saved and to come to a*
> *knowledge of the truth.*

God's people are called to pray for and build the church. This is first in order and priority. In the one hundred year history of Ezra and Nehemiah, we notice when the exiles return from Babylon, they first rebuild the temple. They are empowered by the words of the prophets Zechariah and Haggai. They do this with a spirit of prayer:

> *And I will pour out on the house of David and the inhabitants of Jerusalem a spirit[a] of grace and*
> *supplication... "On that day a fountain will be opened to the house of David and the inhabitants of Jerusalem,*
> *to cleanse them from sin and impurity. 2 "On that day, I will banish the names of the idols from the land, and*
> *they will be remembered no more," declares the LORD Almighty.*
> Zechariah 12:10-13:2

There is much to say here about this pregnant passage. Notice again that prayer is the instrument for rebuilding the temple. When the temple is rebuilt, God will be worshipped and all other gods and idols expelled.

There is great joy in the city when the foundation of the temple is laid;

> *When the builders laid the foundation of the temple of the LORD, the priests in their vestments and with trumpets, and the Levites (the sons of Asaph) with cymbals, took their places to praise the LORD, as prescribed by David king of Israel. 11 With praise and thanksgiving they sang to the LORD: "He is good; his love toward Israel endures forever." And all the people gave a great shout of praise to the LORD, because the foundation of the house of the LORD was laid.*

Yet the worship of God is not fully restored until the walls of the city which surround the temple are repaired and the gates put in place. It is more than seventy years after the temple has been rebuilt! Without city walls the temple lies unprotected from its enemies and uninhabited by God's people. Again, the practice of worship and the integrity of the city are intertwined.

> *"Those who survived the exile and are back in the province are in great trouble and disgrace. The wall of Jerusalem is broken down, and its gates have been burned with fire." 4 When I heard these things, I sat down and wept. For some days I mourned and fasted and prayed before the God of heaven*
>
> Nehemiah 1:3...

It is only after the walls of the city are completed and the gates put in place that the city is filled with worshippers and the full worship of God restored;

> *27 At the dedication of the wall of Jerusalem, the Levites were sought out from where they lived and were brought to Jerusalem to celebrate joyfully the dedication with songs of thanksgiving and with the music of cymbals, harps and lyres. 28 The musicians also were brought together from the region around Jerusalem—for the musicians had built villages for themselves around Jerusalem. 31 I had the leaders of Judah go up on top of[e] the wall. I also assigned two large choirs to give thanks...The two choirs that gave thanks then took their places in the house of God;*
>
> Nehemiah 12

When God's people pray for the church in the city, God will bless them in building the church and he will restore peace and joy to the streets of the city. This is the promise when we pray for the church in the city;

> *"Is not this the kind of fasting I have chosen: to loose the chains of injustice and untie the cords of the yoke, to set the oppressed free and break every yoke? Then you will call, and the LORD will answer; you will cry for help, and he will say: Here am I. Your people will rebuild the ancient ruins and will raise up the age-old foundations; you will be called Repairer of Broken Walls, Restorer of Streets with Dwellings.*
>
> Isaiah 58:6,9.12

In this day and in our cities, we might be few and small. We are in exile. We are a remnant in the city. Yet today we are to pray for the church in the city –for God to restore the foundations of the temple/ church and to empower his people to build her city walls. When we pray for the church in the city in this way God promises to hear. He assures us that he will bless. He will greatly prosper the church. Her gates will be strong and her walls fortified to exclude her enemies. Her gates will be open so the nations can stream in to the temple to pray;

> *"For my house shall be called a house of prayer for all nations!"*
>
> Luke 19:46

When God's people pray for the church in the city- God promises to answer – in part not in perfection. Only in heaven, in the new Jerusalem will city and church be perfectly one:

> *Then I saw "a new heaven and a new earth,"[a] for the first heaven and the first earth had passed away, and there was no longer any sea. 2 I saw the Holy City, the new Jerusalem, coming down out of heaven from God, prepared as a bride beautifully dressed for her husband. 3 And I heard a loud voice from the throne saying, "Look! God's dwelling place is now among the people, and he will dwell with them.*
>
> Revelation 21

Serving the City through Prayer

GOALS: In this lesson we will...
- ❑ Ask for God's heart for our cities and seek how he wants to place the church in the main arteries of our cities
- ❑ Prayer walk our neighbourhood

Introduction   (See DVD Section III: Lesson 10)

As Christianity and the church migrate (or are sent) to the periphery of our culture, there is a tendency for Christians to withdraw, build walls and segregate from the city. We lose our harvest eyes. We become defensive toward the surrounding city rather than compassionate. Jesus shows a different way:

> Matthew 9:36-37, *"When he saw the crowds, he had compassion on them, because they were harassed and helpless, like sheep without a shepherd. Then he said to his disciples, 'The harvest is plentiful but the workers are few. Ask the Lord of the harvest, therefore, to send out workers into his harvest field.'"*

When we lose sight of the city we cease to be 'city soluble'. The church becomes a fortress, all walls and no gates – with a drawbridge that's dropped down for 90 minutes each week. In this lesson we will counter this tendency by learning how to prayer walk. When we walk the city in prayer we grow in our understanding of its brokenness and its need. By putting hands and feet to our prayer life, we physically and personally locate ourselves in the city's greatness and its poverty. Our spiritual passion to others is embodied. We learn to own and love the city and to intercede for her.

City Church San Francisco

For he was looking forward to the city with foundations, whose builder and maker is God.
~*Hebrews 11:10*

This article gives biblical foundations to direct our relationship to and our prayers for the city.

God Is a City Builder

God began history in a Garden, but is ending it in a city (Rev.21). God tells Adam to multiply and develop a civilization that will glorify him (Gen.1:27-28). Adam fails, and God through Christ the second Adam does get a civilization that glorifies him, but Hebrews 3:6 and Revelation 21 show us that this world is urban. The wife of the Lamb is a beautiful city, shining with the glory of God (Rev.21:10-11). When we look at the New Jerusalem, we discover that in the midst of the city is a crystal river and the Tree of Life, bearing fruit and leaves which heal the nations of the effects of the divine covenant curse. This city is the Garden of Eden, remade. The City is the fulfillment of the purposes of the Eden of God.

Is this "only" metaphorical? God is called a Father who is building a spiritual family. That means that, though the earthly family is an institution corrupted by sin, we are to seek to redeem and rebuild human families. So God is a city builder who is building a spiritual city. That means that, though the earthly city is an institution corrupted by sin, we are to seek to redeem and rebuild human cities. As we are to redeem human families by spreading within them the family of God, so we are to redeem human cities by spreading within them the city of God. We know that the power of marriage is such that, as your marriage goes so goes your life. So the power of cities is such that, as the city goes, so goes society.

Why God Builds Cities

1. A place of shelter for the weak and different:

    a. *Under God:* The city was invented as a place of refuge from criminals, animals, and marauders. By its nature, the city is a place where minorities can cluster for support in an alien land, where refugees can find shelter and where the poor can better eke out an existence. The city is always a more merciful place for minorities of all kinds. The dominant majorities often dislike cities, but the weak and powerless need them. They cannot survive in the suburbs and small towns. Thus cities are places of diversity, unlike villages. They reflect the Future City where there will be people of "every tongue, tribe, people, and nation".

    b. *Under sin:* The city becomes a refuge from God, where people with deviant lifestyles can run and hide because of the natural tolerance the city breeds toward those who are different. Also, under sin the diversity breeds anger, tension and violence between the different groups.

    c. *Application:* We will partner with the people of the city in seeking to serve the physical as well as the spiritual needs of the city.

2. A cultural and human development center:

a. *Under God:* The city stimulates and focuses the gifts, capacities, and talents of people, the deep potentialities in the human heart. It does so by bringing you into contact with: 1) people unlike you—very diverse and providing different perspectives, and with 2) people like you who are just as good or better than you at what you do. The concentration of human talent, both by "competition" and cooperation, produces greater works of art, science, technology, culture. The city moves you to reach down and press toward excellence.

b. *Under sin:* the city is exhausting, leading to burn out. Also, now the city leads human beings into an ambition to "make a name for themselves" (Gen.11:4). Selfishness, pride, and arrogance are magnified in the city. Since God invented it as a "cultural mine", the city now brings out whatever is in the human heart, the very best and worst of humanity.

c. *Application:* We must seek to develop a biblical world and life view that seeks to see all of reality through the lens of Scripture, so that we work with excellence but not burn-out of perfectionism, and are able to relax without guilt or laziness.

3. A place of spiritual searching and temple building:

a. *Under God:* the city is the place where God dwells in the center—in the earthly city of Jerusalem, the temple stands as the central integrating point of the city's architecture and as apex of its art and science and technology. Even now, the city's intensity makes people religious seekers.

b. *Under sin:* As in ancient times, the city was built around ziggurats, "landing pads" for the god of the city, so today people are drawn into skyscraper temples worshipping the self and money. Cities are hotbeds of religious cults, idols, and false gods. Since cities breed spiritual seeking, when Christians abandon the cities the seekers fall into the hands of idols and heresies.

c. *Application:* we will look to exposing the idols of the heart with a regular application of the gospel in our preaching, music, community groups, and every venue of the church.

Summary: In every earthly city, there are two "cities" vying for control. They are the City of Man, and the City of God. (See Augustine's *City of God*.) Though the fight between these two kingdoms happens everywhere in the world, earthly cities are the flashpoints on the battlelines, the places where the fighting is most intense, and where victories are the most strategic. Because of the power of the city, it is the chief target of the forces of darkness, because that which wins the city sets the course of human life and society and culture. Therefore, in general, the city is the most crucial place to minister.

Implications for Urban Churches

1. Who we can only reach in the city:

Cities are "population centres." Cities are filled and becoming more filled with people. Soon in the 21st century, more than one half of the world's population will live in cities. These are the people made in God's image whom Christ loves and calls his church to love.

If the Christian church wants to really change the country and culture, it must go into the cities themselves, not just into the suburbs or even the exurbs. Three kinds of persons live there who exert a tremendous influence on our society, and we cannot reach them in the suburbs. They are:

- the 'elites' who control the culture and who are becoming increasingly secularized,
- the masses of new immigrants who move out into the mainstream society over the next 30 years, and
- the poor, whose dilemmas are deepening rapidly and affecting the whole country.

2. Why we can best reach them in the city:

Wayne Meeks of Yale, in The First Urban Christians, points out that Paul's missionary work was urban-centered. He went to population centers, and ignored small towns and the countryside. Christianity spread better in the urban Roman Empire than in the countryside. Why?

a. *Openness:* People in the city are less conservative, more open to new ideas.

b. *Spreading Faster/Global Connection:* Christian evangelists found that in the city the gospel could spread faster into the influence centers—law, politics, arts, etc.—and into diverse national groups. All the ethnic groups came to the cities. Paul could go to Ethiopia for 10 years, learn Ethiopian and reach Ethiopia, OR, he could go to Tunisia for 10 years, learn Tunisian and reach Tunisia, OR he could go to Rome where everyone gathered and use the common language of that city (Latin or Greek) to reach everyone.

c. *Cultural influence:* In small towns the people influence that small town. You can go to a small town and lead some people in media to Christ OR you ca go to a big city (New York, Los Angeles) and influence the entire media profession that is where the companies that own the networks and newspaper reside, where they are produced on a national scale.

The early Christians lived and ministered in the cities. The result was that by the year 300 A.D., over half of the urban centres of the Roman Empire were Christian while the countryside remained pagan (the word paganus means country-man!). The early church was urban. There is no intrinsic reason for urban people to be less religious, only less traditional.

APPLICATION QUESTIONS

For Personal Reflection

1. In what ways has <u>the city</u> helped and/or hindered you a) in finding shelter,
   b) in your personal development, and c) in your spiritual growth?

2. In what ways has <u>the church</u> helped and/or hindered you a) in finding shelter,
   b) in your personal development, and c) in your spiritual growth?

For Small Group Discussion

3. How can the church increasingly help the city become:
   a. a place of shelter for the weak and different,
   b. a cultural and human development centre, and
   c. a place of spiritual searching?
   What different roles would prayer play in this?

4. How is your church currently praying and responding towards growth in these areas?

When Praying On Site Brings Prophetic Momentum

Nehemiah 1:5-10, 2:11-18

1:5 Then I said:

"LORD, the God of heaven, the great and awesome God, who keeps his covenant of love with those who love him and keep his commandments, 6 let your ear be attentive and your eyes open to hear the prayer your servant is praying before you day and night for your servants, the people of Israel. I confess the sins we Israelites, including myself and my ancestral family, have committed against you. 7 We have acted very wickedly toward you. We have not obeyed the commands, decrees and laws you gave your servant Moses.

8 "Remember the instruction you gave your servant Moses, saying, 'If you are unfaithful, I will scatter you among the nations, 9 but if you return to me and obey my commands, then even if your exiled people are at the farthest horizon, I will gather them from there and bring them to the place I have chosen as a dwelling for my Name.'

10 "They are your servants and your people, whom you redeemed by your great strength and your mighty hand. 11 Lord, let your ear be attentive to the prayer of this your servant and to the prayer of your servants who delight in revering your name. Give your servant success today by granting him favor in the presence of this man."

I was cupbearer to the king. ....

2: 11 I went to Jerusalem, and after staying there three days 12 I set out during the night with a few men. I had not told anyone what my God had put in my heart to do for Jerusalem. There were no mounts with me except the one I was riding on.
13 By night I went out through the Valley Gate toward the Jackal Well and the Dung Gate, examining the walls of Jerusalem, which had been broken down, and its gates, which had been destroyed by fire. 14 Then I moved on toward the Fountain Gate and the King's Pool, but there was not enough room for my mount to get through; 15 so I went up the valley by night, examining the wall. Finally, I turned back and reentered through the Valley Gate. 16 The officials did not know where I had gone or what I was doing, because as yet I had said nothing to the Jews or the priests or nobles or officials or any others who would be doing the work.
17 Then I said to them, "You see the trouble we are in: Jerusalem lies in ruins, and its gates have been burned with fire. Come, let us rebuild the wall of Jerusalem, and we will no longer be in disgrace." 18 I also told them about the gracious hand of my God upon me and what the king had said to me. They replied, "Let us start rebuilding." So they began this good work.

QUESTIONS

For Small Group Discussion

5. What was Nehemiah doing as he prayed and walked around the city ruins?
    What was his objective?

6. What did it accomplish for Nehemiah?

7. What did it do for God's people?

PRAYER PRACTICE:
- Confess the brokenness and need that we have, as individuals, as a church and as a city.
- Ask for the Spirit's grace to respond and participate in his redemptive work.

The Reason Why We Prayer Walk
Diagnose Your Relation to Your City

For Personal Reflection

8. Mark an X on the line where you would place <u>yourself</u> in relation to your community:

    involved.................................detached
    recognized............................anonymous
    active....................................idle
    adventurous...........................fearful
    dispersed............................. secluded
    diverse ....homogeneous
    caring...................................indifferent

9. What are the different ways you are involved with your neighbours/neighbourhood?

For Small Group Discussion

10. Mark an X on the line where you would place <u>your church</u> in relation to its community:

    involved.................................detached
    recognized............................anonymous
    active....................................idle
    adventurous...........................fearful
    dispersed............................. secluded
    diverse ....homogeneous
    caring...................................indifferent

11. What are different ways <u>your church</u> is involved with its neighbours/neighbourhood?

Points to consider:

1. Doesn't it seem strange to "leap frog" our immediate community/neighbourhood in order to minister at the church?

2. If we are not involved in serving/praying/sharing on a local level, how will the gospel ever incarnate and come to real expression in the world?

"Your church should be so important to its community, that if you left, it would tear the heart out of it!" ~Randy Nabors

Prayer walking is one way to address the above challenge/crisis for both churches and individuals. It is a tangible way to get to know and serve our community and neighbours.

Reasons for Prayer Walking

"Lift up your eyes. Are not the fields white for harvest?" "Pray to the Lord of the harvest."

"I never noticed my community- as a place of mission until I prayer walked it on my way home for the first time." ~ New York prayer training participant

Praying on site with insight. Praying nearer and clearer.

Prayer Walking: *Why?*

- Praying together (2x2) is powerful.

- Prayer walking roots Christians into a community and gives calling a sense of place. Spiritual 'culture' differs from place to place – even within a city – and each church must have unique expressions of mission for broader city transformation.

- Spiritual mission and warfare becomes immediate/here and now
   - You see the mission field head on.
   - You see the "whole man" in his community, social and economic context, problems.

- Prayer walking takes us out of the cloister into the field and "The field is the world" and the church belongs there!

- Prayer walking is a means to transform ourselves. It opens your hearts and eyes to our community and city – its beauty and its need. It gives you "harvest eyes" rather than "cloistered fear".

- Prayer strengthens Christians and it brings evangelists to a community as we pray for the Lord to send "labourers into his harvest."

- Prayer walking connects our plans and purpose to the plan and purpose of God.

- Prayer walking opens the doors and hearts to the gospel

- Prayer walking *changes*
   - Neighbourhoods into parishes
   - Believers into missionaries
   - Homes into ministry centres
   - Churches into the crossroads of kingdom renewal

QUESTIONS

For Large Group Discussion

14. What other reasons can you think of for prayer walking?

15. What experience have you had with prayer walking?

16. What is your current attitude towards prayer walking (anticipation, apprehension, etc.)? Why?

How to Prayer Walk: Specific Pointers

- Specifics
    - o Go in smaller groups (pairing up is best, but trios work too).
    - o Worship before you go; worship as you walk.
    - o Pray as you walk, out loud, eyes open. ☺ Stop at corners and landmarks.
    - o Pray shorter prayers. Pass it back and forth.
    - o Play off each others' prayer – to focus on a specific need or theme.

- Start with **short prayers of praise**. Remind yourself and the city that **Christ is the present Lord of this community and city.** He is the reigning and coming King!

- Pray for God to give you **harvest eyes** and a **spirit of grace and supplication**. Ask for **boldness** and **open doors** to this city, community, parish. **Confess** fears, weaknesses, lack of concern for those "outside."

- Pray for God to give **insight into his kingdom plans** for this community. Ask to fit into his plan. Pray for ownership of this "parish-community." Rejoice in the opportunity.

- Watch and pray for:
    - o **Critical needs** – Social, Political, Economic, Spiritual
    - o **Crossroads**, critical intersections, nerve centers, *flash points*
    - o **Churches and Christians** to be ministry centres
    - o **Cultural influencers** – public services, schools, galleries, theatres, media
    - o **People** in the community – individuals, major people groups

PRAYER PRACTICE:
- In groups of 2 or 3, go for a prayer walk together following the above guidelines.

DEBRIEF QUESTIONS

For Large Group Discussion

17. What did you see? What surprised you? What encouraged you? What made you uncomfortable? What did you struggle with?

18. What are ways you could prayer walk different communities in your life? *(eg. Work place neighbourhood, church community, local campus or school, major public transit routes/stops, home community, etc.)*

Prayer Mapping: *Why and How?*

- Drawing and referring to a prayer map can reveal and remind you of this: *God has strategically placed you/your church in various communities for his kingdom purposes.* It's a way of "walking and mapping" deeply through your life – to intentionally seek God's understanding to help you see and exegete the people, places and burdens through His eyes, to note these things He has brought into your life and has drawn your attention to.

A. <u>Geographical neighbourhood:</u> *Where do you live? Who's your next door neighbour?*

- <u>Copy or draw a street map of your focus area:</u>
  - For our church the area is approximately 14 blocks by 7 blocks.
  - Use roadways/paths/waterways as key boundaries to identify your 'parish.'

- **Around the church**
  - Note the apparent type(s) of area(s) present: downtown, blue collar, industrial, business, commercial, marginal, etc.
  - Note centres of influence:
    - *Education:* schools, universities, kindergarten, day cares, school boards, libraries
    - *Religion:* churches, synagogues, mosques, cult groups, meditation centres, etc.
    - *Media:* publishing houses/community papers, associated media personalities, etc.
    - *Business:* office buildings, business districts/streets, types of stores and services
    - *Public service:* city hall, government offices, police stations, fire halls, hospitals
  - Note places of cultural importance (arts and leisure):
    - Art galleries/studios, dance or theatre companies
    - Film schools/art schools/dance schools
    - Craft shops, etc.
    - Outdoor sculptures, painting, murals, etc.
    - Cinemas
    - Parks, football fields, hockey rinks, pools, community centres, etc.
  - Note places and centres of need/social disintegration
    - The homeless 'congregate' in certain areas as do prostitutes, drug dealers, etc.
    - Community agencies (private, religious, civil) designed to meet needs: Overnight shelters/rehab centres, emergency food and clothing, literacy, etc.
  - Note beehives of activity, where people like to gather:
    - Strategic crossroads/facilities where different groups people hang or live
    - "Happenin'" places

  - Note the people groups and the extent of social contact between individuals and groups.
    - Ethnic groups represented
    - Social and economic groups

- o Age/life stage: children, youth, families, elderly, single, married
- Note felt needs
  - o Personal illness, loneliness, physical hardships
  - o Insecure housing, property rights, threat of losing personal dwelling
  - o Financial insecurity, poverty
  - o Personal safety and physical insecurity, presence of violence
  - o Other needs…
- **In your 'hood' or parish**

  - Note places and points of need – see above.
  - Note churches and other religious facilities
  - Note community centres
  - Note where other Christians live in your neighbourhood. Your team.

Sample Prayer Map

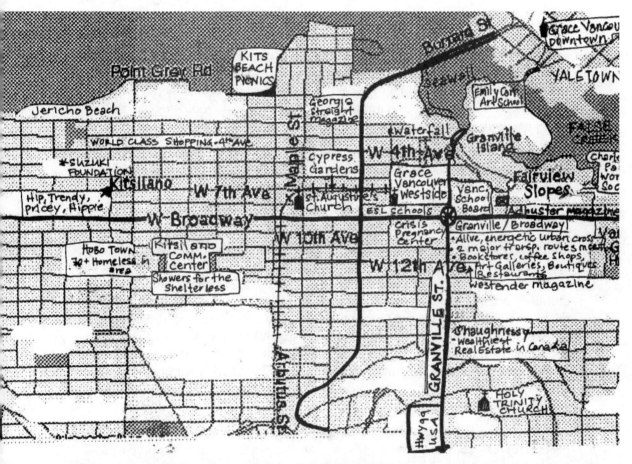

Walking the Streets in Prayer
What happens when we prayer walk
Karla Boy, from a church newsletter

Walking streets in prayer is a helpful testimony from one couple who was richly blessed because as they prayer walked their community.

When the subject of prayer walking is broached, a variety of images probably come to the minds of believers. Maybe a little twinge of fear arises of being "found out." How could prayer walking be explained? Is it espionage? Oh, puh-l-e-a-s-e! The following is our story – the story of a normal, Christian couple who decided to pray for their neighbours in a more intentional fashion.

For many years my husband, David, and I had felt defeated in the area of outreach. Our neighbourhood isn't a swim and tennis subdivision, and folks are at different ages and stages. So, we had no natural conduit to get to know our neighbours. We'd always walked in our neighbourhood, but one day, we decided to begin to pray for each family by name as we walked by their house. And yes, you can pray with your eyes open! As we looked at each house, we prayed for the salvation of its inhabitants and asked God to give us opportunities to get to know the people dwelling there.

Excitement began to build in our spirits as the days and weeks passed because we knew that God would use our prayers. The interesting thing was that God used our prayers to change our hearts. We began to feel compassion for our neighbours and began to have a desire to host a dinner for a few families and to eventually have a block party. These desires became part of our prayers. (As an aside, we would suggest that you start with just the street where you live, so it is more manageable and you have focus.)

About a month after we began prayer walking, breakthroughs started to occur. Our next door neighbour asked if she could walk with us, which threw a welcomed, temporary glitch into our prayer walking routine! On the long walks that followed, we became friends, and she began to inquire about spiritual matters. Shortly after, we began to do a Bible study together. A few months later she began to attend church with us.

Remember the prayer request for a group of families to have dinner in our home? Well, another neighbour asked us to consider having a pre-Thanksgiving meal together with some other families. I replied, "Great~! Let's have it at our house." God was definitely opening the doors for us to walk right through. God answered our prayer for the block party too. The tornado that occurred in the spring of 1998 did a good bit of damage to our street and brought the neighbours out of their homes, allowing them to get acquainted. From lunch appointments and PM Perspectives to baby showers and hospital visits, we were able to become better acquainted with our neighbours and more specific in our prayers for them. A year later in the spring of 1999, my walking friend and I hosted the block party.

Next, we decided to pray about asking some of our neighbours to join us in a mission project. Just last summer, our neighbours and their friends helped us prepare and serve meals at the inner-city summer camp in Summerhill. Our new prayer goal is to walk our street and ask God to give us a core group of families for a Neighbourhood Congregation.

For every outreach gesture we were weak and afraid, but with each victory, our courage and faith increased. God really is "able to do immeasurably more than all we ask or imagine, according to His power that is at work within us, to Him be glory in the church and in Jesus Christ, throughout all generations, for ever and ever! Amen." (Ephesians 3:20-21)

A recent update from Karla

The walking partner mentioned in the article **joined our church along with her husband and had their baby baptized.** She is now in her second year of discipleship, and her husband is in Dave's discipleship group. They live right next door and have become like family to us.

Two more men from the neighbourhood also meet in our home every Monday morning at 6:30. One of them has major problems and is not a believer, but is a regular attendee. He rescued his ex-wife from being an exotic dancer in a strip club in Atlanta. She attended Bible study at our church and prayed with Karla to receive Christ. She now lives in Louisville, Kentucky, and has found a church home there.

The unbeliever mentioned above has a teenaged son who is addicted to drugs, and we've been praying for him. Last week, he came to our home to talk with us and much of the conversation was about spiritual matters. When I told him we'd been praying for him, he had huge tears in his eyes. He is definitely seeking at this time.

Another lady in our street joined Karla's discipleship group last spring. She is planning to reach out to her next door neighbour. The multiplication is starting to occur!

Two other ladies go with Karla to outreach events regularly. One of them has just found out her cancer has returned and seems to be more open spiritually. The other one's brother just passed away, and Dave and I went to visit just prior and prayed with her and her husband at the hospice centre. After the funeral, she asked that Dave and I ride with them to the cemetery.

God has honoured the prayer walking begun in 1998, and we stand amazed at what He has done and continues to do. We follow the Lighthouse Movement's theme of laying the foundation of prayer, showing care, and finally sharing our faith (prayer / care / share).

APPLICATION QUESTIONS

For Personal Reflection

19. What can you learn from this couple regarding how and what they prayed for?

PRAYER PRACTICE:
- Choose one of the communities of which you are a part. Go for a prayer walk this week and write out a vision for what it would look like as God works within it.

HOMEWORK:
- Read through the material for Lesson 12, concentrating on the readings, the personal reflection questions and prayer practice points.
- Clear your schedule for a longer session next time for our day of prayer for the city.

© Pray for the City: Boot Camp for Urban Mission (info@prayercurrent.com)

Prayer and Spiritual Warfare

GOALS: In this lesson we will...
- ❑ Recognize the critical role of prayer as a weapon in spiritual warfare
- ❑ Identify the heart of our cities and articulate a vision for our cities where the gospel breaks through and transforms
- ❑ Pray for each other and for our churches in the spiritual battles of our cities

Introduction   (See DVD Section III: Lesson 11)

In Ephesians 6 Paul concludes his call to spiritual warfare with this challenge: "And pray in the Spirit on all occasions, with all kinds of prayers and requests!". Prayer is an all encompassing defense and advance in spiritual warfare. It is by prayer that we put on the gospel armor. Prayer is also the overarching garment that covers and unites all our artillery. God's work can never advance with mere words and clever strategies. We are in the day of prayer. There is no spiritual advance without prayer.

Understanding the heart of your city is critical in being effective in the spiritual battle that rages on in the place where God has planted you, in the place where Jesus is leading you to reach. In this lesson we will examine the heart of our city – what makes it thrive, what makes it proud and what it holds dearest to its heart. We will consider how Christ addresses its deepest needs and desires. And we will pray for our cities.

We will also learn from Rose Marie Miller who describes the challenge of fear and worry in prayer. She traces her fear to a lack of gospel confidence. She discovers that prayer is the spiritual weapon which restores gospel confidence and brings gospel success as we wage war for Christ's loved ones.

QUESTIONS

For Small Group Discussion

1. *James 4:6-7* But he gives us more grace. That is why Scripture says: "God opposes the proud but gives grace to the humble. "Submit yourselves, then, to God. Resist the devil, and he will flee from you.

   What is the connection between grace and humility to spiritual warfare?

2. *Ephesians 6:10, 18,19* Finally, be strong in the Lord and in his mighty power... *And pray in the Spirit on all occasions with all kinds of prayers and requests. With this in mind, be alert and always keep on praying for all the saints.*

   [19]*Pray also for me, that whenever I open my mouth, words may be given me so that I will fearlessly make known the mystery of the gospel.*

   What does it mean to 'pray in the Spirit on all occasions?

3. *Colossians 2:15* And having disarmed the powers and authorities, he made a public spectacle of them, triumphing over them by the cross.

   Matthew 12:29 How can anyone enter a strong man's house and carry off his possessions unless he first ties up the strong man? Then he can rob his house.

   What does it mean that Christ has triumphed over the spiritual powers and authorities when it comes to mission?

PRAYER PRACTICE:
   - Confess and surrender your weakness to Christ.
   - Confess the power of Christ over all authorities and powers.
   - Confess the power of Christ over the church.
   - Ask to be filled with his Spirit's power.

Quotes on Prayer and Combat

"Jesus replied, 'This kind can come out only by prayer.'" *Mark 9:29*

- Prayer is the power that wields the weapon of the Word. *John Piper*

- To clasp the hands in prayer is the beginning of an uprising against the disorder of the world. *Karl Barth*

- We should not pray for God to be on our side, but pray that we may be on God's side. *Billy Graham*

- We must learn to pray far more for spiritual victory than for protection from battle wounds…. This triumph is not deliverance from, but victory in trial, and that not intermittent but perpetual. *Amy Carmichael*

- Prayer is the very sword of the saints. *Francis Thompson*

- If you cannot win the battle over Satan in prayer, you cannot win it in the ministry. *David Y. Cho*

- The first and decisive battle in conjunction with prayer is the conflict which arises when we are to make arrangements to be alone with God every day. *O. Hallesby*

- Prayer is striking the winning blow at the concealed enemy. Service is gathering up the results of that blow among the (people) we see and touch. *S.D. Gordon*

- To have prayed well is to have fought well. *E.M. Bounds*

- The enemy uses all his power to lead the Christian, and above all the minister, to neglect prayer. *Andrew Murray*

- Pray often, for prayer is a shield to the soul, a sacrifice to God, and a scourge to Satan. *John Bunyan*

- Prayer is warfare. Just getting to prayer is half the battle; staying there is the other half. *Anonymous*

- This is the place of prayer – on the battlefield of the world. It is a wartime walkie-talkie for spiritual warfare, not a domestic intercom to increase the comforts of the saints. *John Piper*

- The one concern of the devil is to keep Christians from praying. He fears nothing from prayerless studies, prayerless work and prayerless religion. He laughs at our toil, mocks at our wisdom, but trembles when we pray. *Samuel Chadwick*

- The Devil trembles when he sees God's weakest child upon his knees. *Anonymous*

- Prayer is our means of involving the omnipotent God of the universe in our personal battle with Satan. *Evelyn Christenson*

- We know that our defense lies in prayer alone. We are too weak to resist the Devil and his servants. Let us hold fast to the weapons of the Christian…. Our enemies may mock at us, but we shall defy them and the Devil if we continue steadfast in prayer. *Martin Luther*

- Our most strategic confrontation is not, first of all, with Satan. Our first confrontation is with the Lord of Glory himself, as we humble ourselves under His mighty hand. *David Bryant*

- Pray or be a prey – a prey to fears, to futilities, to ineffectiveness. *E. Stanley Jones*

- When a Christian shuns fellowship with other Christians, the devil smiles. When he stops reading the Bible, the devil laughs. When he stops praying, the devil shouts for joy. *Corrie Ten Boom*

- The secret prayer chamber is a bloody battleground. Here violent and decisive battles are fought out. *O Hallesby*

- The enemy of our souls is painfully aware of the destructive force of even our dullest and weakest prayers and will go to any length to block them. *Richard Lovelace*

- Prayer is the shout of the fighting believer. *Charles Spurgeon*

- Prayer is a labour above all labours since he who prays must wage a mighty warfare against the doubt and murmuring excited by the faintheartedness and unworthiness we feel within us. *Martin Luther*

- Much of our praying is just asking God to bless some folks that are ill and to keep us plugging along. But prayer is not merely prattle: it is warfare. *Alan Redpath*

- Neglect of prayer is a guarantee that we will not be victors. *Richard Owen Roberts*

QUESTIONS

For Personal Reflection

4. Which of the above quotes inspires you most? How?

5. Which ones challenge you most? Why?

Going Further: Spiritual Warfare

Rose Marie Miller

> *Now have come the salvation and the power and the kingdom of our God, and the authority of his Christ. For the accuser of our brothers, who accuses them before our God day and night has been hurled down. They overcame him by the blood of the Lamb and by the word of their testimony . . . Therefore rejoice, you heavens and you who dwell in them! Revelation 12:10-12*

Miller argues that spiritual warfare is conducted pre-eminently in prayer.

What happens when a deeply suppressed disappointment – and the anger over that disappointment – has been substantially removed from your life? The first answer is . . .You wake up to the fact that you have had the wrong enemies, and you are eager to fight your real ones. I was now deeply grieved in a healthy way that I had seen my husband as my opponent and betrayer for entering the pastorate.

The second answer is . . . You now have a new openness to God and people. For me it meant that my conscience was much more at peace, and I had a new sense of partnership with God and my husband. Now that the fears were gone I looked forward to speaking with my husband Jack in Texas.

Herschel was wearing a big smile when he greeted me at the Houston airport. Herschel was a former seminary student of Jack's, and he had become a zealous pastor, following the development of New Life Church with great interest. He had invited us to speak at a church conference he had organized.

It was to be held in an inner-city church, with Jack, Ron Lutz (Jack's copastor), and me as speakers. Jack was slated to speak first in the San Antonio area, and I had come along to speak for three days to the women – without Jack's shoulder to cry on if things went wrong. Today I did not think about failing. My mind was not really that much on my success or failure but on what I was going to say about Christ. I was to speak several times to the women, telling how grace had so frequently rescued me from a ring of fire. I planned to teach them the truths Jack had presented in South Carolina about justification and the liberation of the conscience.

As we parked near the church in Houston, I looked at the signs of urban blight and thought, These folks have one tough mission field! But the setting had not depressed the spirit of these Christians. When we worshiped together that Friday evening, they were filled with praise for Jesus, and so was I.

When l spoke to the large gathering of women, I led out boldly with my theme. "Freedom," I said, "belongs exclusively to those who are sons and daughters in Christ. It's yours through faith in Christ, not through presumption."

Faces brightened with interest as I talked abut the difference between faith and presumption and illustrated the difference, using my experience in Switzerland. This time I spoke more about the power of Christ and clearly contrasted faith in him with a crippling self-sufficiency. As I talked about Christ's gift of righteousness received through faith, the women responded well. They accepted my teaching stance as a learner-struggler who must give all the glory to Christ because she messes up so often.

The words "in Christ" lingered in my mind after the meeting. "In Christ," I thought, means . . . well, I wasn't quite sure of the full meaning, though l had used the words several times in my talk. I knew Jack would say " 'In Christ' means partnership through faith. We are believing papers with the King!" In his view we praise Christ as the Mediator-King. As a result, we build strong faith in the triune God.

Now my own speaking was giving me a bigger view of Christ: The more I talked about him, the more I became convinced of his reliability, love and power. I thought, Well, if that's what Jack means by faith and partnership, I like the idea a lot. I began to understand that I must submit first to God. When that gets straight, then I have the power to follow Jack. When that happens, we are walking together in partnership. I would lose this concept again and again, but it was beginning to take hold.

During the worship, many of the songs honored Jesus as our Mediator in heaven, who sends his Spirit to work with power on earth. At the close of my presentation, the often hesitant Rose Marie boldly pleaded with these women, "Please pray for my daughter Barbara." After the appeal a number of women agreed to pray for her, and did so right then.

Afterwards, just as I went out the door, a kindly Christian woman shook my hand warmly and gave me a tract. I took it and read the title, "How I Learned to Pray for the Lost" (L.M. Back to the Bible).

It was a pamphlet on praying with biblical authority for the unconverted children of believing parents. The idea of praying for Barbara with authority – well, it was a new thought to me. But it was a natural unfolding of what I had already been learning.

As I read, hope for Barbara's renewal sewed more strongly in me; hope that had almost died in 1972, when Barbara and I had clashed. While meditating on this tract, I did not hear any voice, but I knew God was telling me, Here is something you can do. Come, be a partner with me; I, the sovereign partner and you, the junior partner. Pray not as an isolated individual crying in the night, but as a partner with your heavenly Father. Call upon me; try me. And my Son will defeat the blindness of sin in Barbara's life and free her mind from the dominance of the devil.

On the third day of the conference, Jack arrived. I welcomed him with enthusiasm. As soon as we could, we slipped out of the meetings to walk through the sunlit streets of Houston. As we walked arm in arm in the pleasant weather, I showed him the tract. We then found a park bench and sat down, and I began reading to him.

I said, "Jack, it's talking about praying with authority for lost children of believing parents. Let's claim the authority of Christ over Barbara's thoughts, and on the basis of the shed blood of Jesus, claim her from the dominion of Satan."

Jack listened intently. His spirit resonated to anything that might help Barbara, and he said, "Keep going."

"Matthew 18:19-20 teaches about praying with authority. It begins with two or three people agreeing on an issue and then praying in Jesus' name. The author says that agreeing together about what we want and basing the prayer on the authority of Jesus' name will bring about the working of God. Let's agree on this and pray together against the sins we see in Barbara."

He looked puzzled. "You mean we haven't been doing that?"

"I don't think so. Not in this clear way as partners together when we pray. We often pray for her in a general way, like 'God, save Barbara from her sins,' 'Bring Barbara to Christ,' but we don't pray against specific sins and bondages and in partnership with this promise."

An Introduction to Spiritual Battle

We then identified her besetting sins as deception, lying, excuse-making, and sensualism. Then we worked out the key elements involved in this kind of praying. Here was the order we followed:

Confess unbelief. We confessed our unbelief; that is, that we had been praying for Barbara with a negative image of her future, without praising God for Christ's power to change her. We confessed that our minds had been clouded with doubts fueled by Satan (James 1:5-8).

Claim the sovereignty of Christ over the lost person. We asked for grace to shift our eyes from Barbara and her rebellious behavior to Christ as the triumphant intercessor and ruler at the Father's right hand (Heb. 1:3; 7:25; 9:24). Our plea was Christ's ownership over the children of believers – coupled with a definite rejection of Satan's false claim of ownership of the child.

Agree together to pray against specific sins. We read Matthew 18:19-20, which says, "Again, I tell you that if two of you on earth agree about anything you ask for, it will be done for you by my Father in heaven. For where two or three come together in my name, there am I with them." We agreed to pray against the four specific sins that we had seen in Barbara's life.

Pray against demon influence over these specific sins. In a spirit of oneness, we then prayed simply and quietly for the Father in heaven to overcome each of these sins and to rebuke each demonic being that was blinding her. We prayed against each sin by name. Each time we also prayed in the name of Christ, claiming her from the enemy's territory.

Give thanks: Praise God for the answers then and there. We concluded by giving thanks for God's having already answered our partnership prayer. We thanked him for overcoming each sin we had prayed against, and praised him for the defeat of Satan and his evil powers (Mark 11:22-24).

It was quiet, believing praying, resting in the authority of Christ. We asked the Father clearly and specifically to do what we wanted for his glory. We did it within the context of praise of the sovereignty of Christ and in submission to his person and will. We were relying, not on a formula, but on the astonishing sacrifice of the Son of God as the basis for our intercession and praise.

Surprising Results

About a month later, Barbara walked in the back door and went up to the third floor, where Jack was recovering from the flu. Her face was less clouded, and she smiled as she said, "Dad, do you think you can handle some good news from me for a change?"

Jack quickly forgot about his illness. "Just try me," he laughed. Sitting relaxed at the foot of the bed, she said, "The strangest thing has been happening to me. You're not going to believe this. You know what a liar I am?"

Jack nodded.

"Well, I'm having trouble lying! It makes me uneasy. And I am no longer comfortable cheating and blaming other people. I've even gone down to the IRS and told them I cheated on my income tax last year!"

Jack almost fell out of bed! Our joy went beyond words.

From then on I prayed with a spirit of faith for Barbara, not with a spirit of fear and worry. On a most practical level, I could more dearly see that God was not against me, but for me! The crippling doubts issuing from the powers of darkness were being exposed by the present, working power of the Lord.

Like many parents of erring children, we had been praying a generalized prayer for Barbara's conversion – almost a rote prayer offered repeatedly but with declining hope. Now we were sensing that prayer is partnership with God coming to expression in words; as partners together, we were praying in communion with the King of the universe. We were putting our eyes more on God's authority and less on what Barbara was doing. We were rejecting the sovereignty of Barbara's rebellious attitudes, the sovereignty of Satan, and the sovereignty of all evil over Barbara's life.

The Right Theology

In other words, we were getting our theology straight and finding out what I should have seen all along. Bad theology tones down Christ's sovereignty and often sets in motion an evil emotional chemistry in our inner self. Wrong theology also teaches that you have to contribute a good record to your salvation or you'll never have peace with God. The devil uses that misguided outlook to lead you to think that rejections, disappointments, and failures of all sorts are God's judgment of you – your flawed record – and therefore you have no right to pray with confident authority.

As long as I was ignorant of the biblical theology of grace, my mind was the prey of upsetting circumstances, negative feelings, and circles of despair. I had assumed that my problems were primarily emotional and endless. Actually, till now I was too much like Barbara to help her. But having seen that my basic entrapment was spiritual, I knew Satan had used my sinful nature (fleshly unbelief) to persuade my mind that since I did not deserve to see Barbara saved, and because Barbara was so resistant, there could be no mercy for her. At least not for a very long time.

Why are so many Christians still mastered emotionally by hesitancies about God, and why do they so often question his willingness and power to save hard cases? And why do so many Christians doubt that he loves them with all the deep caring described in Scripture?

The answer is that good theology only helps when it controls the inner life. Today I see more clearly what I only grasped intuitively at that time. Among contemporary Christians, biblical doctrine is often used as a protective shield to keep the inner life away from God's control. I know; I have used it that way. And I have known numerous other people who studied the Bible without any interest in having its teaching change their priorities or bring them into communion with God. They may study the Bible to salve their consciences or to earn brownie points in a spirit of legalistic lawkeeping – not to enter into the life of God.

The Real Enemy

Listen, dear Christian – don't ever forget that without Christ, our inner life is radically self-centered, self-protective, and rebellious. Such a constricted world of self is vulnerable to both Satanic suggestion and condemnation, and is often embittered by unforgiving attitudes toward others. Such an inner life also bristles with self-righteous defensiveness.

But when we submit ourselves to Christ and his will, Christian teaching progressively controls the inner life. And when this happens, biblical truths like sonship and partnership will interpret and transform the whole person.

Another thing happens when we submit to Christ: We learn from him who our real enemies are. This is absolutely necessary before we can battle effectively.

The first "real enemy" in your life is always your own unsubmitted self-life (James 4:1-10). To struggle against your own agendas and passions is at the heart of spiritual warfare. The second "real enemy" is Satan. The one who hates you without compromise is always the power of darkness (Eph. 6:12). Wherever there is self-praising pride, there the devil has much, much influence (James 3:13-4:7).

Why was I so wounded? Because of my mother? My dad's passivity? Jack's sometimes dominance and insensitivity? Barbara's seeming betrayal of us and what we believed?

No, I now saw that the big battle is between Christ and Satan, and that Christ's strategy is to lead us to love and forgive our earthly enemies and pray for them with the hope that Christ would also transform them into sons and daughters. This form of warfare brings glory and mental sanity too, because it fits into reality.

If faith is a primary way that Christ's kingdom power reveals itself in this world, then we are no longer tied up in knots by guilt. Guilt always brings condemnation, but faith in Christ motivates us to pray boldly for the lost. He is not just my Priest-Savior, but he is also my awesome King-Ruler. A big Christ building big faith!

What you know about the power of Christ determines the strength of your faith. Know a little bit about Christ and his omnipotence, and you have weak faith; know more about Christ as sovereign Lord, and you have more faith; know a great deal about Christ, and you are on your way to having great faith (Matt. 8:5-13; 14:22-36).

Over the next months, Jack and I experienced real spiritual warfare as we battled for specific areas in our daughter's life. We learned to recognize answered prayer, and we also learned that prayer must be constant, and that the workings of grace do not eliminate setbacks as the prayed-for person comes to crises and makes his or her own decisions. Here is a rough sketch of our lives during this period.

We began to pray boldly that Barbara would leave her boyfriend, John.

A few weeks later, she decided to leave John; we helped her move home. She got a job as a waitress and enrolled in university classes.

We discovered that she had been seeing John on the sly. Jack and Barbara had a painful confrontation over this. She left to live in her own apartment. This was a blow to us, but I was learning; I didn't fall into despair, as the devil wanted me to. As a family we counterattacked with a strategy of love. Along with Christian friends, we helped her settle into her new living quarters.

More and more I saw the source of this conflict, so when Barbara moved out, I was not discouraged. Any mother can tell you what a breakthrough this new attitude was! My confidence was beginning to shift from what Barbara was doing to what God was going to do. My faith, though, went through some shaky times as I came to know her better.

We discovered that Angelo, the bartender in the restaurant where Barbara worked, had moved into her apartment. By now I had my own sense of partnership with the Father through Christ. Satan's turning up the heat simply drove me to take my shaky self closer to Jesus.

When you have fought the real enemy and have rested in God's sovereign control, then you are free to reach out in love. Angelo was now a welcome guest in our home. At this time Jack asked Barbara and Angelo to read his evangelistic pamphlet "Have you ever wanted a new life?" and give it constructive criticism from a non-Christian's point of view. They responded with useful suggestions about the booklet. His action said to them, "You are my friends, not my enemies." It was also a submitting to them – a showing of respect for their outlook. This humbling of himself led to a new bond of friendship between Jack and the two of them. Jack and I were now drawing them gradually and gently into a partnership with us and with the Father.

Grace Glimpses

Equipped with God's power, we have the ability like never before to come against evil. As sons and daughters of God, we become partners with him in the great battle for people's lives. Through prayers of faith, we allow God to accomplish works of grace in the lives of others.

Prayer: Heavenly Father, teach me to see that my real enemy is not the person who has abused me, but Satan, the great abuser. Help me to fight the devil, not people. In Jesus' name. Amen.

APPLICATION QUESTIONS

For Personal Reflection

6. Where are your prayers typically focused? Mark an X on the line.

   Christ-focused prayer ◄┈┈┈┈┈┈┈┈┈┈┈┈┈┈┈┈┈┈► problem-focused prayer

7. What do your current prayers reveal about your beliefs/theology?

For Small Group Discussion

8. Are the prayers of your church's typical corporate prayers more Christ-focused prayers or problem-focused prayers?

9. What do your church's current corporate prayers reveal about its beliefs/theology?

PRACTICE PRAYER:

- **On your own,** write out a prayer applying Miller's pattern to an area needing breakthrough:
  1. confess unbelief
  2. claim the sovereignty of Christ
  3. agree to pray against specific sins
  4. thank God for the answers
- **In small groups in class,** pray together following Miller's pattern applied to a city need or idol that overwhelms or challenges you as a church.

Just like each individual has a unique personality and heart, each city has a distinctive heart and uniqueness. Being able to recognize and discern what is in a city's heart – both positive and negative – is critical to informing how we pray for it so that our prayers are effective. This is part of celebrating common grace and recognizing the spiritual strongholds in a particular place – strongholds that can only be countered in prayer. Then, as we pray for the heart of the city and for Christ to be revealed there, God reveals to us how he desires to use us as answers to our own prayers and sends us out in specific ways to specific people and places within the city to address its heart's needs.

QUESTIONS

For Small Group Discussion

12. *Describe your city:* If I described my city as a personal friend, what kind of person would they be?

   a. How do they present themselves to the world?

   b. Where do they seek pleasure and comfort?

   c. What do they worry about? What are their dreams?

   d. What issues occupy their thoughts (e.g. what are key issues in municipal politics, what are people talking about on the streets and in coffee shops? etc.)

13. <u>Now summarize the defining character and "heart" of your city.</u>

---

14. Name the idols: What are the things that your city worships and devotes itself to? What does it put above God?

15. Unmask the idols: How are these pursuits and idols weak and destructive, and grievous to Christ?

16. Counter the idols: How does Christ speak to and address these idols?

17. What difference does this make to your church and your city?

PRAYER PRACTICE:

- Pray together regarding the city needs that overwhelm or challenge you as a church.
  1. confess on behalf of the city its sins and confess your own unbelief
  2. claim the sovereignty of Christ
  3. pray against specific sins
  4. thank God for the answers

HOMEWORK:

- Do the "Heart of your City" exercise for your specific neighbourhood.
- Try the "Heart of your City" exercise in praying for the heart of a seeking friend.
- Read through the material for Lesson 11, concentrating on the readings, the personal reflection questions and prayer practice points.

Bringing It All Together

GOALS: In this lesson we will...
- ❑ Practice biblical patterns of prayer for the church in the city

Introduction

(See DVD Section III: Lesson 12)

A spectacular science fiction novel "Ender's Game" won the prestigious Nebula Award. Ender, the main character is a prodigy selected at age 6 to be trained for eventual leadership of the military forces protecting Earth from the 'bugs' which almost destroyed the planet in an earlier invasion. He is chosen because he excels at on-line battle simulations.

During Ender's training he is placed in ever more complex and difficult media simulations. With his own platoon, he engages in boot camp training exercises. Over the few years of training he grows in creativity and strategic insight until no one can touch him- including older children who have been trained for several more years.

Final preparations for actual war take place with increasingly complex, long and grueling media simulations. Ender commands several squads of space soldiers day and night for weeks. It comes down to a final all out, winner take all cosmic battle. (I will let you read the book to find out the conclusion).

There is a stunning twist to the story. The final weeks of training have not been a simulation! Eleven year old Ender is actually commanding the entire allied force in all out war. The casualties are real. So are the victories. It is in order to protect a young Ender from the stress of real battle that his trainers do not let him in on the truth.

We want to you to know the truth. These twelve weeks are more than 'basic training'. Prayer for the city is not a just a workshop – a simulation of reality. Each week we have prayed for ourselves. We have grown in Christ. When we have interceded for our brothers and sisters- the victories and casualties have been real. When we rejoiced and mourned on our knees for our city- The ammunition has been live. The kingdom of God has enjoyed protection and advance as we train in the joys and strategies of prayer to our King.

This week we bring it all together. We are going to pray for a day. We are going to pray the Lord's prayer on our own and together. We will find out how much we have learned about prayer. We are going to continue in prayer. We will learn how much we care those we pray for. The urgency and passion of our prayers will reveal how much we have come to love our city.

It has been a great pleasure for us to be a part of your training. We know it has not always been easy. You have been tempted to give up. "No one else seems to care much about this. Why should I?" You have given valuable to time to prayer and to study. You have found the joy and pain of standing alongside your brothers and sisters to give yourself to a great cause- the greatest cause imaginable. We bless you because you have greatly blessed us by joining Christ's ever growing army of prayer warriors.

With grateful prayer and appreciation,
John Smed and Justine Hwang

The Presence and Prayer of the Church in the City

Robert C. Linthicum

This article expands God's purposes for his people in the city and expands some biblical patterns to guide our prayers for the city.

What is the work in the city to which God calls the church? Scripture is startlingly specific concerning the tasks God expects his people to undertake as the primary means for living out the vocation to which he has called us.

The Urban Christian: Exiled or Called?

Jeremiah 29:1-13 is an often quoted promise in Scripture. "I know the plans I have for you," declares the Lord, "plans to prosper you and not to harm you, plans to give you hope and a future. It we return to the original context of this promise, we find that it is a promise that was made in a city and given, conditionally, to an urban people of God.

This great promise was contained originally in a letter written by Jeremiah the prophet to the Israelites who had been taken as captives to the city of Babylon at the start of the Exile. All that remained of once-proud Israel – the little country of Judah – had been invaded twice by Nebuchadnezzar, the King of the Babylonian Empire. Jeremiah had warned the king of Judah, Zedekiah, that the little nation would be destroyed and the king greatly punished and taste the fury of the Babylonians if he did not surrender.

But because Zedekiah refused to heed Jeremiah's advice, Babylonia viciously razed the city of Jerusalem, burned the temple to the ground, and even spread salt on the remains so that nothing would ever grow there again. True to Jeremiah's prophecy, the Babylonians killed Zedekiah's sons before his eyes, then gouged out his eyes, bound him with bronze shackles, and dragged him as a slave to their capital city of Babylon.

Not only did the Babylonians take Zedekiah into captivity, they also took the best of Israel's leadership into captivity – all the surviving elders, priests, prophets, court officials, even the craftsmen and artisans. It was the policy of Babylonia to export to their country all the people of a conquered nation who could possibly provide leadership to that nation. Only peasants would be left behind to tend the fields and raise the livestock for Babylonia's benefit.

There in that heathen city the Israelite captives began to despair. They grieved for their land, began to lose all hope, and became depressed. It was to those despairing, grieving captives that Jeremiah's letter came. The contents of that letter to those enslaved Israelites is a message that every urban Christian needs to hear.

> This is what the Lord Almighty, the God of Israel, says to all those I carried into exile from Jerusalem to Babylon: "Build houses and settle down; plant gardens and eat what they produce. Marry and have sons and daughters; find wives for your sons and give your daughters in marriage, so that they too may have sons and daughters. Increase in number there; do not decrease. Also, seek the peace and prosperity of the city to which I have carried you into exile. Pray to the Lord for it, because if it prospers, you too will prosper.

> This is what the Lord says: "When seventy years are completed for Babylon, I will come to you and fulfill my gracious promise to bring you back to this place. For I know the plans I have for you," declares the Lord, "plans to prosper you and not harm you, plans to give you hope and a future. Then you will call upon me and come and pray to me, and I will listen to you. You will seek me and find me when you seek me with all your heart. I will be found by you," declares the Lord, "and will bring you back from captivity. I will gather you from all

the nations and places where I have banished you," declares the Lord, "and will bring you back to the place from which I carried you into exile." (Jeremiah 29:4-7, 10-14)

The promise is an urban promise. And it is a conditional promise. It is a promise made to the residents of one city – Jerusalem – who have been taken as political hostages and captives to another city – Babylon. It is a promise of their sons' and daughters' eventual return, but not theirs (for in seventy years, all the original adult hostages would be dead). But it is a promise based on their faithful fulfillment of its condition.

God promises to work for the good of the exiled Israelites if "you will call upon me and come and pray to me… You will seek me and find me when you seek me with all your heart" (Jer. 29:12-13). His blessings on them in captivity and their consequent return to the Promised Land are conditional, for these are based on their receptive response to God. But how are they to seek after God? Where will they find the Lord?

They will find God in the city – not in the city of Jerusalem, but in the enemy city, the evil city, the heathen city – Babylon! God will bless the Israelite exiles if they seek after the peace and prosperity of Babylon!

The pivotal passage in Jeremiah's letter is that famed Scripture:

> "Seek the peace and prosperity of the city to which I have carried you into exile. Pray to the Lord for it, because if it prospers, you too will prosper."
> (Jer. 29:7)

Were the Hebrews "exiled" or "sent" to Babylon? The Hebrew word actually contains both meanings. It would be translated most accurately with the awkward phrase, "I have caused you to be carried away captive." The word means "exile" – that is, "forced removal from one's country." But it also suggests what happened to the Israelites was not simply circumstance; they were "sent" into exile by God.

"You have been *sent* by God to this city," Jeremiah is also suggesting in his letter. You are not in Babylon simply because of the exigencies of war or the particularly repressive policies of the Babylonian Empire aimed at emasculating a conquered nation. It is that God, in the Lord's infinite wisdom, needs you in this city. God needs the presence of his people in this city. You Israelites are in Babylon because God wants you there. The repressive policies of the Babylonians were the tool God used to get you there! You are sent by God into the city – that is his *design*!

I suggest that this is a message, not only to Jews exiled to Babylon, but to all urban people of God. Why are you in the city in which you live? You may have been born there. You may have decided to move there. You may be in that city because you took a job there or have built a career there. You may have come to that city to be educated or to retire there. But none of those reasons are why you actually live in that city. Those are simply the *circumstances* God has used to bring you there.

Why are you in the city in which you find yourself? You are there, Jeremiah suggests, for one reason and one reason alone. You are in your city because God has *called* you there. You are in your city by God's design, by God's will. Whether God's plans for you in that city turn out to be plans for your peace and not for your disaster depend upon whether you can see yourself as being called by God into your city, and then whether you can seek to live faithfully according to that call.

"Seek the peace and prosperity of the city to which I have carried you into exile," says the Lord. Christians in the city have a destiny and purpose to be there, because they are there by God's design and will.

Where then, do we seek God? In the city – where God has called us. That is where we will find God. But how do we live into God's urban call to us? How does God expect God's people to work for the peace and prosperity of their city?

Praying for the City

Pray to the Lord for [the city], because if it prospers, you too will prosper. (Jer. 29:7)

When the psalmist joins Jeremiah in urging God's people to pray for the city, his instructions are to "pray for the peace of Jerusalem" (Ps. 122:6). This is the biblical writers' essential call to God's people for urban prayer – to pray for the peace or shalom of the city. The Hebrew *shalom* means contentment, fulfillment, unity with one another, accord, prosperity, and a genuine commitment to each other's good. But what does it mean to pray for a city's peace?

When Christians pray for a city, we tend to pray for it in one of two ways. Either we pray that the city will be reached by the Gospel and that many people will be redeemed, or we pray for the well-being of the Christian enterprise in that city (that is, praying for ourselves, our families, our own church, and the body of Christ in that city). Scripture calls us, however, to much more comprehensive prayer than for the success of the Christian enterprise in that city. Let's look at some biblical insights on praying for the city.

Psalm 122 provides an essential model for urban prayer.

> Pray for peace in Jerusalem:
> "Prosperity to your houses!
> Peace inside your city walls!
> Prosperity to your palaces!"
> Since all are my brothers and friends,
> I say, "Peace be with you!"
> Since Yahweh our God lives here,
> I pray for your happiness (vv. 6-9)

Pray for the city's economic health

First, the psalmist calls us to pray for the economic health of the city: "Prosperity to your houses!" Here is a cry for the city to be a city of economic well-being, not simply for the wealthy but for all the city's inhabitants. No one in the prosperous city is to be poor, rejected, marginalized, or cast off by society. God wants our prayers to be prayers for the economic well-being of the city and for all its citizens.

Pray for the safety of the city

Pray for "peace inside your city walls!" (Ps. 122:7). The Psalmist further instructs us to pray for the safety of the whole city, for both its internal fabric of common life and its external life.

We should pray for the safety of a city's citizens: safety from conflict, from violence, and from crime against individuals and property. The very nature of shalom is one of "every man [sitting] under his own vine and under his own fig tree, and no one will make them afraid" (Mic. 4:4). If the crime of a city is not being reduced and is not kept under strict control, then no citizen feels safe. When the citizenry of a city lives in fear, then that city is in the midst of psychological collapse.

There is another dimension of prayer for a city's safety: prayer for those who commit its crimes. Scripture repeatedly calls upon God's people to pray for those in prison and to become their advocates. "Remember those in prison as if you were their fellow prisoners," the author of Hebrews advises the church, "and those who are mistreated as if you yourselves were suffering" (Heb. 13:3).

It is easy for humans, particularly the frightened and intimidated, to become vindictive. There is no place for that in the Christian community! Therefore we are to pray for those in prison, both for their salvation and for their rehabilitation. We are to pray for the police, that they will flee both corruption and unjust practices. We are to pray for the judicial system, that it will be uncompromisingly just and fair to all its citizens rather than showing favouritism toward those accused of "white-collar" crime or those who hold significant political or economic power.

We are to pray for our city's safety.

Pray for the political order

Pray for the "prosperity to your palaces" (Ps. 122:7). If there is any focus for prayer stressed in Scripture, it is prayer for the government. Thus Paul advises Timothy, "I urge, then, first of all, that requests, prayers, intercession and thanksgiving be made for everyone – for kings and all those in authority, that we may live peaceful and quiet lives in all godliness and holiness" (1 Tim. 2:1-2).

God's people are to pray for a reformation of the political process, so that it creates peace instead of strife, justice instead of a party spirit, and prosperity for all its people, including economic redistribution for the poor.

We are to pray for our political leaders: not that they be successful, but that they be just; not that they build power for themselves, but that they empower the commonwealth. We are to pray that our city's politicians "defend the afflicted among the people and save the children of the needy… [and] crush the oppressor." We are to pray that they are transformed (converted) into authentic leaders whose primary concern will be to "deliver the needy who cry out, the afflicted who have no one to help… take pity on the weak… and save the needy from death." Rather than accruing power and prestige personally or for the political party, or consorting with the economic powers of the city, the governmental leader is to be compassionately concerned for the city's hurting, marginalized, poor, and powerless. "Precious is their blood in his sight."

Pray for the people

> Since all are my brothers and friends,
> I say, "Peace be with you!"
> Since Yahweh our God lives here,
> I pray for your happiness (vv. 6-9)

The psalmist reminds us to pray for the people of the city – the ordinary folk, the "little people" who make up the great populations of each city. We are to pray shalom upon them all, no matter who they are, what they believe or do not believe, whether or not they work for the good of the city, whether or not they recognize that we are working for the good of the city. We are to pray God's peace upon them all: economic peace, the peace of safety, the peace of justice.

Isaiah develops this theme in a passage written in the face of the Israelite jingoism of his day.

> Let no foreigner who has bound himself to the Lord say,
>> "The Lord will surely exclude me from his people."
> And let not any eunuch complain,
>> "I am only a dry tree."…
> "To the eunuchs… I will give within my temples and its walls a memorial and a name
>> better than sons and daughters…
> And foreigners who bind themselves to the Lord to serve him…
> these I will bring to my holy mountain
>> and give them joy in my house of prayer.
> Their burnt offerings and sacrifices
>> will be accepted on my altar.
> for my house will be called
>> a house of prayer for all nations" (Isa. 56:3-7).

We are to pray for the happiness of all the people of the city – foreigner as well as Israelite, eunuch as well as parent – for God welcomes all to god's holy mountain (i.e. Jerusalem). God's temple is to be a house of prayer for all nations; the common factor of the people of God is not a bloodline, but a relationship with God.

Why should we pray for all the people of our city, even those who are not like us? For one simple reason: "Since Yahweh our God lives here, I pray for your happiness" (Ps. 122:9). Because God lives in our city, this makes all the city's residents my urban brothers and sisters, whether or not *they* recognize that reality. I am to pray for their happiness and joy. I am to pray that they will discover God's shalom. And I am to pray for no other reason than that they happen to live there with me!

Pray with Importunity

Scripture not only shows us how we are to pray for our city; it shows us with what seriousness we are to take on this responsibility. In Isaiah 62, the prophet instructs the people of God:

> I have posted watchmen on your walls, O Jerusalem;
>> they will never be silent day or night.
> You who call on the Lord,
>> give yourselves no rest,
>> and give him no rest until he establishes Jerusalem
>> and makes her the praise of the earth (Isa. 62:6-7)

What Isaiah dreams about and what the psalmist encourages, we see actually carried out through one city's praying community of believers. The earliest Christians in Jerusalem gathered in desperate prayer upon the arrest of Peter and John, the church's most pivotal leaders. These apostles were being confronted by the Jewish Sanhedrin who were looking for a way to put them away permanently.

Because the leaders of the Sanhedrin could not decide what to do with Peter and John, however, they warned the men not to preach any longer in the name of Christ. Then the Sanhedrin let the men go, but Peter and John gathered with that praying community of believers and shared with them how the chief priests and elders had to release them. "When [the people of the church] heard this, " Scripture tells us, "they raised their voices together in prayer to God" (Acts 4:24).

Praising God for his miraculous deliverance of Peter and John, the little band of believers prayed, "Now, Lord, consider their threats and enable your servants to speak your word with great boldness. Stretch your hand to heal and perform miraculous signs and wonders through the name of your holy servant Jesus" (Acts 4:29-30). Then, just as they had prayed, God immediately worked in and through that little community of faith in amazing and very specific ways. Luke tells us:

> After they prayed, the place where they were meeting was shaken. And they were all filled with the Holy Spirit and spoke the word of God boldly. All the believers were one in heart and mind. No one claimed that any of his possessions was his own, but they shared everything they had. With great power the apostles continued to testify to the resurrection of the Lord Jesus, and much grace was upon them all. There were no needy persons among them. For from time to time those who owned lands or houses sold them, brought the money from the sales and put it at the apostles' feet, and it was distributed to anyone as he had need. (Acts 4:31-35)

It is intriguing to note what came out of that little prayer meeting. As a result of the prayers of God's people for the city of Jerusalem and its leadership:

- The Christians were filled with the Holy Spirit.
- They preached the word of God boldly.
- They became united as a church.
- They cared for each other's physical, economic and social needs.
- They built a life together that was a sign to the inhabitants of the city of the corporate and individual way of life that they coveted for the entire city.
- They testified openly to the resurrection of Jesus Christ.
- "Much grace was upon them all."

Scripture calls us to steady, insistent prayer for the city. We are not to take lightly the privilege given to the church to pray for the city. This is prayer which is not to be focused on the Christian nor on the church, but on the totality of that city, in all its economic, political, judicial, social, and spiritual dimensions. Only such intentional praying will reach the city and change the church. It is only upon the intentional praying of God's people that a city can be built "whose architect and builder is God" (Heb. 11:10).

Prayer is both absolutely necessary and strategic. But it is not sufficient. The church has not fulfilled its call to city ministry by praying. How does God expect his people to work for the peace and prosperity of that city?

Being God's presence in the city

> "Build houses and settle down; plant gardens and eat what they produce. Marry and have sons and daughters; find wives for your sons and give your daughters in marriage, so that they too may have sons and daughters. Increase in number there; do not decrease" (Jer. 29:5-6)

"Build houses and settle down; plant gardens and eat what they produce" (v. 5). Enter your city's economy and contribute to it; purchase a home in the city and settle into your neighbourhood. Marry, have children, raise them to adulthood, see them married, and enjoy being a grandparent. Make an investment of yourself and your family in Babylon, Jeremiah insists.

"Increase in number there; do not decrease" (v. 6). The prophet seeks to teach the discouraged people: become God's presence in the city which has been given to you and the city will be blessed by your presence. Live and move and have your being, as God's people, in the city where he places

Jeremiah advises the Israelite exiles in Babylon to live into God's urban call to them by becoming a godly presence in their adopted city (see Jer. 29:5-6, quoted earlier). God says the same to God's people today. Whatever the circumstances might be that have brought you to your city, what God most wants out of you as a Christian in that city is to live fully into your circumstances.

Buy a house or rent an apartment, God instructs you and me. Find your vocation and enter into your city's economics. Buy and sell. Give and take. Love your neighbourhood; commit yourself to its people. Laugh and cry with them. Celebrate and mourn with them. Make an investment of yourself and your family in your city.

Be God's moderating presence wherever you might be in the city – flavouring all of life with the beauty of your life, preserving your city from spiritual decay, shedding God's light on the lies of your city's powerful, exhibiting to all around you the quality of life God means for all to live in the city. Become God's transforming presence at your work, your school, and your community as your life becomes an aroma pleasing to the Lord. Live and move and have your being, as God's person, in your city. And in this gentle and unassuming way, become God's profound blessing to your city, your neighbourhood, your working place, your family and yours.

As the church in the city, God has not called us to be above our city, fellowshipping only with God's people while singing, "This world is not my home; I'm just a-passing through." Nor are we simply in the city, committed to our own welfare without contributing to the city's good. As children of God, we are called to be for our city and with our city, casting our lot with this city. We are to pray for our city. We are to work for justice for our city's powerless and proclaim the Gospel in our city.

Underneath it all, however, we are to be the people who live our lives joyfully and hopefully and profoundly in the city, being the very presence of God to the loneliness and fear and deep hunger of our city's people and systems and principalities. For only as we so live into God's call to us in our city will God fulfill his promise to us: "I know the plans I have for you, declares the Lord, plans to prosper you and not to harm you, plans to give you a hope and a future" (Jer. 29:11).

APPLICATION QUESTIONS

For Personal Reflection

1. Think of the typical content of your prayers. How do your prayers compare to the patterns for prayer described in Jeremiah 29:4-14?

2. Why are you in the city in which you find yourself? Why do you think God has "sent" and called you to be here?

3. What are one or two concrete and intentional ways that you can pray to become and act as a transforming presence in your city this week?

For Small Group Discussion

4. How do the typical themes of your church's corporate prayers compare to the patterns for prayer in Jeremiah 29:4-14?

5. Why is your church/ministry in the city in which it is located? Why has God sent you here? What mission does he have for your church to the specific surrounding city?

6. What are one or two practical areas of city life that your church can increasingly become and act as a transforming presence?

PRAYER PRACTICE:
- Pray for God's transforming presence to increase through his people in the city.
- Pray for your city's economic, political, judicial, social, and spiritual health.
- Pray for your church's outreach to the cultural elite, immigrants and the poor.

Fasting and Prayer

Edith Schaeffer

Edith Schaeffer shares from her own vast experience of spiritual transformation in starting a house for spiritual retreats called L'abri. Her words compel us to commit to the biblical discipline of prayer and fasting in order to progress in gospel freedom and power.

As Fran and I mailed that letter resigning from our mission board in early June 1955, we looked at each other with a measure of dismay! In the letter we said we were going to live by prayer. We were going to set forth to answer honest questions with honest answers, insofar as God would give us wisdom and His help. We would not try to get people to come; we would not ask for money for food and expenses. We wanted to demonstrate God's existence, not only by showing the logic of truth being true, but also by His provision in the simple and observable things of everyday life.

What had we done? There was Priscilla at the University of Lausanne. True, Swiss universities do not cost more than a few dollars, and she was scrimping on food. There was Susan in bed with rheumatic fever and working on a correspondence course from Calvert School. There was Debby in school, just nine, and Franky, two and a half, just starting to get back to walking after polio. What had we set out to do anyway? How serious were we about prayer? Would there be a difference in using time? We knew we had been clearly brought to this particular place, not just geographically but also in our seriousness about not wanting to "sell Christianity as one would cornflakes." We wanted a real work that would not be our wisdom, but wisdom and knowledge given by God as to the next step. What would we do?

"Mummy," said Susan as I took her lunch tray into her room and sat on the edge of the bed (which took up the whole narrow room), "Mummy, let's have every Monday be a day of prayer. Look, I've made a chart with the hours divided up from seven in the morning until seven in the evening. You have to work, cooking and washing clothes and taking care of Franky and everything, and no one of us can pray *all day right now.* But if we are going to live by prayer, don't we have to pray more? Let's have twelve hours of prayer every Monday, but divided up so that we pray one after another!"

"Good idea," I said, and from that week on, Monday became our "day of prayer." I printed, by hand, a sheet of paper with verses that had helped me to have that two-way communication. I then wrote some spiritual requests, some material requests, some requests for each of us and whoever had come to be with us that day in areas of physical need and need for strength and direction. We made that sheet, a Bible, a notebook, and a pencil available so that each one could add something he or she wanted the rest of us to pray for. We stayed in the room praying until someone came to relieve us, feeling like a watchman on a wall! We were not in the room at the same time, but the feeling of togetherness and taking responsibility was very real. Perfect? No. But real.

About twenty-two people in America had asked if they could take responsibility to pray for us as we were now alone – to pray for the people of God's choice to come, people who would need help in their search for answers, search for truth, search for understanding. These praying people received copies of what we then called the prayer list, which they read and prayed over, read and prayed over with us. Of course, they continued to read also in heir own Bibles and to listen to God. We wrote them, "Dear Praying Family," and I do believe that only God knows who did the most effective work, because intercession is *work.* Each member of the Praying Family promised (all of their own volition) to pray on Mondays, as long a block of time as each one could, and to pray for a half-hour or hour each day for L'Abri.

A few weeks passed, and we were deluged. No electrical appliances worked; everything had to be done by hand. Fran was clearing refuse out from under hedges and digging a vegetable garden. We came to feel that we needed something more than our Monday of divided time and our own personal times of prayer, the prayer in our Sunday services, and our family prayer times, We felt a great need for something more. What could that be? Only one thing – a day of fasting and prayer with all of us taking part.

There is a wonderful passage in Ezra telling about the people of Israel preparing to go back to Jerusalem. King Artaxerxes had let them go and was making it possible for them to go back to worship "the God of Israel whose dwelling is in Israel." In Ezra 8:21 comes this (Ezra speaking):

> There, by the Ahava Canal, I proclaimed a fast, so that we might humble ourselves before our God and ask him for a safe journey for us and our children, with all our possessions. I was ashamed to ask the king for soldiers and horsemen to protect us from enemies on the road, because we had told the king, "The gracious hand of our God is on everyone who looks to him, but his great anger is against all who forsake him." So we fasted and petitioned our God about this, and he answered our prayer. (NIV)

This serious fasting and prayer, bowing humbly before God with repentance and concern for His mercy, took place in the context of practical need – for protection and guidance, for help in choices and for the supply of material things. This day of fasting and prayer was not separated as a kind of retreat aimed at achieving a spiritual high; it was a part of the warp and woof of a hard time in family life. It was an intensely important time in the next step of Ezra's responsibilities.

They asked for a safe journey with their children and with all their possessions. The asking was to be a demonstration of their trust that God could do it and that they were not going to the king for help. (This fits in with the command of God to NOT go "to Egypt" for help.)

Is fasting ever a bribe to get God to pay more attention to the petitions? No, a thousand times no. It is simply a way of making clear that we sufficiently reverence the amazing opportunity to ask help from the everlasting God, the Creator of the universe, to choose to put everything else aside and concentrate on worshiping, asking for forgiveness, and making our requests known – considering his help more important than anything we could do ourselves in our own strength and with our own ideas.

When the news of the breaking down of the walls of Jerusalem and of the suffering of the remnant in captivity came to Nehemiah, he responded with sorrow and fasting and prayer.

> And it came to pass when I heard these words, that I sat down and wept, and mourned certain days, and fasted, and prayed before the God of heaven, and said, I beseech thee, O Lord God of heaven, the great and terrible God, [or awesome God], who keepeth covenant and mercy for them who love him and observe his commandments: Let thine ear now be attentive, and thine eyes open, that thou mayest hear the, prayer of thy servant, which I pray before thee now, day and night, for the children of Israel, thy servants, and confess the sins of the children of Israel, which we have sinned against thee; both I and my father's house have sinned.… Now these are thy servants and thy people, whom thou hast redeemed by thy great power, and by thy strong hand. O Lord, I beseech thee, let now thine ear be attentive to the prayer of thy servant, and to the prayer of thy servants, who desire to fear thy,name; and prosper, I pray thee, thy servant this day, and grant him mercy in the sight of this man. For I was the king's cupbearer. (Nehemiah 1:4-6, 10-11 KJV)

Nehemiah has first fasted and prayed for some days, obviously including others with him in this intercession, in preparation forgoing to the king with his request to rebuild the walls of Jerusalem. He takes a long time of prayer and fasting, confessing sin and preparing for the Lord's answer, which he expects. It reminds us of the Lord's telling Joshua to have the people sanctify themselves in preparation to see the Lord's answer to their entering Jericho. It is a solemn thing, an awesome thing, an overwhelming thing to ask and then receive an answer whether the answer is sufficient grace to go on in the midst of affliction, or whether that an answer is a fantastic opening up of a path in the wilderness in some form.

Fasting along with prayer is meant to be a means of seriously asking for cleansing, not only in the Old Testament, but also after Christ's death has cleansed us. We need to realize that although we come to God our Father, in the name of Jesus Christ who told us to come this way, we ourselves need to ask for preparation to make requests. Sometimes that preparation should be in the midst of fasting; other times we call out to Him as we are dropping in a parachute, scuba diving, rolling in a car down a snowy embankment, sitting all night by a baby who has croup, or waiting for word from the operating room. There are moments of extreme need when we can scarcely form words, let alone sentences – moments of crisis, moments of impending tragedy or sudden fear. At such times only a brief prayer can be lifted in a cry or, a whisper, *Lord, Your mercy and Your strength, please.*

It needs to be pointed out that some people have diabetes and need proper amounts of food every two hours; others have low blood sugar for other reasons or get severe headaches if they go without food or juice or a hot drink at set times. Of course, any who have these problems need to provide food to take along with them if they are going into the woods to pray for a whole day or if they work in the hospital as nurses or doctors. Also those who are anorexic need to be to eat and pray as an important help in their reluctance to eat for one reason or another. At L'Abri through the years I have prepared a picnic of some small sandwiches, an apple, some biscuits for ones whom I felt needed to eat and pray on the day of fasting and prayer. In every day of fasting and prayer we would assign someone to put out soup and bread so that people could quietly come and take something if they felt faint or could not concentrate because of a headache. However, we asked (ahead of time of course) that no one linger and talk at that time. The food was there between one hour and another which had been announced, a simple soup and bread, and could be taken away to eat.

These are simply practical notes for those who might feel they have failed to do "the right thing" because of a need for food. It is good to re-read that portion of Revelation in which Jesus says, "Behold, I stand at the door and knock. If anyone opens the door, I will come in and sup with him." This speaks to the unsaved as an invitation, but also to the Lord's people who would in a very real sense pray quietly as they eat alone.

Back to Nehemiah. After he is in the presence of the king, the king asks, "For what dost thou make thy request?" Nehemiah prayed to his God in Heaven and then answered the king. He does not stop calling on God at the end of the days of fasting and prayer. His communication is natural and has a continuity of faith and trust.

As you read on through to the end of the sixth chapter you will see that prayer was a basic part of the rebuilding of the wall, but prayer did not replace hard work, nor did it replace being prepared to fight the onslaught of the enemy with weapons. The reality of continued prayer and trust that God would fight for them did not remove the need to blow the trumpet on the wall to ask for others to come and help at a particularly dangerous place, at a particularly dangerous time. Trusting God to answer our intercessions and requests does not make it wrong to call for help as the floods rise, the earthquake hits, the fire burns our barn, or hail ruins a field of crops. There is a lifelong lesson to be learned, over and over again, that we are not self-sufficient. We need God's help. We need to accept and give "servant-like" help to each other, as well as to work hard and to fight "the enemy" who is attempting to break down the wall we are building.

Yes of course moral and cultural breakdown and the difficulty of finding an absolute that could roll back the multiplying and terrifying results is troubling people. Rebuilding, repairing the broken walls in these areas will take hard work accompanied by very serious fasting and prayer by individuals as well as the gathering of some to intercede together. It requires a combination of prayer, slogging work, calling each other to help at some point on the wall, and then doing what is needed in the way of fighting when attacked.

Yes, they were told to have weapons as well as trowels with which to put the stones together with mortar. It is a very definite combination of hard work, prayer that our God will fight for us, calling to others for help, and keeping our swords by our sides. Read Nehemiah 4:17-20:

> They who built on the wall, and they who bore burdens, with those that laded, everyone with one of his hands wrought in the work and with the other hand held a weapon. For the builders, everyone had his sword girded by his side, and so builded. And he who sounded the trumpet was by me. And I said unto the nobles, and to the rulers, and to the rest of the people, The work is great and large, and we're separated upon the wall, one far from another. In whatever place ye hear the sound of the trumpet, resort ye thither unto us. Our God shall fight for us. (KJV)

God's fighting for us does not exclude the responsibility to be prepared for battle both in the area of strategy and in equipment. Trusting God completely in prayer believing that He is able to do all things, does not remove the need to pray for His strength in our weakness and then to do, to take action in His strength to accomplish what He has prepared us to do! We are to do what He is unfolding for us to do, fulfilling what God is giving us strength to do, acknowledging that it is His strength and not ours. It is a truly active passivity, not a false whirling humbleness that says, "I can't do anything; I'm too weak."

Day by day we face local, national, and international battles. The battles need a balanced involvement. We need to fight the killing of the unborn who would be the next generation; we need to fight the spoiling of the land and be God's stewards whether by planting more trees or purifying the air in other ways. We are faced with scandals on every side in medicine, government, business, sports – increase of crime or the removal of any moral base for the teaching in schools. The battle for truth is not simply someone else's business, but something we need to pray about as to what the Living God, our Heavenly Father, would have us do.

Yes, we are to turn the other cheek as people do things to harm us personally. But in injustices internationally, nationally, and in our towns and villages, we need to be brave enough to fight for the protection of the weak, to fight for liberty for others, and for the next generation. To fast and pray in the midst of considering what we are meant to do in a practical way, today, tomorrow, this week, this month in the now of history is important indeed.

It is not always another organization that is needed, with a big name and offices and vast buildings. Sometimes we must be willing to "pray in the closet alone," to go out into the mountains or woods, fields, or parks, by streams lakes, into a woodshed or empty kitchen and really pray for courage, direction and willingness to be where He would have us be. That place may not be visibly apart of anything other people may observe. It may be a willingness to go on filling teeth as a dentist; cooking and scrubbing clothing and floors and reading aloud to children as a mother; painting, drawing, or sculpting as an artist; doing what we do well, with excellence, to be beside the person who needs us to say the right word. What person? The patient, the client, the actor, the cameraman, the woman cleaning the washroom, the driver of a taxi. Who is going to be in our place "on the wall" if we are not there? That is what being a light not hidden under a bushel is all about. There are no bright lights announcing that our place today is the most important place in the whole piece of today's history. We are to be serving each other as servants as if we were serving the Lord, knowing He is perfectly fair and just.

We need to read Ephesians in the midst of Nehemiah's building and preparation for battle. As we listen to the Lord as we read the whole of this epistle during our days of fasting and prayer or at other times, we see, as in a mirror, our sins and shortcomings, realizing our need of prayer for help.

> Finally, my brethren, be strong in the Lord, and in the power of his might. Put on the whole armour of God, that ye may be able to stand against the wiles [schemes] of the devil. For we wrestle not against flesh and blood, but against principalities, against powers, against the rulers of the darkness of this world, against spiritual wickedness in high places [against rulers, against authorities, against the powers of this dark world, and against the spiritual forces of evil in the heavenly realms]. Wherefore, take unto you the whole armour of God, that ye may be able to withstand in the evil day, and having done all, to stand, Stand therefore, having your loins girt about with truth, and having on the breastplate of righteousness, and your feet shod with the preparation of the gospel of peace; above all, taking the shield of faith, where with ye shall be able to quench all the fiery darts of the wicked. And take the helmet of salvation, and the sword of the Spirit, which is the word of God. (Ephesians 6:10-17 KJV)

Clearly what is outlined here is an ongoing battle. It is the conflict of the ages, of all the centuries since Lucifer rebelled against God and gathered other angels to rebel under his leadership. It is a conflict, a battle, which will not end until the Lord Jesus Christ returns to have the final victory, to defeat death itself, for the last enemy to be destroyed will be death. Yes, we are in the midst of battle, and whether we are persecuted and killed for the sake of the truth of the gospel, as were the martyrs through the ages and present-day martyrs, still we are to stand firm, working hard to build the wall with a trowel in our hands.

…

Prayer is an essential part of the practical fighting in the ongoing battle in which we all are involved – the battle for truth when the very existence of truth is being denied!

As in any day of history, prayer has to be interwoven into every part of the day and week and month. But we, as well as people in past ages, need a whole day of fasting and prayer at times. We cannot have any unbroken time otherwise; we cannot have freedom to read and think, to consider our own sin in the light of Ephesians 4:26-32:

> Do not let the sun go down while you are still angry ... Get rid of all bitterness, rage and anger, brawling and slander, along with every form of malice. Be kind and compassionate to one another, forgiving each other, just as in Christ God forgave you. (NIV)

We need a long period of time, either fasting from conversation and food preparation and eating, or fasting from sleep and other good normal parts of life, to be able, to search our memories and our consciences to ask forgiveness for our sin. We are not to blithely make a list of requests without having time to prepare for prayer. In our reading and praying, this follows along very strongly. A central place must be considered for unbroken times of prayer, as well as for the snatched moments.

Ephesians 6 goes on with Paul asking for intercession for himself:

> Pray also for me, that whenever I open my mouth, words may be given me so that I will fearlessly make known the mystery of the gospel, for which I am an ambassador in chains. Pray that I may declare it fearlessly, as I should. (vv. 19-20 NIV)

Paul does not ask prayer that the chains may be removed; he asks prayer that he would declare the mystery of the gospel fearlessly. He is already in chains for doing that very thing, but he is asking prayer for courage and persistence in continuing without fear of what might happen to him is asking that the truth of what he is communicating may not be hindered by any hesitancy in his speaking. In the *King James Version* the word used is *boldly:* "Pray ... that I may open my mouth boldly as I ought to speak." His call is for help in continuing the battle.

The battle does continue. The immediate focus changes as history goes on. The need to pick up the stones out of the dust and carefully place them again in "the wall" continues all through every change of history. Russian Christians have a new freedom to worship and to receive Bibles openly as the amazing change has come in the overturn of the power of communism. The Baltic countries have a new measure of freedom also. But as for these people in having a worldview which will give them a base for formulating new laws and a new pattern of life, it is evident there is much building to be done.

In the battle for teaching and living on the basis of right rather than wrong, truth rather than lies, there is now and always will be opposition. Anyone rebuilding the shattered stones and giving a base for morals and ethics will be attacked. Understanding that an attack may come from two sides at once is very important in living practically in our present-day undertakings that are similar to Nehemiah's restoration of the wall of Jerusalem.

What do I mean?

…As believing doctors speak to these issues, there is need to pray they will be heard but also that the fierce opposition that arises may not become the norm for rules and regulations governing the practices of the medical profession. Whether the issue is euthanasia, or genetic engineering, or infanticide, or the definition of the quality of life, these battles are not theoretical, but very practical, and affect many people now and in days to come.

In facing the rapid changes in many parts of our children's world, we have responsibility to pray for a wider number of people, our doctors – the believing doctors we know and the medical people and scientists who struggle with choices and decisions. We cannot simply criticize without praying seriously and doing some practical things to help.

Abortion is another practical place where we need to be involved in some way. Marches, rallies, voicing objections in various ways to the disregard of human life? Yes, but also to have true compassion and desire to help people who need help during the months of waiting for a baby. Young girls? Yes, but also mothers who need help with an unexpected pregnancy. When someone feels she is being criticized, disapproved of, and in a desperately impossible situation, she needs human compassion, someone to "rush to that place on the wall" with some warmth of pitching in to help. But also there are false "helps" being offered, being insisted upon, being pushed, being whispered into ears, being flashed on a screen, being suggested as the only way to rid yourself of a problem. "Friends" or medical people or family members may be saying that there is no absolute. There is no right and wrong, because everything is relative anyway, and this collection of molecules is not a human being. We cannot do everything that needs to be done in this world at this time, but whatever area we ask God to give us strength to be involved in needs prayer, positive building, fighting the enemy, and blowing the trumpet to get others to come to this spot where we are being hindered or attacked in putting the dusty stones of "ideas" back in place again. Some are needed on a hot line, others to open their homes, others to start a crisis pregnancy home.

Yes, we usually take a day of fasting and prayer in the midst of urgent needs in our personal and family lives, in the midst of our work. It is often taken where there is an enormous question mark about what comes next. On such a day, we also need to give about serious attention to sorting out what issues and areas we want to involve ourselves in our private prayer, what practical ways we can help, which battles we must be willing to serve in! As we serve each other in our lives, sometimes that will mean aiding each other in a battle as someone's attempt at putting the stones of correct ideas into place is being fiercely attacked, and the enemy seems to be overpowering! *Lord, give me a sensitive ear to hear the trumpet being blown for help.*

There is also the kind of need that people have when they are caught up in something that they really want to get out of, but find the desire to remain in it is stronger. Such a one needs help intensely... Very great weakness needs a calling, a blowing of the trumpet, for someone who understands to come to that one's place "on the wall" with a comprehensive insight of the struggle going on, encouragement that what seems impossible is possible, and a willingness to help, to spend energy and time to be available when needed. What am I talking about? Alcoholism, drugs, the gay life style, and other areas of need not so frequently recognized....

We are finite and limited in our time for fasting and prayer. Even when we take a whole day of prayer or a night of prayer, the hours slip by, and we find we have not covered everything we wanted to pray about. However, just as we are admonished to 'bear one another's burdens, so we are clearly told to pray for one another. In our time of fasting and prayer, when we have a longer periods of time, a part of that time should be spent in really praying for any we know who are struggling with their own temptations or difficulties or for some who are sacrificially giving time to helping others in some area of struggle. We can't just shrug our shoulders and pull away from involvement.

APPLICATION QUESTIONS

For Personal Reflection

1. What struck you most about the examples from Ezra, Nehemiah and Paul? Why?

2. Are there any areas where you need to a deeper commitment to prayer? Where do you need God's strength for battle? Where do you need God's direction?

For Small Group Discussion

3. What is the relationship between prayer, fasting and action?

4. How do the exhortations from Schaeffer, Ezra, Nehemiah and Paul call you to respond?

5. Are there any current issues or battles in your church/ministry or city that needs this kind of deeper commitment to prayer?

PRAYER PRACTICE:
* Spend some time praying about a local, national or international battle for which you feel burdened. Surrender it. Ask the Lord to fight the battle. Ask him to reveal to you how you/your church may be called to respond and be involved.

But I, by your great mercy,
Will come into your house;
In reverence will I bow down
Toward your holy temple. -Psalm 5

Prayer is the slender nerve that moves the muscle of omnipotence.   ~Charles Spurgeon

Jesus did not pray about things, he brought things about by prayer.   ~Armin Gesswein

If you would never cease to pray, never cease to long for it.
The continuance of longing is the continuance of your prayer.   ~Augustine.

We have found that organized, planned days of prayer in which people lead us through periods of thematic prayer that correspond to the Lord's priorities – which contains times of both personal and group prayer – to be quite helpful. Here is a sample template.

I Opening session:

Opening prayer

Intro: The Purpose of a day of Fasting and Prayer:

1. A special and **intimate time of talking things through with God and renew our intimacy and fellowship with God,**. Letting him reveal spiritual and relational needs to you (through the Word).   I call this **percolating my life** through prayer and the Word.

    The moment you wake up in the morning all your wishes and hopes for the day come rushing at you like wild animals. And the first job each morning consists in shoving it all back; in listening to that other voice, taking that other point of view, letting that other, larger, stronger, quieter life come flowing in. ~CS Lewis.

    Thomas hand, in his great study <u>Augustine and Prayer,</u> put it this way:
    Prayer is the articulation of our love for God; it is the affectionate reaching out of the mind for God. But while the desires of our heart find expression in prayer, our prayers in turn are the breezes that fan the flame of our love. It is prayer that develops our desire, and enlarges our heart until it is capable of containing God's gift of himself. "Ask, seek, insist," exhorts Augustine; "by asking and seeking you grow big enough to receive."

2. We fast in order to **renew our love for his children, and our compassion for our neighbor:** Notice how our relationship to God and to our neighbor is tightly related:

    Is not his the kind of fasting I have chosen; to loose the chains of injustice and untie the cords of the yoke, and to set the oppressed free and to break every yoke? Is it not to share your food with the hungry and to provide the poor wanderer with shelter- when you see the naked to clothe him...Then your light will break forth like the dawn,...Then you will call, and the lord will answer; you will cry for help, and he will say; Here am I.....

➢ God promises that **real and manifest changes** will begin to happen in your life and substantial healing in the world around you when you prioritize your relationship with God and with those in need…

If you spend yourselves in behalf of the hungry and satisfy the needs of the oppressed, and then your light will rise in the darkness…he will satisfy your needs in a sun-scorched land and will strengthen your frame….Your people will rebuild the ancient ruins and will raise up the age-old foundations; you will be called the Repairer of Broken Walls, Restorer Streets with dwellings…then you will find your joy in the Lord…Isaiah 58

2. To bring special requests and urgent needs to God when nothing less than **his direct intervention and answer** is needed

I proclaimed a fast, so that we might humble ourselves before our God and ask him for a safe journey for us and our children, with all our possessions. I was ashamed to ask the king for soldiers and horsemen to protect us from enemies on the road, because we had told the king "The gracious hand of our God is on everyone who looks to him, but his great anger is against all who forsake him." So we fasted and petitioned our God about this, and he answered our prayer. Ezra 8:21

Examples: Crucial decisions and major crossroads.
Chronic sin and addictions.
Lack of a thirst for God.
Spirit of dissent and bitterness.
Broken relationships in the home/ church. (Family custody etc)
Needing a job.

<u>Take some time by yourself to pray to God about this day of prayer</u>.
- Ask him to bless you and all of us in this time.
- Meditate on these scriptures, Try not to force things so much as listen, reflect and respond to the word.
- Pray for a spirit of 'grace and supplication' (Zech. 9).
- Speak to God about your relationship with him.
- Begin to download your urgent needs (as noted above) and ask for humility, courage and openness to see your faults and needs.

<u>Now get together in groups of three</u>:
- Each share briefly your hope and expectation for this day.
- Pray for each other by name – for God to deeply bless them and the whole church in this special day. Ask God to help them have open ears and an open and willing heart before God.

> **Prayer time alone**: anywhere in the building or go for a walk. Let this be a special time with just you and God. Try to spend all of this time alone – without interacting or discussing with others. Bring your Bible along. Use the following outline and scriptures from the Lord's prayer to guide your time.

1.   OUR FATHER IN HEAVEN (The gospel and prayer petition)

You have free and immediate access to God in prayer through Jesus!

> Since we have a great high priest who has gone through the heavens, Jesus the Son of God,…Let us boldly approach the throne of grace, so that we may receive mercy and find grace in our time of need. (Heb.4)

He is eager to hear you and willing to answer:

> O you that hear prayer, to you shall all flesh come. (Psalm 65)
> Ask and it will be given to you. Seek and you will find. Knock and the door will be opened to you. Matthew 7

You could not be more loved. He loves you with the intensity and character of his love for his only son…

> Because you are sons, God sent the Spirit of his Son into our hearts, the Spirit who cries out "Abba" Father.

- **Think about this.** Take some time to let this joyous and rich truth percolate into your soul. Think of the perfect father and his joy in his children. Love being loved. Feel it. Say thanks. Come boldly!
- Pray for a 'spirit of grace and supplication' and a heart felt desire to be near to God in prayer. Pray for good prayer habits and discipline.
- Pray for prayer ministries and prayer training classes/conferences, for those who are leading, who are being trained and other churches in other cities, and YOU!

2.   HALLOWED BE THY NAME

The old English means: "Let your name be held as holy in all my life and worship and words". These words constitute an opportunity to worship and at the same time a time to confess coldness of heart, lack of praise and thanks, words or thoughts that are neglectful or dishonoring of God.

> *You shall not misuse the name of the Lord your God, for the Lord will not hold anyone guiltless who misuses his name. Exodus 20*
> *Worship the Lord God and serve him only. Luke 4*
> *True worshippers will worship the Father in spirit and truth,.. John 4*

- ➢ **Talk with God about your heart affections towards him.** Download about your thoughts and attitudes in worship services and personal prayers. Ask yourself (and Him) how much God is at the heart of your thinking. Has he been distant and foreboding or near and warm?
- ➢ **Pray about our worship ministries.** Thank God for the leaders and others who work hard in this area. Pray for the gospel message to be clear and bold in all our worship. Pray for yourself and them to be filled with the Holy Spirit and Gospel of grace.

Break

3. THY KINGDOM COME

Here we ask God to manifest his present and coming rule and reign in us and to other who know him not. This petition refers especially to the great commission and to the preaching of the Good News here and throughout the world. (Matthew 28:16-20)

Form in groups of 3

(i) **Start by sharing / praying for <u>one key person who you want to come to Christ</u>.**

(ii) **Continue by praying for <u>outreach efforts</u>:**

- Pray for God's word and message of Christ to go forth in power and increasing force. Pray for the ministries of <u>preaching and teaching</u> in your church.

- Pray for <u>new church plants and the leaders</u> of those plants in your city/region/country.

- Pray for other <u>churches</u> in your area.

- Pray for God to give us boldness in <u>reaching our neighborhood</u>, including:

  -residents (singles and families in homes, condos, as well as the homeless, etc.)

  -businesses and workers in the area.

- Pray for <u>your own neighbors</u>, key contacts, friends, relatives.

- Pray for God to <u>open doors to men women and children's hearts</u> to hear and receive the gospel.

- Pray for <u>outreach ministries</u> including seeker Bible studies/discussion groups like Alpha or Christianity Explored, campus ministries, senior's care, arts outreach, etc.

(iii) **Thank God for <u>Seekers and new converts</u>**

- Pray for the <u>seekers</u> that are in contact with your church and with members of your church. Pray for God to <u>bring in the harvest.</u>

- Pray for <u>Satan to be bound and crushed</u> so that this word will not be hindered. His Kingdom is here. It is coming in full force soon. We pray for this time to be short and for the present harvest to be great.

(i) Prayer walk in groups of three or four for next hour. Concentrate this hour on praying for the church and personal outreach to the needy and for personal outreach.

4, THY WILL BE DONE ON EARTH AS IT IS IN HEAVEN (Mercy & Social Justice)

This has special reference to a life of obedience and piety- of love and good deeds in the here and now of our lives. We want the harmony, holiness love and joy of heaven to visit this world through God's people as they minister the gospel in word and deed.

What good is it, my brothers, if a man claims to have faith but has no deeds? Can such a faith save him? Faith without deeds is useless….James 2.

In that you did it to the least of these you did it to me…Matthew 25

- Pray about **your own heart** towards those in need. Think of the poor, other **ethnic** groups than your own, non-Christians in general. Ask God to change your heart to be like his. Ask to be RAW – ready, available and wise. Ask God to show you where, when and how you should be involved.
- Pray for our **neighbors,** local businesses, art galleries, apartment dwellers, as you pass by them.

(ii)   Stay in your prayer walking group:
- Pray that God will help us in developing and existing **mercy ministry** of his choosing.
- Pray for God to pour out his grace so we can move into more rehabilitation and **social** issues.

5. GIVE US THIS DAY OUR DAILY BREAD

Finance Thanksgiving and request: includes praying with thanks for all that we require in the way of governance, food and lodging, and peace to enable us to serve God as he intends. This includes, for example, praying for our parents, those in authority over us, our jobs and our bosses/managers/ as well as for our financial needs.

- Ask that God will **give you all that you need so that you may be generous** with your time and money to those in need and the ministry of the church.
- Pray for a right attitude towards possessions, for a **spirit of simplicity and generosity** in giving to others needs.
- Pray for your **church's needs.**
- Praise God for his **faithfulness in provision** to date.

6.   FORGIVE US OUR DEBTS AS WE FORGIVE OUR DEBTORS

Confess your sins to one another and pray for each other so that you might be healed. James 5:16
We pray for peace and unity in our homes and in the church. This unity comes about through confessing our sins and receiving forgiveness from God and each other.

In groups of 3:
- Pray for God to help **you be a peacemaker** – to not receive or make gossip about anyone. Rather to speak kindly or be silent.
- Pray for **unity** within the church, especially within the leadership.
- Pray for our **small groups**/home/fellowship/neighbourhood groups to grow in grace and love.

7.   LEAD US NOT INTO TEMPTATION BUT DELIVER US FROM EVIL

We always need to pray for the grace of perseverance – to keep up the fight and not quit – and for courage to stand against temptation, and to withstand the many trials we face.

- Pray for **spiritual protection** especially for yourself and leaders who are on the front lines.
- Pray for those in your midst **struggling with addition.**

CONCLUSION: Share a song, testimony of how God spoke and worked today, and prayer.

evaluation of outcomes

GOALS:
- ❏ Evaluate personal prayer progress and identify new attitudes, understanding and skills developed during our training
- ❏ Develop a plan for implementing prayer action points for further growth

All learning involves a change in understanding content, attitude adjustments, and skill development. Please summarize the changes you have experienced during this learning experience.

NEW UNDERSTANDINGS: List 2 new concepts that have gripped you during these sessions.

1.

2.

ATTITUDE CHANGE: List 2 changes in attitude, either positive or negative, that have occurred in your heart during these sessions.

1.

2.

SKILL DEVELOPMENT: List 2 new skills that have been awakened or highlighted for development in your life during these sessions.

1.

2.

NEXT STEPS: Normally follow-through in concrete action does not occur unless specific steps are outlined. List two actions you plan to take in the next two weeks. What will you do to apply what you have learned?

1.

2.

Who will you share this with to hold you accountable and to pray with and for you?

What impact do you potentially see resulting from incorporating the principles and practices you have learned from this training?

This evaluation is important in improving and validating teaching methods and for gaining feedback on course content. Thanks for your input!

*All learning involves a change in **understanding** content, **attitude** adjustments, and **skill** development. Please list changes you've experienced during this training:*

What new **understandings/concepts** have gripped you?

What **attitude** changes (positive or negative) have occurred in your heart?

What new **skills** have been awakened or highlighted for growth in your life?

What is the most significant thing you will take away from this training?

What contributed most to your learning?

What would you change (add, remove, do differently) to improve this training?

Any additional comments or suggestions?

How can we support you in passing your learning on to others and in your own **growth** process?

Please turn this page over

Topics & Tools

Poor---------------Excellent

Priorities of the Lord's Prayer	1 2 3 4 5
Paul's prayers for himself in reaching the world	1 2 3 4 5
Paul's prayers for others' spiritual transformation	1 2 3 4 5
Prayer Progress Evaluation (personal/corporate)	1 2 3 4 5
Prayer walking	1 2 3 4 5
Prayer list	1 2 3 4 5
Missional prayer partnerships	1 2 3 4 5
Calling and prayer	1 2 3 4 5
Discerning the heart of your city	1 2 3 4 5
Bringing kingdom prayer into your church	1 2 3 4 5

Content

Learning outcomes were clear	1 2 3 4 5
Learning outcomes were achieved	1 2 3 4 5
Content was relevant and practical to my life context	1 2 3 4 5

Delivery and Format

Questions were encouraged and addressed	1 2 3 4 5
Participation and collaboration were a key part of the learning process	1 2 3 4 5
Learning activities/tools helped achieve objectives	1 2 3 4 5
Exercises were practical in building skill	1 2 3 4 5
Discussions were helpful and relevant	1 2 3 4 5
Materials were accessible (easy to understand/use)	1 2 3 4 5
Training was well-paced	1 2 3 4 5
Time commitment was appropriate for the objectives	1 2 3 4 5
Scheduling of course was accessible	1 2 3 4 5

Facilitator(s)

Communicated concepts clearly	1 2 3 4 5
Shared from their passion and experience and are practitioners of the subject area	1 2 3 4 5

General Impact

My desire to learn and grow in this area has increased

1 2 3 4 5

I have grown in practical skill in this area due to this training

1 2 3 4 5

This training will help me in *my own journey* in
knowing and loving God more fully   1 2 3 4 5

This training will help me to be more effective in
my mission to love others in my life context more fully 1 2 3 4 5

I feel I will be able to take what I've learned here and pass it on to others

1 2 3 4 5

Would you recommend this training to others?   Yes____ No____

Bibliography

Boy, Karla. "Walking the Streets in Prayer." Atlanta: Church Newsletter and Personal Correspondence, 2005.

Cook, Jerry and Stanley C. Baldwin "The Church as Force." Love, Acceptance and Forgiveness: Equipping the Church to Be Truly Christian in a Non-Christian World. Ventura: Regal Books, 1979, pp. 35-54.

Edwards, Jonathan. A Humble Attempt to Promote the Agreement and Union of God's People Throughout the World in Extraordinary Prayer For a Revival Of Religion And The Advancement Of God's Kingdom On Earth, According To Scriptural Promises And Prophecies Of The Last Time. <http://www.graceonlinelibrary.org/etc/printer-friendly.asp?ID=112> March 9, 2009.

"God's Love for Cities. God is a City Builder." San Francisco: City Church San Francisco, 2009. <http://www.citychurchsf.org/citylove/citylove.htm>

Jeffrey, David Lyle (ed). "Introduction." A Burning and Shining Light: English Spirituality in the Age of Wesley. Grand Rapids: Eerdmans Publishing Co., 1987, pp. 1-52.

Keller, Tim. "The Centrality of the Gospel." New York: Redeemer Presbyterian, 2000. <www.redeemer2.com/resources/papers/centrality.pdf>

Keller, Tim. "The Idol Project." New York: Redeemer Presbyterian, 2000.

Keller, Tim. "Preface to Galatians." School of Servant Leadership. New York: Redeemer Presbyterian, 2000, pp. 17-20.

Keller, Tim. "A Simple Way to Pray." New York: Redeemer Presbyterian, 2000.

Keller, Tim. "Son or Slave Project." New York: Redeemer Presbyterian, 2000.

Kelly, Douglas F., Philip B. Rollinson, and Frederick T. Marsh, "Questions 98-107." The Westminster Shorter Catechism in Modern English. Phillipsburg: P&R Publishing, 1986, pp. 22-23.

Linthicum, Robert C. "The Presence and Prayer of the Church in the City." City of God, City of Satan. Grand Rapids: Zondervan, 1991, pp. 145-162.

Luther, Martin and Archie Parrish (ed). A Simple Way to Pray: Martin Luther, the 16th Century Reformer, Tells His Barber How to Empower His Prayer Life. Okahumpka: Serve International, 1999.

Miller, Rose Marie. "Going Further: Spiritual Warfare." From Fear to Freedom: Living as Sons and Daughters of God. Colorado Springs, Waterbrook Press, 2000, pp. 109-118.

Mueller, George and Fred Bergen (ed). Autobiography of George Mueller. London: J. Nisbet Co., 1906, pp. 152-54.

Murray, Andrew. "The Power of United Prayer." With Christ in the School of Prayer. New York: Fleming H. Revell Co., 1885. <http://thebiblerevival.com/teachings/books/0013/p15.htm> September 1, 2003.

"New York City Prayer Meeting: Selected Stories and Teachings from the History of Revival." Adapted from <http://www.knoxvillerevival.com/Revivals/worldwiderevival.htm> and <http://www.truthkeepers.com/prayer1.htm>. October 1, 2008.

Schaeffer, Edith. "Fasting and Prayer: Part One." The Life of Prayer. Wheaton: Crossway Books. 1992.

Smed, John. "Prayer and the Sequence of New Testament Mission." Vancouver: Grace Vancouver Presbyterian, 2008.

Smed, John. "Priorities in Prayer." Vancouver: Grace Vancouver Presbyterian, 2005.

Smed, John. "How to Pray for Revival in the Church and City." Vancouver: Grace Vancouver Presbyterian, 2009.

"William Wilberforce." Washington: Trinity Forum, 2000.

Order *Prayer Current* Resources

Prayer Current helps people navigate life through prayer. Whether someone is just entering the waters or is an experienced traveler, Prayer Current provides inspiration and practical tools to grow in prayer, and to "pray it forward" by helping grow others in prayer. Designed for life in the city and for personal or church use, Prayer Current engages people in a balance of reflection, interaction, study, actual prayer practice and mission.

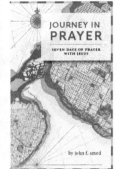

Journey in Prayer: 7 Days of Prayer with Jesus. The secret to growing in faith and the key to reaching the world are found in the Lord's prayer. This book explores Jesus' simple but purpose-filled pattern for prayer. He invites us to pray it personally. He calls us to pray it in community. Each chapter explores the implications and impact of each petition on our lives and world. *Great for seekers who want to learn to pray, believers who are beginning in their prayer journey, or for Christians to introduce a seeker friend to prayer and Jesus.*

Journey in Prayer: 7 Days of Prayer with Jesus with STUDY GUIDE. This study explores the Lord's prayer, with each chapter expanding on the implications and impact of each petition on our lives and world. Includes an integrated study guide to help you develop a regular habit of prayer that goes beyond daily urgencies – to one that reflects the vast priorities of Jesus' prayer. This study guide offers a practical and simple prayer list method for personal daily prayer based on a seven day structure, with one petition each day. *Great for Christians who want to develop a deeper, more regular/daily habit of prayer. Excellent for use in small groups.*

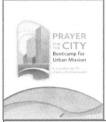

Prayer for the City Bootcamp for Urban Mission. This workbook and DVD is a 12 lesson group study in training yourself and others in gospel centred, missional prayer. Featuring key readings on prayer, questions for personal reflection and group interaction, and prayer points to guide prayer practice, you'll be challenged to come back to the heart of prayer, the gospel and mission. Each lesson contains practical tools in developing new or deeper prayer habits, personally and corporately, including biblical prayer patterns, prayer lists, prayer walking, prayer maps, prayer progress evaluations, prayer groups, fasting and prayer, identifying prayer needs of your city, and tips in training others and building a culture of prayer. *Great for training churches in prayer (use this to first train your leaders who can then lead others in prayer). Excellent for church planters to train core group members in prayer and mission.*

Resource Title	Quantity	Unit Price	Subtotal *(Cdn $ or US $ the same)*	
Journey in Prayer: 7 Days of Prayer with Jesus		$10		Please fill
Journey in Prayer: 7 Days of Prayer with Jesus with STUDY GUIDE		$15		
Prayer for the City: Bootcamp for Urban Mission		$30		
Pack of all 3: One copy of each Title		$45		
Less Discount *(5% on 10+ copies, 15% on 50+ copies, 20% on 100+ copies)*				Office use only
Plus Shipping and Handling (Bulk cost)				
TOTAL				

Would you like to receive more information on upcoming training opportunities? Yes_____ No_____

Billing Address:

Name:_____Organization:_____

Address:_____City,Prov/State:_____

Postal Code/ZIP _____ Phone:_____ E-mail:_____

Shipping Address (if different from above)

Name:
_____Organization:_____

Address: _____City,Prov/State:_____

Postal Code/ZIP _____ Phone:_____ E-mail:_____

Payment: _____Cheque payable to The Grace Project _____ Visa _____ Mastercard

Name on Card_____ Card # _____

Expiry_____ Signature_____

Please send orders to: Prayer Current, 106 – 1033 Haro Street, Vancouver, BC, V6E 1C8 CANADA
Credit card orders may be **phoned** to 778-987-0274 or **faxed** to 778-588-7528 or **emailed** to: info@prayercurrent.com

Prayer Current

Navigating Life Through Prayer

Prayer Current helps people navigate life through prayer. Whether someone is just entering the waters or is an experienced traveler, Prayer Current provides inspiration and practical tools to grow in prayer, and to "pray it forward" by helping grow others in prayer.

Designed for life in the city and for personal or church use, Prayer Current resources engage people in a balance of reflection, interaction, study, actual prayer practice and mission.

www.prayercurrent.com